Redeeming SARAH

ELIZABETH HAMILTON

Redeeming Sarah

Elizabeth Hamilton

First published 2019

© Elizabeth Ryan

All rights reserved. No part of this printed or video publication may be reproduced, stored in or introduced into a retrieval system, or transmitted, in any form, or by any means (electrical, mechanical, photocopying, recording or otherwise) without the prior written permission of the publisher and copyright owner.

Editor: Elizabeth Hamilton

Cover Designer / typesetter: WorkingType Design

Printed by On Demand Printing

ISBN: 978-0-6485893-9-6

Table of Contents

Acknowledgements v
Introduction 1

PART ONE: THOMAS BRADSHAW
& JANE FAIRBROTHER
From the Midlands of England to the Gold
Fields of Australia
1847 — 1913 3

PART TWO: SARAH
England: 1850 – 1852
Australia: 1852 – 1913 131

PART THREE: WILLIAM HAMILTON
Australia: 1873 — 1969 265

Conclusion 301
Notes to the reader 393

Acknowledgements

In many ways this book has been a team effort. I am deeply grateful to the following, without whose help, it could never have come to fruition.

To Mauri Hamilton whose skills as a researcher and enthusiasm for the task kept me going when it all seemed too hard.

To Gabii Ryan and Peter Ryan for their excellent proof reading and editing, as well as their brave suggestions for structural changes.

To Peter Jackson in Priors Marston without whom none of my English research would have been possible. It was Peter who put me in touch with Dot Brown and Barbara Flint, the latter who lives in 'The Butcher House,' where Thomas Bradshaw grew up and who graciously opened her house to us.

To Pam Hicks in Byfield who enabled me to see that the Fairbrother name was one to be reckoned with in the parish of Holy Cross.

To Joan Hamilton who began the research into William Hamilton's birth family and who alerted us to the 'mysteries' surrounding the search.

To my family, all of them the legacy of Sarah Hamilton, I thank them for putting up wih my obsession for the last two years.

To John, Nancy, Jessie and Alan Wilson, Elsie Stratton and Joy and Jim Hamilton whose acquaintance I have only just made but who have helped with information about the Hamilton family. I am only sorry Jim couldn't hang on to read the story of his father's family.

And finally to my Bamawm friends, Chris Cleary and her late husband Brian, whose friendship of almost fifty years made me a frequent visitor to Bamawm. I never knew that Thomas Bradshaw's property was just a stone's throw away from where I had spent so many happy hours or that Sarah was buried nearby in Rochester. I know now, why I always felt at home there, as if I belonged.

Introduction

I am walking through the Rochester cemetery
The grave is here somewhere
I have a map -
Row 9, grave no.14 – Anglican section

Here it is, a piece of dirt, indistinguishable from any other
Beneath this dry, cracked earth lie two people
Without one of them, I would not be here

Her name is Sarah, I have only just discovered her
Buried here in 1913, over a hundred years ago. She was 62

She is calling to me. I need to bring her to life

Sarah, this book is for you

PART ONE

THOMAS BRADSHAW & JANE FAIRBROTHER

From the Midlands of England to the Gold Fields of Australia, 1847–1913

THOMAS — BAMAWM

Christmas Eve, 1913

I am an old man looking out over the dry, flat Bamawm Plains, realising this is where I will die, a realisation that both scares me and arouses me. I imagine my body returning to the dust of my adopted country, enriching it with the sum of my life.

There is some sort of commotion going on, out there, beyond the veranda. The boy is screaming about me forgetting to close the paddock gates and he and Marriott are working with the dogs to get the wandering animals back where they belong. Was I in that paddock this morning? I can't remember. I have been forgetting so much lately. It worries me. Marriott hurries back to the kitchen, making sure he doesn't look in my direction. He is a good son. He doesn't want to hurt my feelings. The boy is walking towards the veranda. He looks at me with a mixture of anger and sympathy. He flings himself into the chair beside mine and sticks his long legs out in front of him. "You left the gate open again," he says not looking at me. I nod in acknowledgement.

Together we sit. The old man and the young boy. He has his life ahead of him, mine has almost finished. We both love this brown, unforgiving country. Marriott wants me to sell and go to live with him in Torrumbarry. I don't want to go. Bamawm has been my home for forty years. I know people here and people know me. Who will know me in Torrumbarry?

The boy has calmed down and is asking me how the funeral went. After we came home from the cemetery, he hung around, sensing my despair, making excuses to be close to me. I sensed he just wanted me to talk. But I couldn't talk. Not then, anyway.

The funeral. Was it only two weeks ago? I didn't want to go but Marriott insisted. "She's your daughter, Father. You have to go."

Sarah, my daughter, my only daughter, a half sister to Marriott, my little girl, born in England to two people whom I no longer recognise. She died before me. Where is the sense in that? I am 88 years old. I don't understand life at all.

The boy often asks me about my early life. When I talk, he listens as if he is really interested. He's a curious young fella; a bit strange, but hard working and should make a good farmer given the right opportunity. He reminds me a little of my grandson, William, who lived with me for a while after his father died. But I am much more gentle with the boy than I was with William. I have learnt that at least.

I think he is grateful that I took him out of the orphanage and he has made himself at home with me. When Marriott comes, he tells him stories and I hear the two of them laughing out loud. Marriott has the knack of making people laugh, no matter who they are. It annoys me that he doesn't take life more seriously.

I would like to hand over the farm to the boy and just close my eyes forever. There are too many memories and lately they have turned into demons.

"Father, are you with us?" Marriott has joined us on the veranda. I open my eyes and look at him. He winks at the boy. "You were off daydreaming again."

Daydreaming! Is that what he calls it when an old man would rather live in the past than in the present. I was a child again, back in England, on the green and wet pastures of Priors Marston. How different from the heat and parched land I see around me today.

Would that I could fly over the seas and lay to rest in the grounds of St Leonard's Church next to my mother and father, and my father's father and so many Bradshaws through the ages. But of course that is not possible. I am a world away — a little boy again, running from the schoolroom into the churchyard and hiding behind the graves where the writing has faded on the Midlands granite. "Coming, ready or not." Lots of Bradshaws were enjoying their final rest amidst the overgrown tombstones scattered randomly but they didn't concern me. My family was alive and well and I had no need for the dead – that is, not until now when I am almost among their numbers.

The Lebanese Cedar trees, planted when I was a child, now protect and shelter all who have their final rest there. I loved those trees. I watched them grow and spread their shade over those who had spent their allotted time on earth in a place known as Priors Marston, a tiny dot on the map of England, but to them, their entire world. The boy has never heard of Lebanese Cedars. All he knows are gums, wattles, willows and the occasional oak. I told him they had names, Trafalgar and Waterloo. He scoffed at the notion that you would name a tree after a place.

It was Mr Hart, our headmaster who thought it would be a good idea to commemorate the battles of Trafalgar and Waterloo, so he took the whole school into the Churchyard and formed us into two groups. He called one group Trafalgar and the other Waterloo. I was in the Waterloo group. I was only seven years old and took my turn with the spade although the older boys did most of the hard toil. "Where is Lebanon?" we asked when we got back to the classroom. Mr Hart would flip down the map which hung from the blackboard and point to Lebanon. He was good at making places come to life and by the end of the day we were all determined, one day, to go to Lebanon.

Twenty years later, I left Priors Marston to travel, but not to Lebanon, rather a much greater distance, to Australia. Before I left, I visited St Leonard's churchyard and saw that the cedars were already tall and stately. Years of growth had cemented their place as the key focus of all the dead who were resting peacefully. "You've seen the painting of the trees in my bedroom," I said to the boy without looking at him, not knowing whether he was listening or not. "My sister, Mary sent it to me before she died. It's what they look like now, towering, magnificent giants, grown from seeds planted by a few small children."

The church bells would summon us into the Sunday service with admonishments from Mother and Father to behave. Father was strict but I believe he understood our impatience with the dry, long sermons. I secretly think he and Mother were anxious for the service to end so that they could catch up with the weekly news and gossip afterwards. People would stay for ages in the grounds talking while we children would chase each other around knowing trouble awaited us for dirtying our good clothes.

It's not the same here in Bamawm. The very landscape is the antithesis of the Midland's landscape. We didn't even have a church when I first moved here. We had to go into Rochester where the dry and withered grounds of the church worked against prolonged social gatherings. When they built the church nearby in Lockington, it was better and I loved to see Marriott and the local children playing in the dusty paddocks like I used to as a child.

Many of my neighbours and friends didn't worship at the same church as I did and so there was a divide to start with. My Catholic neighbours did not share with me the religion I had grown up with. I missed the fact that we didn't worship at the same church. I also missed the gravestones in the church yard. There was none. When you died you were taken to the Rochester cemetery miles away on the Kyabram road or to Echuca. All connection to your church was lost. The Rochester cemetery is huge and everyone is buried there no matter who they are, where they come from and which God they believed in.

The boy asked me how the funeral was. Did I answer his question? It was dreadful. Watching while my only daughter was committed to the hard, cracked ground, I didn't want to be there. it seemed every fly in the universe was invited, annoying the hell out of us. There wasn't a patch of green grass and when the flies weren't in our eyes the dust was.

I thought I had banished Sarah from my life but there she was, torturing me in death even more than she had in life. I loved her and it was as if it were me in that coffin.

Marriott and I settled under a shady tree where we could see the proceedings but keep our distance at the same time. I knew people would be watching me, to see how I behaved. They all knew of the differences I had with my daughter. Was I ashamed of her? Did I feel as if she had tarnished my reputation? To be honest, yes I did, but there, with the coffin resting on the dry dirt, knowing that I would never see her again, I felt ashamed. Not of Sarah. I was ashamed of myself.

Six of her seven children were there, my grandchildren, all except for Annie and no-one knows where she is. She may not even know her mother is dead. Just disappeared one day. Went to Melbourne and no-one's heard from her since. Seven grandchildren! I suppose a man should be pleased about that but I don't see them very often. I used to, but not since their mother and I had a falling out, and they took their mother's part.

They look at me now as if I am some sort of monster.

A falling out? Is that what it was? No it was more than that. Can a father be expected to forgive a daughter for breaking God's law, not once but three times? Was that how she repaid me for what I did for her? I gave her a house, paid for her children to attend school and provided her with whatever she needed but that wasn't enough for her. I tried to tell her that losing a husband was unfortunate but she just had to get on with it and not feel sorry for herself. God knows, I should know. I told her she had to snap out of it.

Well she did that all right! Pregnant three times and wouldn't tell me who the father or fathers were. I had my suspicions but could not risk confronting him because he was a married man and I couldn't afford to make unnecessary enemies. I told her that she had made her bed and she could lie in it, at the same time withdrawing my financial support and suggesting she ask her man friend for money.

Do I regret that? Do I regret that I didn't visit Sarah on her deathbed? I don't think so. A death bed reconciliation would have been redemptive but it was not going to happen and I think my appearance would have made things worse. I know how angry she was and probably hurt as well but what I did was right. I know it was.

It was strange seeing William again after all these years. My oldest grandson. He looks very different from the headstrong and confused young boy who came to live with me at the age of 11 because of his health. Looking at the strong, robust man he is today, you would never believe he was a frail boy. We exchanged polite words, about his work as an accountant, his family and the area in Melbourne where he lives. It is one of the better areas, one where I could never aspire to live. I had the feeling he was trying to impress me as he didn't think I had much of an opinion of him.

But he was wrong. I was fond of William despite what he believed. He just needed strong guidance and I knew his mother couldn't give him that. I suspect he holds it against me that I was so hard on him, but without a father, what hope did he have? He was a good boy but had some rough edges and needed discipline. He blamed me for taking him away from his mother and he blamed his mother for letting him go. He could never accept the fact that a move from Melbourne was necessary for his health

Two weeks since the burial and I can't get the scene out of my mind. My youngest grand-child, Nellie, kept staring at the grave as if she couldn't believe that her mother was gone. At eighteen, with her anaemic face and slight build, she hasn't fully recovered from the rheumatic fever she suffered some years ago and the death of her mother will not be easy for her. Strange how thoughts go through your mind. I imagined her tears falling on the dry dirt and producing some grass in that God forsaken cemetery. Seeing Nellie, I wanted to reach out to her but what use am I now? I hardly know her. I suspect she will go to live with her older sister, Agnes.

The boy is listening intently. What have I said? Have I told him any secrets I meant to take to my grave? I wonder whether I should have taken him with me to the burial. I know he likes to feel part of the family after having been with me for years. He has a sensitivity not common in young boys and is curious about Sarah. I suppose he has heard the rumours around town. He asks me about her mother and wonders why I never talk about her.

When he mentions Jane, I surprise myself. I don't want to bore him but for some reason I want to talk about her, the woman I loved and brought to Australia, only to deliver her to her death. It's ages since I talked to anyone about her. I ask him to go to my bedroom and get my green cushion. If I'm going to be sitting here for some time, I need to be comfortable.

The boy returns with the cushion and a book. I snatch it from him. I ask him where he found it. He looks hurt and tells me it was on the floor under my bed. He had obviously looked inside the cover where in big letters are the words:

JANE FAIRBROTHER,
Byfield 1847.

He asks me if it is her diary

I want to be angry with him but it's too late for anger. How can I tell him that although I have had Jane's diary in my possession for almost sixty years, picked it up and tried to read it many times, I have never got past the first page?

I nod, and then I ask him to read it to me.

Why not?

He reads well for a lad who has had very little education. I smile and think about Jane and her excitable nature. Reading her diary will be a challenge for him.

JANE – BYFIELD, ENGLAND
April, 1847

Mrs White gave me a diary for my birthday. I have never kept a diary before but I think I like the idea. After I am dead, someone will find it and publish it and I might be famous, like Jane Austen.
It could be a novel. A romantic novel about Jane Fairbrother.
I will write my name in big letters on the cover.

JANE FAIRBROTHER – Byfield, 1847.

Firstly I should introduce myself. I am almost twenty five, just finished training as a milliner, the oldest in a family which stretches back as far as anyone can remember in this village. Carrying the name Fairbrother is quite a responsibility around these parts. You don't want to misbehave!
What do I want in life? I want to get married and have children and hope to meet someone like Mr Rochester in Jane Eyre, a wonderful new book by Currer Bell, that all my friends are reading. It's the story of a poor girl who is a governess for a Mr Rochester and she ends up marrying him It is ever so romantic.
I suppose I had better tell you what I have been doing for the last twenty five years.
My first 17 years were just like every other girl who grew up in Byfield. Work, school and play. The same, day in and day out. Then, when I turned seventeen, Father and Mother asked me whether I would like to become a milliner.
I most certainly would, I said, unbelieving that they could afford to

buy me an apprenticeship. I was the oldest and I thought that Mother would want to keep me at home.

"It will give you a trade," said Father, "the boys will have the farm and we have the two servant girls to help your mother. When your sister is older we will do the same for her."

I was overcome with joy. I knew that to do an apprenticeship, I had to go to the city of Luton and how exciting that would be. Father later told me that he had sold some of his land to the railways and made quite a profit. I also think he didn't see me as likely to get married at any time soon. I hope he's not right about that!

That was seven years ago.

I started my millinery apprenticeship with two other apprentices, both named Elizabeth, the same name as my little sister. We lived together in a room above the shop and were apprenticed to a respected milliner named Mrs White, (She is the one who gave me this diary) a widow with five children who survived because of her skill at making bonnets and hats. There was no shortage of demand for her product as no woman would venture outside without a bonnet.

Mrs White was a kind woman but had high expectations of her apprentices. She did not tolerate mistakes and each of us was on the end of several tongue lashings which were not at all pleasant, I can tell you. She treated us well, however, and gave us more free time than she was obliged. The girls and I became good friends and we spent many an hour dreaming our girlish dreams.

In 1845 I received my trade certificate. Unfortunately, the two Elizabeths had moved on. One had married and gone with her husband to Daventry as they were expecting their first child. He was certainly no Mr Rochester but she seemed happy enough. The other Elizabeth had gone home to nurse her mother who was ill and had not finished her apprenticeship. I felt sad for her as she had worked so hard and had nothing to show for it. I hope she will continue to make bonnets and that people will pay for her skills. But I suspect that won't happen.

I agreed to stay on and help Mrs White for at least a year as she was finding it difficult to cope with the demand. It was a welcome change to be paid for my work and I was able to send money home to Father to pay him back for my indenture. Father has not been well and the younger boys have been carrying the load on the farm. I hoped the money would provide relief.

Luton was the centre of the hat trade in Great Britain. We made hats, not just for the local people but for people all over England, even fulfilling orders for stylish people on the Continent. Handmade hats, each with its own personality which rich people were happy to pay for the privilege. They looked like little girls in a sweet shop as they left the shop parading their new purchase. We used to laugh at them.

The youngest of the White Family, Elijah, was the sweetest boy who would give me pictures he had drawn of me. I was touched and told him he would be a great artist one day. He said that when he grew up he wanted to marry me! Maybe one day he will make someone a fine Mr Rochester. At least I can tell everyone I have had my first marriage proposal!

After twelve months, however, I knew I had to move on to further my experience, so with an excellent reference from Mrs White, I obtained a position on the other side of town at one of the premium, and much larger establishments called The Hat Box. I start there after I have had a few weeks home with my family.

So here I am, back in Byfield, a different woman from the young girl who left all those years ago.

My family is proud of me and tell their friends in the village that I will be earning "lots" of money and making hats for rich people, maybe even for the new queen! Wouldn't that be something? She is so small that she would have to have a hat that didn't make her disappear!

My father does not look well and his cough is horrible. I lay awake at night listening to him try to get his breath and wish I could help him. I don't ask what the doctor has said as I'm not sure I want to know. When I gave him all the money I had saved and thanked him for giving me an opportunity to become a milliner, he was overcome.

"Well I didn't think you'd be the type to marry young," he said. "You always seemed a restless girl, not satisfied with just being in one place. We thought this might give you a chance. Mind, I'd love to see you married now and have some little 'uns.'"

I hugged him and told him that I would love to marry but hadn't met the right person. Secretly I am not quite so cofident and have been worrying that I might never meet anyone. After all I am almost 25. I had some suitors in Luton but knew that if I married, I would have to give up my profession and I was not prepared to do that. I wonder if it is too late for me.

Tomorrow I will take the two day coach ride back to Luton. The new railways can't be built fast enough as the Coach is bumpy and tedious

And you, Diary, will come with me.

THOMAS — BAMAWM

Christmas Eve — 2013

The boy paused. He said Jane sounded like lots of the girls he meets, romantic and ditzy. He looked at me as if he couldn't believe she had chosen me.

Hearing those words read to me brought Jane alive. Yes, she was 'romantic and ditzy' but intelligent and strong as well as loving and amusing. And to think, the little girl we had together is now in the ground. Life, you are so cruel. In a way I am glad Jane is not here today to bear the grief of seeing her daughter lowered into the grave.

Jane and I adored our little Sarah. I can still see her as a little girl tugging at my sleeve asking 'Where's mummy? I want mummy!'

What could I tell her? My little girl. That her mother, my Jane, was never coming back, that because she wanted to give Sarah a little brother or sister, death was the consequence; that her little sister lasted just 4 days and was buried with her mother that night; that I did not try too hard to keep her little sister alive? No I couldn't tell her any of this so I told her nothing. That was left to others.

Could I have saved her little sister? The baby was obviously suffering from dysentery, the doctor giving her little hope. If I had paid more money for a decent wet nurse? If I had moved my Jane earlier away from the squalid conditions of Melbourne? IF, IF, IF...

Jane died because of the dreadful conditions, conditions worse than she would have experienced at home in Woodford, Byfield or Priors Marston. She died because we had no money when her family was swimming in it at home.

Before they carried her body out the door of our North Melbourne house, I shut down. I was no longer husband to Jane and father to Sarah. I belonged to no-one. Jane was gone, and the baby. Now I wanted Sarah gone. Seeing her was just too hard.

"Papa," she cried, holding her hands up to me. I pushed her away. It was Helen Little who spoke:

"Come with me, Sarah. You can come and stay with us for a while."

I didn't argue. In fact, in that moment, I wanted nothing to do with Sarah. All I could think of was that I would never see Jane again and the thought was all consuming.

How could her mother back in England forgive me? Thank God her father had died not long before we left or else I would be answerable to him as well. My friends were sympathetic but I pushed them away. I wanted no sympathy. Just oblivion.

The boy asks me if I want him to continue. It's painful to hear Jane's words after all this time, but yes, I do want him to continue reading.

JANE — LUTON
February, 1848

I have been remiss in my writing as I have had very little time.

Should I write in chapters like a real book? Then I could call the chapters after my adventures. This one could be called 'Jane starts as a milliner,' or is that too prosaic?

The new job is hard and I miss the easy going atmosphere at Mrs White's. I like Luton though. It is buzzing with life and everywhere you look, there are new buildings. The older people are moaning about how things are moving too quickly but you don't hear that talk from my friends. We love the excitement and the railways mean that we can travel to all parts of England. It's marvellous.

Travelling from Byfield by coach seems to last forever although the slow travel does make you appreciate the changing countryside more and the cramped towns that the coach rattles through and even the overnight stop at the inn. On my last journey I felt very grown up when we arrived at our accommodation and the other two young girls on the coach looked positively frightened.

"'You'll survive, girls," I said, "just don't trust too many people." I took them under my wing. They were most grateful.

When the coach pulled into the station mid-afternoon, the familiar essence of Luton entered through my nostrils, my eyes and finally my ears. It was smelly, dirty and loud but I was glad to be back. How easy it was to merge into the cacophony of this city and become completely anonymous. I was no longer a 'Fairbrother' but just another human being.

I found Lancrets Path and wandered along the lane till I found The Hat Box, *a smaller frontage than I imagined, dark green with a diagonal* blue sash across the window. I liked it. Inside I saw different styles of hats, positioned on a pink wall and in the window were models of women wearing the most beautiful bonnets I had ever seen. Whoever did the window dressing had flair. I hope I can learn from such an artist.

I introduced myself and was informed where my lodgings would be, twenty minutes' walk along George St. I was to share a room with one of the other workers at the shop, an older woman named Elsbeth. Elsbeth would take me to my lodgings at the end of the shift. I must say I was disappointed that my roommate was not the same age as I was.

My employer is not friendly like Mrs White. She is not even a milliner but rather a business woman. She takes the orders and the money and doles out wages to the seven milliners who work in a huge room at the back of the shop.

Her name is Jemima Allen and I was told to call her Miss Allen. She is a big woman — her bosoms are the first thing you notice about her and the first time I met her I wanted to giggle as they wobbled under her dress. I wouldn't dare laugh though and wondered if she ever smiled. I was introduced to the other girls and wondered which one did the window dressing.

They weren't very friendly, and I longed for my old life. Mother told me to be prepared to feel lonely and I dismissed her as I had never before felt the pangs of loneliness. But in those first few days at The Hat Box I remembered her words. I was determined not to cry, telling myself that a Fairbrother does not give in. I held my shoulders back and my head high and found a working position in the right hand corner of the room where I could see the street from the single window. The view is different from the other side of Luton. Here there is considerably more construction happening and the noise of shouting tradesmen drifts through the open window. The girls find amusement in the conversations drifting through the windows and are quite sure much of it is meant for them.

The hours are long but the work is interesting and gradually the other *girls have taken me into their confidence, especially after I praised their craft. They take pride in their work and when a satisfied customer expresses delight in the intricate workings, they glow with satisfaction.*

Some of the women who order hats are exceedingly rich and live in houses like the manors back home. They have so many hats that they're never seen in the same one twice. I can't wait to write and tell them at home about the clientele we have. Ladies who have always been rich and those who have married rich men. I prefer the former as they are not trying to impress everyone, have always had money and accept that they are entitled to the best hats available.

To my surprise, Elsbeth has turned out to be quite a satisfactory roommate. She has been married but a great tragedy befell her. Her husband, Edmund, fell off a horse and contracted gangrene a few months after their wedding. He died a horrible death with Elsbeth by his side and since then she has developed a permanent sadness in her demeanour. She must have been quite old when she married as she would be close to 40 and her husband has only been dead two years.

After the tragedy she returned to her profession of millinery. Work is now her life and when I discovered that she was the one who did the window dressing, I was delighted. To think that this plain looking, drab dressing woman could produce such works of enticement.

Sometimes, on a Sunday, after church, we go to the tea rooms and just sit and chat. Considering our age difference, we manage to converse amazingly well. I feel guilty that I judged Elsbeth because of her appearance before getting to know what a courageous woman she is. I have never known suffering like Elsbeth has — to lose your husband, the love you expected to be with for the rest of your life and to have children with. This is beyond my imagination. If it happened to me, I would surely die.

"The pain stays with you, Jane, all the time but you learn to live with it and life happens through and around it. I am not the same person as I was before Edmund died but life can still be good. "

" But don't you want to marry again, Elsbeth," Perhaps this was insensitive of me. I hope I didn't offend her.

"I am happy with my work, Jane. I have no desire to marry again."

Elsbeth would become like some of my old aunts at home who never married. As children we would make fun of them. How childish that seems now. I still think I would die if something happened to MY Mr Rochester.

The daily grind of creating hats and bonnets has become routine. We work long hours and sometimes we're too tired to do anything but just fall into bed at night. I have learned about supply and demand and pricing. The wealthy of Luton care nothing for price, ordering what they want regardless. I find this hard to understand as one hat made for a lady from one of the manors of Luton would cost as much as my father needs to pay a worker for a month.

THOMAS — BAMAWM

Christmas Eve, 1913

I had forgotten about Elsbeth. She was a champion. I wonder what happened to her. Did I ever write to tell her about Jane? Probably not but she would have heard from Jane's sister I'm sure.

The boy asks me who Jane Austen is and I tell him that I don't think he would like her books. I can tell he likes my Jane though and the way she looks at life. He thinks I am a crotchety old man but I try to make him understand that I was young once and adventurous — bringing my wife and daughter on a sailing ship from England. He is fascinated and says he would like to go to sea. I tell him that ships are very different now from what they were in 1852, and when I explain what it was like for the passengers, and the number of shipwrecks, he looks at me as if I was mad, to risk our lives like that.

I tell him about the England that I left, a powerful, rich country that didn't look after its own. Landowners and industrialists who became rich on the backs of the labour of the poor. Even my own father had to pay a 'tax' to the Lord of the Manor to cross the green outside his house

He liked that story, after I told him what a 'green' was. He asked me if I had any brothers and sisters, as he has no family of his own – that he knows of. I told him I hadn't seen my family since I left England more than 60 years ago.

My brother, Johnny was four years older and Mary, a year older. Mary and I grew up as close companions while our father bestowed his attention on Johnny. It was Johnny who would accompany Father to the shop, Johnny who would learn how to kill a sheep, Johnny who would watch while Father strung up the carcass in the butcher shop on the circular hook which covered the perimeter of the room. It was Johnny who went to the sales with Father and chatted about the experience on his return.

I did not begrudge my brother and the closeness that he and Father experienced but I, too, wanted to make Father proud of me and he seemed not to notice me at all. He wanted me to go into the family business with Johnny. He could see the sign above the door, *Bradshaw & Sons*. I told him I really did not want to be a butcher and he was angry. I didn't like it when Father got angry because it didn't happen often.

After many arguments, however, he knew that there was no point in pushing me. He did not want an unwilling apprentice. I think my mother convinced him of that.

The new sign would be simply Bradshaw & Son!

The house we grew up in was known as 'The Butcher House.' It had a thatched roof and a staircase leading up to the bedrooms from which we could see towards Napton on the Hill, three miles away, past the twenty-five acres where my father grazed the sheep that would end up on the tables of the people of the village. He used to kill the sheep in the yard and I would come home from school and see the animal hanging from the hook in the front room. On the other hooks would hang assortments of meat, sausages, legs of lamb and it was nothing to walk under pounds of sausages towards the kitchen where Mother would be making a cake for tea or pastry to enfold the scraps from Father's sales.

My mother came from a village nearby, Woodford. Her father was a butcher too so it ran in the family. Not long after their wedding, Mother discovered she was carrying a child, my brother, Johnny. It seemed her life was perfect. Father worked hard and when Johnny came along, the villagers of Priors Marston got used to a toddler running round the butcher shop as they waited for their meat to be prepared. Little Johnny spent a great deal of time in the shop as Mother recovered from the miscarriages which beset her after Johnny's birth.

Two miscarriages and a still birth took their toll on Mother. She felt sad and wondered if they would have any more children. The birth of Mary, quickly followed by me in 1823 and 1824, restored her spirits somewhat but she was still sad. She didn't know what was wrong with her. She felt tired all the time and couldn't seem to enjoy anything anymore.

Mary and I grew close, like twins.

"I'm never going to be a butcher," I said to Mary one day as we walked to the Smithy to pick up a newly shod horse. "I don't want to spend the rest of my life here in this village."

I remember that day. I was about ten, I suppose. Mary had dark, brown hair plaited down her back and a mischievous turn of mouth. I thought she was the prettiest girl in the village.

"I would love to travel and see something of the world but I don't think it will happen," she said as she stretched to pick an apple off the nearby tree, took a bite and said, " I will probably marry Seth Brickhill and have 20 children and live unhappily ever after."

We both laughed as Seth Brickhill was a sad little boy that no-one would play with.

"But Thomas, you are a boy," continued Mary, "and boys can do whatever they want. You can do all sorts of exciting things, and you can write and tell me all about it so I can share your adventure."

"Well, wherever I go," I promised, "It will have plenty of sunshine, and I will write long letters to you and send you some of that sunshine."

She grinned, knowing that she would never move far away from where she now stood. I think she knew, however, that I would not be happy staying in Priors Marston.

I had always been good with my hands. I was never happier than when I was using old bits of wood to construct something useful.

Father, once he became resigned to my never becoming a butcher, arranged for a carpenter's apprenticeship in nearby Byfield. At least, he thought, I would become a skilled artisan.

Byfield was little more than three miles from Priors Marston, but I knew that an apprenticeship would be all consuming of my time and I would see very little of my family during that time. I was also fearful of how hard masters could be on boys studying a trade.

My friend, Edmond, had shown me a copy of the agreement he had to sign when he became apprenticed as a cobbler. I quoted part of it to the boy word for word:

The said apprentice shall serve his Master; his secrets keep. He shall not waste his Goods nor lend them. He shall not contract Matrimony within the said term. He shall not play at cards, dice, tables or any other unlawful games. He shall not haunt taverns or playhouses nor absent himself from his Master's Service, day or night, unlawfully.

The boy couldn't believe that I would agree to such conditions. It was a different world then. No doubt about it, the apprenticeship was hard and many times I felt like walking away. My master was tough and seemed anxious to break my spirit. I often wonder whether he enjoyed seeing me work to the point of exhaustion. I had no love for him nor he for me but I completed my apprenticeship and when I returned home to Priors Marston, I was no longer a boy. My sister, Mary, noticed the difference in me.

"Thomas," she said "you are quite grown up."

In my absence, we had written copious letters, telling each other the local news with me entertaining her with stories of the girls I had met although I had to keep their acquaintance secret from my Master. I never told her about the times when I would cry myself to sleep, nursing bruises from the beatings.

Mary had written about a man she had met, Richard Hyatt, not a local. He was from Addington in Gloucestershire and had moved to Charwelton to take up an offer of land. She thought him strong and handsome.

"You'd like him, Thomas," she said, "he likes to talk about 'things' and 'plans'. He's a dreamer like you."

I did like Richard, very much, and we enjoyed an easy friendship. It was he who suggested my move to Luton when work became scarce in Priors Marston.

"It's not far from London, Thomas, but a better place to live. I hear that they're crying out for good carpenters."

I knew he was right. It would be hard to leave Priors Marston, especially as Mary and Richard had just had a little boy, Robert, my godson, and my father and I were on better terms, but I needed to make money if I wanted to follow my dream of travelling.

"You know, Father," said Marriott who was still on the veranda with us, "I have never heard about your time in England. All these years, I never knew that your father was a butcher."

I told him there was a lot about me he didn't know.

JANE — LUTON
April, 1848

Wait till you hear what this next chapter is about. The novel (and my life) is getting interesting.

Today, I met a man who may just be my Mr Rochester. What do you think about that? I have been walking round the house dreaming of him. He is taller than me, that wouldn't be hard, and has the most beautiful wavy hair. His eyes are blue and ever so cheeky. He has huge hands, not surprising I suppose for a builder, but they are kind hands. Does that sound stupid?

I met him as I was walking to work this morning. It was raining, nothing unusual for Luton, and I knew the puddles and mud to avoid on my walk which is so familiar by now. I test myself on which building is around the corner and memorise my surroundings. I'm sure I could reconstruct them exactly if I were asked to and any change to a building, like a painted door or sign in the window, I notice immediately.

Luton is alive with new boarding houses catering for the many new people arriving looking for work. Some of these houses look rather inauspicious and I wonder that unscrupulous landlords are taking advantage of the newcomers. It makes me grateful for our humble but satisfactory rooms.

But I digress and want to return to my meeting with this most handsome of men.

The new Town Hall is the talk of the city. It will reflect the grandeur of the town and is due to be finished in less than a year. Everyone is aghast at the magnificence of it. Inside will be County Courts, a Savings Bank, and a hall used for public lectures or concerts. We can't wait to see it finished.

"You're early, Miss" a voice said, "I thought I was the only one to start at the crack of dawn."

I knew where the voice came from and knew I shouldn't respond. The women at The Hat Shop had been complaining about the remarks made to them on their way to work by the labourers, some which are nasty and crude. I didn't know who this man was but at least he had not insulted me. Instead of ignoring him and walking on, I turned and looked at him. Did I know him? There was something familiar about him. I decided to stop and engage in conversation. My mother would be disgusted.

"I start early," I offered, "I make hats." I wondered why I added that last bit.

"Do you fix them as well?" He was turning his cap in circles.

"Not at the shop," I said, "but I could do it at home. What's wrong with your hat?" I think I may have been flirting as I wiggled my hips a little as I spoke to him. Was that wrong?

"It's my cap. It's come away from the lining and I feel lost without it. Could I give it to you to fix? I'll pay you of course."

I could not believe that I agreed to fix his cap. What had come over me? Don't worry, I told myself, It's just a job and I'll accept his payment. But I knew it wasn't 'just a job' and I continued to flirt. My feet were rooted on the spot and I didn't want to leave him.

He seemed so confident. Yes, that was what it was. He exuded a confidence that was nigh impossible to resist.

"All right, give it to me and I'll see what I can do."

He smiled as he placed his cap into my hands. There was something about his smile that I still can't identify, almost as if he had won a victory.

I will fix his silly cap but I can't wait until I see him tomorrow morning. Maybe I am making something out of nothing but he is very handsome and he seems most agreeable.

I can't wait till tomorrow. Oh, I hope I can sleep.

THOMAS — BAMAWM
Christmas Eve, 1913

The boy asked me if I remembered that day. He was settling in for the long haul. Marriott had reluctantly left to prepare dinner and there were just the two of us and the ghostly presence of Jane.

Of course I remembered that day. It was like the world had opened a new door and it was filled with bright lights. I had not been long in Luton and was on an early shift. I watched this woman walking past, hurrying, maybe late for work. I know that woman I told myself. She's a Fairbrother from Byfield. I wonder what she is doing here.

I had seen her years ago in Byfield when I did some work with her brothers on their farm. I thought then that she was pretty, quite small, with long dark hair and smooth, almost olive skin. I remembered the rumours about her mother, Maria, and how she had gypsy blood. There was a scandal when she got pregnant and married William Fairbrother thereby incurring the disapproval of his family. They said she had 'trapped' him into marriage.

Although Jane was small, she walked with a resolute stride, as if she were ready to take on the world. I wanted desperately to talk to her and I devised a plan for us to meet. The next morning, as she walked past, I just happened to be in her path. We almost bumped into each other.

I concocted some story about my cap coming to pieces and she agreed to fix it for me. Did she recognise me as the boy who worked with her brothers? I wasn't sure. But my plan worked. I went home that night with a spring in my step.

The next morning she gave me my repaired cap. I suspected that she may have guessed my strategy but she didn't let on. She accepted my money and turned to go to work. Go on, Thomas, I said to myself, make your move. I was about to speak when she halted her step and looked at me."

"I feel as if I know you," she said. "Have we met before?"

I introduced myself. "Thomas Bradshaw, from Priors Marston. I did some work with your brothers last year."

She seemed pleased. And that was the beginning. We talked and talked until she realised she would be late for work and hurried off but not before we had arranged to go on a picnic on Sunday, chaperoned of course by her room-mate, Elsbeth. For the rest of that day, I couldn't stop thinking about her. She was a local girl, she was pretty, she was easy to talk to and she seemed to like me.

Maybe…just maybe!

The boy smiled. Perhaps he saw in me a reflection of that young lad who decided to talk to a pretty girl.

JANE — LUTON

April, 1848

The chapters are getting more and more interesting. And so is my life. At this rate I won't have to make anything up!

At work I could think of nothing else but my 'Mr Rochester.' He has asked me to have a picnic with him on Sunday. I can't believe it. He has a name, Thomas Bradshaw and he is a Priors Marston Bradshaw. We are practically neighbours!

This morning he was there waiting as I came past. I decided to act very matter of fact, as a decent woman of breeding would. I held my head high and strode past in a decisive way. Some of the girls and I have practised this walk. It's meant to make men curious.

"Ah, my saviour," he said and I could hear the smile in his voice. "Have you fixed my cap?"

"There was not really anything wrong with it that you couldn't have fixed yourself," I said as I handed him his cap and took his payment. I was tempted to charge him nothing but I didn't want him to owe me anything.

"I'm good at building Town Halls," he said, "but useless with a needle and thread."

He was about to say more when I spoke.

"I feel as if I know you, sir. Have we met before?"

He seemed pleased that I was prolonging the conversation.

"Indeed we have, Miss Fairbrother, my name is Thomas Bradshaw."

Then it came to me. He was an apprentice carpenter at Byfield and had worked with my brothers. My heart gave a flutter. He remembered me and knew my name even though I had only met him once or twice.

"Of course," I said, "You are from Priors Marston. Your father is a butcher!"

"Yes," he said, "and your father is a farmer and your mother a great cook!"

Once I knew he was from home, I relaxed. I don't know why but it was almost as if he were family. Some of the people I have met here in Luton seem to be from a different planet. They don't understand my humour or my way of speaking.

It was so easy talking with him. He told me that my mother used to bring tea and cake to the fields where he worked with my brothers. He said he never had the same cake twice. Good old Mother. She loves feeding the workers and she is a good cook.

"I think sometimes Mother finds it hard being a Fairbrother. Cooking and sewing have been her way to acceptance."

Thomas laughed. He knew exactly what I was saying.

"It's a bit like that being a Bradshaw," he said. "That's one good thing about the city. No-one knows you from Adam."

The time flew as we exchanged so much of our lives and our feelings about coming from a small village. With much chagrin I realised I would be late for work if I didn't cut short the conversation. As it was, the workers were arriving with their bagged lunches and banter. If I stayed any longer I would be subject to their comments and considering myself a lady of breeding, I told him I had to go.

"So you're being a real Fairbrother now," he mocked, but he understood that I was uncomfortable. He suggested a picnic on Sunday with my roommate, Elsbeth whom he had seen with me sometimes.

"Have you been spying on me Mr Bradshaw?"

"Yes," he said cheekily, "and please call me Thomas, Mr Bradshaw sounds like my father."

Having Elsbeth as a chaperone would mean that we could get to know each other better. I only hoped that Elsbeth would agree. It wasn't much fun being the chaperone to two people who might want to be alone.

"A picnic would be lovely," I paused, "Thomas. I will ask Elsbeth tonight and let you know tomorrow morning, and my name is Jane."

"Until tomorrow morning, Jane," he said and touched his newly stitched cap.

I noticed no buildings from that point until I reached The Hat Box. I must have walked in with a smile on my face as the other girls teased me in their good natured way as we were all sensitive to the ups and downs of each other's romantic aspirations. I don't remember much about the rest of the day in The Hat Box except that on my walk home, the dreary weather seemed to give way to rays of sunshine.

Elsbeth has agreed to our picnic plans. She is such a darling. She tells me that she wants me to meet someone as life can be very lonely when there is no-one special in your life. Some women would be bitter after life had dealt them such a blow but Elsbeth is not one of them. My opinion of her goodness continues to soar. I can't wait till Sunday.

THOMAS — BAMAWM
Christmas Eve, 1913

The boy had never heard of Luton. Well, why would he? England is as far away from him as the moon. The only city he knows is Bendigo. He's never even been to Melbourne! When he asked me if Bendigo was like Luton, I laughed at him. "Nothing like it son," I said, "nothing at all."

To a boy from Priors Marston, Luton was a shock! Cities are cold places and I missed the friendliness of home where people knew me and where I belonged. At the same time, it was freeing, being a nobody.

I worked hard and was able to save a bit of money. Some of the men wasted their money on gambling and brothels, but not me. I wanted to travel and travelling meant money. Each week, I would deposit money in the Luton Savings Bank and watch it grow.

The boy understood this. Unlike many his age, he doesn't waste his money.

Meeting Jane was an antidote to the misery of the city, the dirtiness, crowding and shameful acts of indecency. I shiver when I think of the poverty and the misery of that city. It was like those early days in Melbourne, the crowded conditions and lack of sanitation. The villages were emptying into the cities; the crime was out of control and the conditions were appalling.

While I was in Luton, millions were starving in Ireland and the influx of poor, Irish migrants, especially to the northern cities of Liverpool and Manchester created ill-feeling amongst people. The immigrants didn't worry me but the newspapers were full of anti-Irish sentiments. I thought the newspapers unjust as England was not blameless in the cause of the Irish Famine, but I was careful where I voiced my sentiments.

The boy knew all about the prejudice against the Irish. He was Irish himself and had been called all kinds of names. He said that he was quite old before he realised that his name wasn't really Paddy!

"They're taking our jobs," was the cry in England with little or no sympathy for their plight. Workers were angry and finding their voices against everyone really, the Irish, the factory owners and especially the land owners.

The boy gets impatient when I stray into politics in my raving. He wants to get back to the story of Jane and me.

The picnic with Jane was a great success. It was Spring and the Common was in its full splendour. Elsbeth, whom I was nervous about, was delightful company and I could tell she had a good brain. I brought a bottle of local cheap wine, thinking she might disapprove, but she accepted a glass willingly.

"Do you read, Mr Bradshaw?" She wasn't so much testing me as curious.

"When I can, but to tell you the truth, I'm so tired when I get home that I haven't the energy."

"Well, why don't you two sit down on the grass and I will read to you. I have the latest edition of *Bentley's Miscellany* with a chapter of Mr Dicken's *Oliver Twist*."

Elsbeth was quite the presenter. Between sips of the wine, she play acted Mr Dickens making us giggle at her renditions of Mr Bumble and The Artful Dodger. I think she enjoyed herself immensely. I had not read Dickens before and loved it. The clever and humorous way he presented English society opened my eyes to the many injustices surrounding us. Perhaps I loved it even more, as I got to sit side by side with Jane, our hands finding each other, making my heart beat fast and when Elsbeth took a break from reading to go for a walk, we kissed. It was magic.

I saw the boy squirm in his seat. I don't think he could ever imagine me kissing anyone. I'm surprised I even mentioned it.

Our picnics became a regular event with Elsbeth insisting on reading. It suited us and I think she knew that. Dickens was the favourite but other times she would read Jane Austen and I must admit I am not a fan and would stop listening to the ballroom antics of the upper class and dream of the woman I was with, on the Luton Common.

Later, here in Australia, I would read the serialised story of *For the Term of his Natural Life* by Marcus Clarke in the *Australian Journal* to my grandson William. He loved it so much I lent him my copy of *Oliver Twist* which he devoured. He couldn't wait for the latest edition of *The Bulletin* for the bush poetry section. He would memorise it and recite it as he went about his work on the farm. He had a memory like an elephant, that boy.

Elsbeth's walks lengthened in duration. It was like a game. We all knew the rules. Jane and I explored each other more and more, relishing the hours we spent together, both of us knowing that we never wanted to be parted.

The boy looks up from his reading. He is enjoying it, I can tell. I think Jane's diary is the first romantic book he has ever read. He's usually not interested in any books except those on farming and machinery.

JANE — LUTON
April, 1848

Who needs to imagine romance when it is happening to you in real life. My life is better than any Jane Austen or Currer Bell novel.

These past few days have been so wonderful. O dear God, have I met the man of my dreams? Is it too good to be true?

Thomas was there waiting for me the day after I gave him his hat and he looked pleased to see me. He reminded me that I had agreed to picnic with him on Sunday.

"I will bring the bread and cheese," he said, "and you can bring something sweet."

"All right," I said wondering what I could make. I am not the cook my mother is.

"And I'll bring the ginger beer," he said as he helped me over the construction area.

"What if it rains?" I said hoping against hope that it would be a pleasant day.

"Then I will bring the sunshine as well," he said and we both laughed.

It was a wonderful picnic and I doubt if I shall ever forget it. It didn't rain. Instead it was an unusually sunny day. Was that an omen? I made a Bakewell pie which turned out rather well. To my great surprise, Thomas and Elsbeth liked each other, enjoying talking about the unrest in England. Elsbeth can talk about such things whereas I am ignorant when it comes to world issues. The two of them seemed to agree about everything so I just leant against a chestnut tree and felt happy that these two special people in my life, as I know Thomas will be, could be friends.

"This isn't ginger beer!" I said as I tasted the drink he gave me

"It's wine," he said.

I didn't like it but didn't want to tell Thomas that. I had never tasted wine before and know nothing about it, being a Fairbrother, a family of teetotallers.

"I want to grow my own grapes and make the best wine in England." He declared enthusiastically.

He has a zest for life which I have never met before. When he speaks of agriculture and the economy and the many problems Britain is facing, it's describing a world I have never thought about. It's as if he is standing on the edge of the world ready to take the plunge into its bottomless ocean. He is intoxicating.

"Is it hard to grow grapes?" I said weakly, anxious to show interest as I surreptitiously tipped the wine under the nearby tree and covered the red stain with leaves. Thomas took one look at my feigned expression, chose not to answer the question and moved in so close to me that my heart screamed in response.

"Your cheeks are red," he said mischievously, "Is it something you ate?"

I couldn't speak as his two hands embraced my face and he kissed me.

The kiss. It's with me still, a moment stopped in time. It penetrated my soul, my whole being. I am flying, on a cloud. Nothing can make me feel ordinary again.

I don't remember even packing up after we had finished eating. I don't remember anything after that, except Thomas' eyes as we parted from the kiss. I was floating.

As Elsbeth and I walked home from the picnic, I risked asking her what she thought of Thomas, nervous that I might be disappointed with the answer. I knew she liked him but that didn't mean she thought he would make a good husband. "He's a man who is too big for Luton," she said. "Probably even too big for England."

THOMAS — BAMAWM

Christmas Eve, 1913

I chuckled as the boy read about Jane tipping her wine under the tree and covering it up. I had no idea she had done that. I suppose I should have realised that a well bred girl like her would not have been used to wine.

The boy wasn't impressed with the sentimental parts of Jane's diary. He liked girls but I knew he found it hard to talk to them. I hoped he would find a girl just like Jane one day and then he would know what it is like to surrender your whole self to another person so that you feel incomplete without them.

For Jane and me, the Spring and Summer of 1848 was a magical time, walking in the meadows, picnicking on the Common, swapping childhood stories, comparing dreams and ignoring the growing unrest we saw around us every day.

I knew that Jane was the woman I wanted to spend the rest of my life with. I loved everything about her, the way she walked, her head on the side when she asked a question, her olive complexion but most of all her warmth. When I was with her, it was as if nothing bad could ever happen and I knew she thought I was wonderful. What a feeling that is, to know that someone sees only the good in you.

I wanted to protect her for the rest of my life, and hers. Oh, if only I had known!

Some months after we met, we were walking home from a play that we had gone to see with some of the girls from her work. As we passed the Town Hall where we had first met, I pulled her into the laneway where we couldn't be seen. We kissed and with my arms strongly around her waist, I was going to ask her to marry me but some of the girls came up behind us and the moment just wasn't right. It would have to wait.

It wasn't until the following Sunday that the moment presented itself and I nervously asked her if she would become my wife.

I don't think she was surprised.

"Yes, Thomas, I will marry you," she blushed and giggled at the same time, then gave me a short peck on the lips. "Can we do it today?"

We both laughed in delight.

"It will have to be in Luton," I said, "I can't get time off work to go back home."

For a second, I thought I saw a look of disappointment on her face but after a pause, she said,

"I don't care if it's in the stables, Thomas. I am just so happy."

St Mary's Luton it was. According to the rites of the Church of England, wedding banns were to be publicised at three consecutive morning services in the local church, before we were free to marry. This was to give people the opportunity to declare any impediment. It was usually just a formality, but as we sat in the pew of St Mary's listening to our names being read from the pulpit, we had to stifle a giggle.

"Wouldn't it be funny," she whispered, "if someone stood up and protested against our coming wedding like they did in Jane Eyre."

"How could they," I replied, a little too loudly, "when we are such perfect people?"

The woman in front of us turned with a disapproving scowl and we hung our heads to stop from laughing. I was happy to marry in St Mary's. I loved its cruciform design and the fact that it had been added to so tastefully over the centuries. I admired the sheer audacity of such a magnificent building and enjoyed pointing out various features to Jane as she sat beside me towards the back of the Church. I don't think she was all that interested in the architecture but at least she listened to my ravings and made appropriate comments.

I do miss those ancient buildings. I grow tired of the makeshift, new buildings around here, in Rochester and Bamawm although I felt privileged to have worked on some of the more beautiful and more solid buildings in Melbourne which will stand the test of time. The Town Hall in South Melbourne looks magnificent and last time I was there I felt a pride to have been involved in its building.

But I am rambling and the boy is looking at me in that quizzical way of his. He is seeing a different side of Thomas Bradshaw, that's to be sure. Once I would have felt uneasy about this, but somehow I am glad. I have an inexplicable need for this boy to know who I am.

JANE — LUTON
February, 1849

I am now Mrs Thomas Bradshaw. Doesn't that sound marvellous? Ever since I started this pursuit of writing, life has been magnificent.

I have not written in this diary for so long because I have been blissfully happy and there has been so much to do. I cannot believe it is only eight months since I met Thomas and now we are husband and wife.

How do I sum up the last eight months? I just read over my last entry about our first picnic and our first kiss. I thought then that Thomas and I were meant for each other. It's like we were two stars in the universe coming together, having spent our whole lives searching for the other.

We had picnics every week until the weather changed. Sometimes his friends or my friends would join us and we would have quite a party. Thomas continued to bring his bottle of wine but I finally felt comfortable enough with him to tell him that I didn't like it.

"All the more for me," he said as his friends tossed down the local ale. Not many of them liked wine either and they used to tease him about his 'strange tastes.' Some of them drank too much and became very loud. I didn't like that as I had grown up disapproving of people who couldn't hold their drink.

I never saw Thomas drink too much. He savoured the wine, drinking slowly, and I respected him for that. We would find ingenious ways to be alone. I enjoyed the kisses very much but I was nervous that Thomas wanted more. I kept thinking about my mother giving birth to me a few months after they married. She told me the story and warned me against it happening to me.

"Your father had to marry me," she told me not long before I left home, "and the people in the village condemned me, not him but me. It's taken years for me to be accepted, especially as I am an outsider."

It was hard not to give in to Thomas. I felt mean and just hoped the wedding day would hurry up. It was our last outdoor picnic. The leaves were beginning to change on the oak trees near our picnic spot. They were red, yellow and orange with a few stubborn green completing the kaleidoscope of colour. The light was fading and it would not be long before darkness closed in. All our friends had long gone and we were alone.

Thomas poured me a drop of red wine and just as I began to say I didn't want it, he put a finger to my lips.

"This moment, Jane, I want you to share everything with me. Please?"

Suddenly I knew what was coming and I could hardly breathe.

"Jane Fairbrother," he was holding both my hands, kneeling beside me, "Will you marry me?"

I remembered Elsbeth's words about him being too big for England but did not hesitate. I would go to the ends of the earth with this man.

"Yes, Thomas, of course I will marry you."

Thomas Bradshaw, my Mr Rochester.

Was it Thomas who pulled me into the shadows of the nearby oak or was it I who pulled him. It didn't matter. We were entwined in each other's ecstasy, our bodies shouting for joy. I knew Thomas wanted to consummate our union then and there and, yes, I wanted it too, but we had come this far, I had to be the strong one. My mother's words were ringing in my ear.

I told Elsbeth everything when I got home. She had been worried about me, out after dark and searched my face for any evidence of impropriety.

"Thomas makes me feel as if I can do anything, Elsbeth. I never believed it possible to be this happy."

I think Elsbeth is sick of me talking about how wonderful he is, although I know she is fond of him.

"I'm very happy for you both, Jane, I know you'll be very happy."

Was there a hint of sadness in her voice? Oh how insensitive I am not to think that our love would be hard to witness for someone who had lost love so violently.

"Elsbeth, you are my truest friend and I love you very much."

We sat in the kitchen for what seemed like hours and we talked. Not about Thomas this time. Just two girlfriends swapping stories and laughing. It was late when we finally went to bed. My last thought before I closed my eyes in sleep was of the drop of red wine and how it stayed in my glass the whole time until we were packing up. I grabbed it and tossed it down my throat thinking, If he's going to make wine, I had better learn to like it!

I had not known that Thomas had returned to Byfield to ask my father for permission to marry his daughter. We were both old enough not to need permission but for both of us, family approval was important.

"Your father thinks it a good idea that I take you off his hands," said Thomas as he playfully grabbed me on the grass after the proposal.

"Maybe I'll be one of those wives who makes their husbands give up all pleasures."

"I'd like to see you try."

It was banter, meaning nothing as Thomas didn't have any sinful pleasures and I wasn't the type of woman to dominate anyone, let alone a strong man like Thomas. But it did make me wonder how well we knew each other and wonder if he would he always be so considerate and loving.

Initially I was disappointed that we couldn't marry in Byfield, being a bride in my home village with all my girlfriends and family there, but I knew it wasn't possible and didn't dwell on it.

It was a blissful time preparing for the wedding. In November, Thomas and I went to St Mary's to listen to our wedding banns being read out for the third time. He kept talking to me about the architecture of the church until I told him to be quiet as people around us were looking disapprovingly.

I always feel small in churches and although I appreciate the magnificence of St Mary's, I find it intimidating. During the sermon which droned on, I pictured myself walking down the aisle in my wedding dress towards Thomas waiting for me at the altar. I was in a white dress similar to those I have seen in the shop windows of the bridal shops on Lancrets Path. My hair was swept upon my head with a hat made by my friends at The Hat Box and on my feet were the most beautiful silver shoes.

I knew the reality would not be so grand but there was no harm in dreaming. I wondered how many other young couples had been married in this centuries old church and whether they had all been as full of hope as we were. Where were they now? I thought of the weedy cemetery outside with the names of the dead fading on the local stone. This thought sent an involuntary shiver through me which made Thomas turn in response. I smiled at him and he smiled back. You silly girl, I thought, just enjoy what you have at this moment.

The day of the wedding finally came. I thought it never would. My girlfriends fussed about me and when I looked at myself in the mirror, I couldn't believe plain old Jane Fairbrother looked like the bride of my dreams.

The church bells rang. I walked to the church on a carpet of blossom which Elsbeth had laid from the road to the front door of St Mary's, ensuring a happy path through life, a custom I loved. My two milliner friends from my apprenticeship days, the two Elizabeth's had designed my bonnet which everyone commented on. It was exquisite, green and gold with a black, velvet ribbon. My dress was one my mother had worn, decorated with a white ribbon, flowers and silver leaves. Truly it was a wonderful moment.

The sun shone on us even though it was December. Jane Austen or Jane Eyre would have been jealous that day of Jane Fairbrother.

PART ONE   THOMAS BRADSHAW & JANE FAIRBROTHER

England and Ireland might be in a Depression but Thomas Bradshaw and his new wife are ready to take on the world.

THOMAS — BAMAWM
Christmas Eve, 1913

The boy said he is not going to get married and have children. That doesn't surprise me. He hasn't had the best experiences in life. I know he likes Jane by the way he smiles as he reads. I wish he'd met her.

That year, 1848, was the happiest I have ever been in my life. I spent every minute I could with Jane and we planned our lives together. We talked about the children we would have and the places we would go. As we strolled along the Green, our happiness was complete. The world was collapsing around us but we were happy.

When I look back to that time, I wonder that life is merciful and allows you those moments when you don't know what is around the corner. The dark places, the grief and the ongoing sorrow. I wonder about the boy. What is round the corner for him?

For nigh on sixty years, I have survived on the memory of that year. Certainly there were good times later, not least another marriage, a son, a new beginning as a farmer, grand-children and a new community here in Bamawm. But I have never come close to that happiness I felt with Jane and I have never come close to the sorrow I felt when she died.

I asked the boy to get me a book from my room and when he returned I showed him a picture of St Mary's and explained to him about the cruciform and various other aspects of this most wonderful church. I thought he would be interested as he has a builder's eye.

But to him, churches have nothing to recommend them. They remind him of when they were 'herded', yes that's the word he used, 'herded,' into churches and belted if they spoke or couldn't repeat what the priest said in the sermon. The orphanage must have been horrible.

I was surprised how much I enjoyed the wedding. Because it was in Luton and we didn't have most of our family present, I thought it would be over and done with and we would just get on with our lives. Jane's mother and sister made the journey and so, too, my mother. I missed Mary and Richard who couldn't attend but many of my work chums turned up after work and we adjourned to *The Fox and Hounds* where we celebrated well into the night.

Jane and I became husband and wife that night and the world could have slipped off its axis and we wouldn't have noticed. The shyness we felt with each other quickly dissipated and we became as one. It was what we both had longed for and as we lay in each other's arms we wondered if it were possible to die of happiness.

She was everything I hoped for in a wife. Beautiful, funny, adventurous, cheeky and most of all, she loved me. The next day, my head ached and as I dragged myself out of bed, I made two resolutions: firstly that I would do everything in my power to provide for Jane and secondly that the wine I made would be a hell of a lot better than the wine we had at the wedding!

JANE — LUTON
June, 1850

I didn't think much beyond the wedding day. I wonder if many girls do. My unhappiness and loneliness took me by surprise. When I told Thomas that we were going to have a child, he was overjoyed and I have to admit I was excited also, but the excitement has been tempered by my sickness. I have lost weight and can't seem to hold any food down at all.

My marriage meant the end of my work at The Hat Box and I missed it terribly. I missed the girls. We would talk about our designs and creations and how lucky we were to make the most adorable hats for the wealthy women of the city. Every Monday morning, we would gush over Elsbeth's newest window decoration and every Saturday afternoon we would remind Mrs Allen that the clock had already struck three and it was time to close!

I liked Luton then. I thought it exciting but now that I have finished work, what once was exciting now seems tedious and unsafe. I have grown tired of it and long to be back in Byfield. This is not the place to bring up children. The noise and crime of the city, together with the horror of another cholera outbreak such as we have just had, fills me with dread. We all know people who were fit one day and fatally ill the next, and many were young and strong. The opening of the new cemetery on the north of the town boundary is a horrible testament to the death toll.

I could bear all this but the distance that seemed to have grown between Thomas and myself, I could not bear. The foreman has been pushing his men to finish the Town Hall and I have hardly seen Thomas *in the last few months. He hardly talked when he came home, ate and went to bed.*

BUT

Today I am like a nightingale that wants to sing her song of joy over the rooftops of Luton. All because of what happened last night.

I heard Thomas coming up the stairs and I thought it would be another night ending with me feeling disappointed and guilty as has been my wont of late. I have given up preparing imaginative meals as he hardly seems to notice so there was just potted pork and potatoes on the table. The sight of it turned my stomach.

Imagine my surprise when as soon as he was through the door, he pulled me close to him and said he had something to say.

"I have been thinking, Jane. The building on the Town Hall is coming to a close and the word around some of the chaps from Northampton is that they are desperate for good skilled workers to work on the railways in Banbury. The tracks will eventually go through Chipping Warden and Woodford so they need structures to be built down the line. It would mean we would be living closer to our families. What do you think? "

He said he had been worried about me, getting so thin and that I needed country air and fresh fruit and vegetables.

"And some of my father's meat," he added.

I hugged him tight. I had thought he had not noticed my unhappiness. Now I know he does care for me.

"Thomas," I kissed him, soaking him with my tears, "you do love me?"

"How could you doubt it, Jane. You ae everything to me and I want you to be happy."

Life is so strange. While I condemned Thomas for his lack of sympathy, he was working out ways to make me happy.

For the first time in months, last night, we talked excitedly about the future and the things we looked forward to such as having family around to support us and our coming child, living closer to Mary and

Richard and their two young children, and being closer to our childhood friends, people who have always known us.

"I want our children to know their cousins, Thomas, especially Mary and Richard's children. I like Mary, she isn't stuffy like John and Georgina."

Thomas laughed. The thought of his older brother being 'stuffy' was amusing as he didn't think he was anything like that.

"Dinner with the Bradshaws means a freshly killed lamb, with all the trimmings."

"Dinner with the Fairbrothers means pear and apple dumplings," I laughed

"This baby will be the fattest baby in all the universe, " said Thomas patting my tummy.

I climbed into my bed rejoicing that we had recaptured the magic of that first picnic.

THOMAS — BAMAWM

Christmas Eve, 1913

The boy couldn't believe that although I had noticed Jane's failing health, I hadn't noticed her loneliness. He would have. He observes things like that, just as he has worked out that I need someone to talk to. He knows what it's like to be lonely. He asked me if the child Jane was having was Sarah. I told him it was.

I was overjoyed about the coming baby and hoped it would be a son called Marriott after my mother's family. My father would expect me to call it Thomas or John but I was always close to Grandfather Marriott and thought I would honour him by calling our son after him. If it were a girl, however, we would not be stopping at one and the name would keep. Becoming a father was a responsibility. It changed everything.

The thought of bringing up a child in Luton, in our cramped lodgings, surrounded by squalor and unrest was not an appealing one. I wanted him to grow up in the village, with his grandparents and cousins. I wanted him to breathe fresh air and to eat good food.

I know I should have talked to Jane and told her of my thoughts and misgivings but since she finished at *The Hat Box*, she had changed and lost some of her spark. She told me she missed the other girls but I'm afraid I wasn't too sympathetic. Wasn't I enough? After all, wasn't this what women did? Looked after their husbands, and the house and had babies? Jane seemed to be constantly sick and listless. Wasn't child bearing supposed to be natural?

"My sister, Mary, was never sick when she was carrying children," I said rather cruelly to her one day. "Maybe you're giving in to yourself too much." I remember the hurt look on her face. She muttered something about all woman not being the same but I know how hurt she was. Sitting here sixty years later, I do regret that.

My work on the Town Hall was coming to a close so I asked around about other work. "They need skilled workers on the railways near Banbury," said the foreman who was purring with pride at the completed Town Hall. "Woodford is preparing to be part of the venture so you could try there. It's close to home isn't it?"

Woodford would be perfect. My mother's family was there and so, too, some of Jane's relatives. It was only a few miles from Priors Marston and also from Charwelton where Mary and Richard lived. I knew I would have no trouble getting work.

I didn't want to tell Jane until I was assured of employment. It didn't take long, however, as the foreman mentioned me to a friend who was visiting. "So you're from that district, are you? We try to get locals as they don't just up and disappear like itinerants."

I told him of the forthcoming baby and the desire to return home.

"You're hired," said the contact with a shake of the hand, pleased he had snared a good carpenter. "You start in two weeks."

Jane's reaction to the news surprised me. She hugged me so tightly that I couldn't breathe. I had no idea that she missed Byfield so much, and later, while we were having supper, she told me how lonely she had been with me working such long hours and her not really knowing anyone except the girls at work who had simply gone on with their own lives without her. As I glanced around the tiny room, I began to see things from her point of view. Would I like to be cooped up here for most of the day, only getting out for the time it took to go to the market and back?

I was glad I was born a man.

JANE – WOODFORD
March 1852

When I first started writing my story, I had imagined it as straight forward and like a fairy tale. But life is not like that. I have discovered things about myself that I would never have believed when I first started out. Then, life was uncomplicated and I just drifted in my own little world. But everything has changed. So much to write about. So much.

I am a mother! Can you believe that? We have a little girl called Sarah. Thomas wanted a strong biblical name and I liked the sound of it, so Sarah it is. I am writing this while Sarah is playing around my feet. The feeling of love I have as I look at her pert, little face catches me by surprise. I want to pick her up and hold her close, feel her squirming in my arms in a desire to get down and keep exploring.

I hear my own mother in the kitchen preparing a meal for us. Yes, that's right, we are home, back in Woodford and I am surrounded by familiar places and people. It makes me realise how lonely I was in Luton. We are living in the newer part of Woodford. The villagers have named it Hinton. Grandfather bequeathed this house to Father when he died in 1838 and since the tenants recently gave notice, Father permitted us to lease the cottage as long as Thomas did some work on its upkeep. I love it. It is small but warm and cosy. And it is ours!

Sarah is fifteen months old, walking and trying to say some words. She says 'Mama' and 'Papa' and each time I pick her up from her cot, I long for the smiles she gives me. She is a delight. From the time she wakes until her sleep time, she is on the move, running and jumping and laughing at everything.

Who does she look like? She has my colouring and the way she holds her mouth is like me. But I suspect she might have Thomas' personality, the curiosity she has about everything.

Childbirth was different from what I expected. I was scared. I had known of women who had died having children. Would that happen to me? Could God be so cruel as to take me away from Thomas? I kept telling myself that it was natural to feel frightened and because I was healthy and under the care of the best midwives in Warwickshire, nothing bad could happen to me.

Well I didn't die, but the pain was like nothing I have ever experienced. I didn't really know what was happening and must admit, I was frightened. I felt like I was going to break in two. The midwife didn't say much but Mother was with me and kept mopping my brow and saying. "It will all be over soon, Jane." Just when I thought I couldn't take any more, the head showed and our Sarah made her entrance — healthy and beautiful. What a moment it is when you hold your child for the first time. I have done something magical, I thought, something magnificent.

Thomas was working nearby and I knew when he heard the news that it was a girl, he would be disappointed but from the time he entered the house and held Sarah, his pride in his daughter was pleasing to behold. He was so happy. I suppose he had been worried also. I don't think I will ever forget that moment, with the two of us hovering over a tiny bundle wrapped within an inch of her life. We looked at each other and Thomas smiled.

"We're a family now," he said. "We have another little person to take care of." He couldn't take his eyes off her and the way he looked at me made me feel as if I had performed a miracle. "Thankyou."

I don't know what it's like for other women but for me, the time following Sarah's birth is a bit of a blur. That's why I haven't written in my diary. Every day is filled with feeding, bathing, washing and cooking. I climb into bed in the evening wondering if I could possibly feel more exhausted and if this feeling of tiredness would ever end.

I thank God that Sarah is a good baby and sometimes I just sit on the floor with her and play. She loves it and so do I. It is our special time together and I hope I will always remember how special it is. My mother thinks I spoil her but I don't care. She is the one shining light amongst all the drudgery.

My body has healed completely and I am able to go for walks around the village with Sarah in the pram, even managing to push it up the hill to the main street where I meet other young mothers doing their shopping. Sometimes she begs me to let her walk but the hill is so steep, she doesn't last long. Thomas' cousin Alfred Marriott runs the butcher shop there and loves to see Sarah. He gives her titbits to chew on while he serves his customers and she loves it.

The village is bursting at the seams with the railway buildings popping up anew and filling with workers. Alfred is happy. He sells as much meat as he can kill. I like it too. It brings in different people from all over England, making for a bit more variety than usual, although there are some undesirable elements as well and we try to steer clear of them.

It's eighteen months since we left Luton. Without doubt, it was the right thing to do and after that night when Thomas said we were coming home, I presumed we had turned a corner in the way we treated each other and everything would be back to the way it was when we first met.

Was I naïve? Is any marriage like that?

After the initial joy of Sarah's birth, Thomas again seemed to drift apart from me. I thought I was imagining it and gave myself a good talking to but I couldn't help feeling sad. He seemed to lose interest in me. That night in Luton, he pledged never again to keep anything from me but I knew something was worrying him. What is it about menfolk that they can't seem to tell you what's wrong?

Of course I never discussed how I felt with him as I thought it was all in my head. Sometimes, the black cloud would descend upon me and I felt like a butterfly trapped in a cage. Did Jane Eyre ever feel like this after she had married Mr Rochester? I tried to remember the good times and looked forward to the time when I could tell Sarah the story of how Thomas and I met and the trick he played on me with his cap. I dreamed of filling her head with lovely stories and taking her to Luton to show her where we married.

It all came to a head last Saturday night when we visited Mary and Richard in Charwelton. I was very much looking forward to a night away and talking to Mary, whom I love like a sister. There was a parish census and we all had a giggle filling out the forms trying to remember where we were born and how old the children were. I am sure there is a lot of inaccurate information on those forms, especially after partaking of Richard's home brew.

Thomas teases him about it and says they could use it to power the new rail engines. Richard just smiles and tells Thomas he's sick and tired of hearing about his intention of making good wine and tells him to get on with it.

"When are you going to make this great wine, Tom. You talk about it enough. I think we'll be too old to enjoy it by the time it actually eventuates!"

Thomas doesn't like being teased and told Richard that he needed time and money to make wine, neither of which he had at this time in his life, but that, one day, he would show them all.

Richard poured him another beer and slapped him on the back. I like Richard very much. He is even tempered and kind and I think Mary has chosen well. He works hard, loves his wife and enjoys his children. I hope that our family can be as happy as theirs and our children as free spirited.

Although Thomas and Mary are as close as a brother and sister could be, they are different. She is far more practical, fun loving and her common sense is a breath of fresh air. Her little Sarah is a few months older than our Sarah but Mary seems to know exactly what to do and someday I hope to be like her. She is kind, also, and seems to sense that I am finding everything difficult. I almost cried when we talked about the lack of sleep and the work involved with a small child but managed to fight off the tears.

"It gets better," she said after hugging me. "They don't stay little for long."

Mary's rabbit stew was delicious. With Thomas' father and brother being butchers, mainly of lamb, it was refreshing to have a change.

"There's much talk about the goldfields in Australia, Thomas. Thought you might be interested."

Thomas looked at me with the strangest look

"I don't think so, Richard. I've got a family to think about now. Going to Australia would be irresponsible."

It was like someone had turned the lights on in my mind. It dawned on me that Thomas saw married life as the end of all his dreams. Was this why I had married him, so I could be with someone who didn't take risks? Did I want a husband who stayed in the same village until the day he died and took up space in the church graveyard? Was this what was behind his moodiness and seeming disinterest in me? Had Thomas become a stranger to me because I had stopped him from doing what he most wanted to do? Did he think that now I was back home, I wanted to stay here forever?

The months of moodiness, the shortness of temper. It all became clear to me. He felt trapped.

I wanted to talk to him about it but there was no opportunity as we were all going to Priors Marston the next morning to St Leonard's to attend the christening of John and Georgina Bradshaw's little girl, Mary. All through the service, I planned what I would say when we had a chance to talk. I felt as if a weight had lifted from my shoulders. What sort of a wife was I to Thomas if I didn't urge him to pursue his dreams? He was a good man who would always do his duty but why couldn't he pursue his ambitions as well?

We had all filed into the church for the christening but I wasn't paying much attention to the service when suddenly a tap on my shoulder made me turn. Thomas whispered in my ear.

"I'm taking Sarah outside, she's driving everyone mad."

THOMAS — BAMAWM

Christmas Eve, 1913

The boy asked me whether the English villages were like Bamawm and Rochester. I told him they were in some ways, but vastly different in others. For one thing they seem to have existed forever, whereas everything in Bamawm and Rochester is new. And there aren't the strong family lines. I'm one of the oldest residents in Bamawm and I've been here less than fifty years whereas the Bradshaws in Priors Marston can trace their ancestors back for hundreds of years.

The boy said that the blacks have been here longer than any of us, and of course he is right. He talks to the tribe of black fellas that live along the Campaspe and has a real sympathy for their plight. I tell him they're not like us but he just glares at me and says they're smarter than some of the white fellas he knows. He also asked me if I was aware of how miserable Jane had been since Sarah's birth. I confessed that I did not. Having said that, I suppose I suspected something of the kind and this may explain my reluctance to read her diary until now. I was frightened what I might read.

I thought once we were back in Woodford and Jane was surrounded with family and friends, she improved her spirits and put on weight. But maybe I saw what I wanted to see. If she wasn't happy, I felt powerless to do anything about it. Her mother was always at our house and fussed too much but I didn't mind as I was very rarely there. I liked Mrs Fairbrother and thought that Jane would be just like her when she got older.

Maria Fairbrother wasn't like the other women in the district. The village folk had not accepted her at first but she had won them over with her abilities as a seamstress. She made the most exquisite clothes and found herself in demand when people wanted something special, even those who had been most enthusiastic at spreading rumours about her in the early days of her arrival in the village. A 'gypsy' they called her.

She had high hopes for her daughters and I admired the way she and Mr Fairbrother organised professions for Jane and Elizabeth. So many families enslaved their daughters in the family home, cooking, cleaning and caring for younger children until they were married but they seemed genuinely enthusiastic for their daughters to have a profession.

My work preparing for the railway to go through Woodford was constant and I earned far less than in Luton. Because of the people who held the purse strings, and politics which I didn't understand, Woodford would be one of the last places to have a railway. The foremen were incompetent and lazy and the lack of direction was such that often we didn't know what we were doing. I wasn't happy and sometimes felt a monkey could do my job as well as I could.

I worried about Jane giving birth as I thought of all those stories of women dying. I didn't know what I would do if that happened to her. I know, now, that I should have talked to her more about my concerns but that's something I found very had to do. A man does not admit weakness.

I do remember the day Sarah was born, though. I remember it well. It was one of those biting, winter days when any uncovered part of you feels the icy fingers of the wind when I was walking down the hill towards Hinton. My hands were under my coat to keep them from freezing, when Mrs Fairbrother, uncoated and in an excitable demeanour, met me in the lane, about fifty yards from the front gate. She was puffing from exhaustion in the cold.

"You have a daughter, Thomas,"

"And Jane?"

"They're both well, but she's tired, Thomas. It was a difficult labour."

I left Maria hunched over trying to get her breath and raced to the bottom of the hill, hurdling the fence of our cottage and stumbled, breathless through the door of our bedroom. Jane was sitting, propped up in bed with the baby cuddled beneath her arms. I have never seen her look more beautiful.

"It's a girl Thomas. Are you disappointed?"

I kissed Jane and told her I loved her. Was I disappointed it wasn't a boy? Initially I was but as I took the tiny bundle of perfection and looked into her eyes, I could never wish for anybody else.

"What will we call her?"

"Sarah. She looks like a Sarah."

"Hello Sarah, I 'm your papa."

After the exhilaration of the first few weeks, things settled down. We had a lot of adjustments to make and Jane was getting very little sleep. Sarah cried a lot and Jane seemed withdrawn. Was she merely exhausted or was it something else?

I tried to make her happy but to tell the truth, with the difficulties at work, I couldn't muster enough energy to cope with her moods. As the months went by, a strange kind of melancholy descended upon me and I couldn't 'taste' the joy of anything. Mary commented on it and asked me if anything was wrong, but I brushed her concerns aside.

My happy place was by myself, working on the cottage, making things, fixing things and not having people demanding things from me. I left Jane and Sarah to themselves and hoped that Jane's mother would give them what they needed.

I couldn't bear the thought of spending the rest of my days within the boundaries of the Midlands. I felt as if I were in a cage. I longed to travel, to see what was out there and what possibilities there were. Richard had spoken of Australia and I found myself wanting, really wanting, to explore the possibilities.

I reminded myself that I was now married and had responsibilities. Was my dream of travelling gone now that Sarah had arrived? Could I ask Jane to leave her family and travel with me? Could I take Sarah away from Maria and William and my parents? It all seemed impossible.

All the talk at the pub was about Australia. Some of the lads were boasting that they would make the trip but I knew they would not have a hope with what they earned. I joked that they should commit a crime and be sent there on a convict ship. They didn't think that was very funny. "Do you really want to live amongst murderers and thieves?" I played the devil's advocate.

"It's the gold," they said, "People can become rich overnight. Lots of ordinary people are going and they will outnumber the convicts."

" Anyway, I heard they are going to stop sending convicts as of next year." This from one of the better informed member of the drinking crew.

Even while I was teasing them, I secretly sympathised. Not so much with the desire to find gold. I wasn't stupid enough to believe the wild stories of miners falling over nuggets of gold as big as a turnip, but rather the excitement of what a gold rush would bring, the opportunity to be a pioneer in a new society and the chance to get away from the boredom of a place that was stuck in days gone by. Certainly the railways had been an enriching development in Britain but the people hadn't changed. Life went on the way it always had. The rich got richer and the poor were still poor.

My brother, John, thought I was mad when I mentioned it to him. He was happy taking over the butcher business from Father and for him, his wife and four children were all he ever wanted. When I mentioned my desires, he disapproved and said if I went I would most likely never see the family again. Did I want that? I was torn between Australia on the one hand and family on the other.

The boy dropped something he was fiddling with. I had almost forgotten about him. Had I been talking or just dreaming? I wasn't sure until he told me he didn't think it was a hard choice at all. I was lucky to have a family. Why, when I had a family where I belonged, a large, extended family in a country that I had an affection for, why did I want to leave? He said that if he had a family, he would never leave them.

Does he not know that I have asked myself that same question over and over? Does he not know that when Jane died, I regretted it so much that I had left England?

I can hear Marriott crashing about in the kitchen. He likes to experiment with food but he is a messy cook. He is probably trying to tempt me with some of his rabbit stew. I heard him and the boy out shooting last night. Confounded rabbits! My sister, Mary, used to make a delicious rabbit stew. The smell of Marriott's stew makes me sad to think I never saw her again after I left England. And now she is dead.

Marriott certainly hasn't inherited my work ethic. I think there is too much Irish in him. He likes to sit around and tell stories and drink. Even preparing a meal is hard work for him.

Immediately following Sarah's birth, I admit to feelings of jealousy. Sarah had all her mother's attention and Jane hardly noticed me. She didn't ask about work or make my favourite meals any more. I wanted things to go back to how they were. I spent more time than I should have in the *Fox and Hounds* enjoying the company of the chaps who were all abuzz about the goldfields in Australia.

"Remember Tommy Makepiece? His sister had a letter from him and he has found so much gold he's built 'imself a grand house. Even sent money home to his mam."

"Sounds like a tall story," said one of the doubters who had no hope of ever leaving Woodford. "If it's that easy, why doesn't everyone go to Australia?"

"Well I heard them blacks don't take too kindly to Englishmen and roast them for their supper!" said another enjoying the looks of horror on the younger men's faces, "You won't catch me going."

I listened to the banter and I joined in but all the time I was thinking how I could make it happen. How could I get to Australia?

With the coming of Spring and the unusually warm summer, my melancholy subsided somewhat and my attitude to Sarah changed. She began to smile, crawl and communicate her affection towards me. It was like I fell in love with her and surprised myself how much I enjoyed being a father. I couldn't wait to come home and see the changes in her. She was always so pleased to see me and 'papa' was her first word. I would bounce her on my knee and she would say, *more, more,* and then I would tip her upside down to hear her giggle the most infectious giggle. Sometimes as I watched her in her cot, I would feel a surge of protectiveness and couldn't imagine losing her. She had come into our life and we couldn't remember a time when she didn't exist.

"News from Luton came through at work today, Jane. Thousands have died of the cholera epidemic."

"I heard," said Jane, " some of the girls from *The Hat Box*, Anna and Imogen were victims. I just can't believe it." Jane reached out for Thomas' hand. "I'm so glad we left. Imagine if I lost you." I was pleasantly surprised by this rare display of affection. It gave me hope.

"Mary and Richard have asked us to spend the night with them on Saturday. There are parish census forms to fill out."

"That's wonderful, Thomas, but didn't we fill out those forms last year?"

"These are just for the Parish, and it could be fun."

"Everything is fun with those two, Thomas."

The trip to Charwelton was not a long trip but as the cart rattled along, we realised it had been ages since we had had an outing. It felt good. We laughed a lot as we filled out the census forms. Richard's home brew probably didn't make for complete accuracy! I'm glad Jane remembered it in the same way. It was a good night.

"How old are you now Thomas?" said a slightly tipsy Richard as he wrote a number down.

"Well, I'm eighteen months younger than Mary, Richard but you've got us as the same age. Hadn't you noticed we're not twins?"

The children had gone to bed but had to be spoken to several times as their excitement at being with their cousin Sarah kept them from settling. The conversation turned to immigration.

"Are you interested Thomas?" said Richard.

"I've heard stories of men finding nuggets of gold big enough for them not to have to worry about money again"

I saw Mary and Jane exchanging glances.

"If we didn't have three small children, we might consider it," said Mary, "but it is so far and we might never see our families again"

I thought I saw a look of terror on Jane's face but having heard what she wrote in her diary, I see that I completely misunderstood her. It wasn't going to Australia that she was frightened of, it was losing me. Oh, why is it so hard for two people to understand each other?

JANE – WOODFORD
March — 1852

My last entry finished rather abruptly as I was called away but so much has happened since, I can't wait to write it all down. You know, diary, you've become like a friend, a friend I can tell anything to. Maybe I don't want my life published after all!

Thomas had disappeared with Sarah during the service at St Leonard's. I'm not sure it was necessary to take Sarah out but I think his father might have said something about her unruly behaviour. Maybe Thomas just wanted an excuse!

Everyone spilled out into the grounds after the service and congratulated Georgina and John on the christening of little Mary. I was politely introduced to people I had never met before and joined in the conversation as much as I was able. Out of the corner of my eye, I saw Thomas and Sarah coming from the side of the church. Sarah had acorns in her hand and I noticed a scratch on her wrist.

Thomas politely conversed with his relatives about whatever they wished to speak about, the state of the country, the price of food and the growing unrest in the industrial areas, before whispering in my ear: "I need to talk to you about something when we're alone," then he picked Sarah up and said to the circle of people. "She's a handful, this one. She seems to have no fear at all."

People chuckled obligingly, fussing over Sarah, although I knew many disapproved of her tomboyish behaviour, and then gradually took their leave. Thomas and I ambled along School Lane to the 'Butcher House' for our meal with the growing Bradshaw clan. Sarah delighted in picking the flowers which grew up beside the road and presenting them to us.

We had a handful each before she grew tired of that game and Thomas picked her up on his shoulders.

"Why don't we go to Grandma and Grandpa's house, Sarah? Would you like that? And we will see your cousins, Thomas, James, John and little Mary Bradshaw, and Robert, Mary and Sarah Hyatt."

John's wife, Georgina, is distant and I feel as if she looks down on me. We don't talk much. John is very different from Thomas, very proper and his father's favourite. John carves the meat, John directs the conversation, whatever John says is listened to. They have four beautiful children: Thomas, James, John and Mary, all beautifully behaved whereas Mary's children: Robert, Mary and Sarah are more mischievous, and at times, quite naughty. Maybe I find their naughtiness appealing. I was conscious that Sarah was not as well behaved as John's children but Mary just smiled and said,

"She's only a baby, Jane. Plenty of time to learn manners."

All through the meal, I couldn't keep my mind off what Thomas had whispered to me. Was it a coincidence that I had resolved to speak to him about feeling trapped in marriage and now he wanted to speak to me about something mysterious? It had to be the stars aligning in a particular direction but exactly what that direction was, I wasn't sure.

At one stage, he looked across the table and grinned, not just a smile grin but a grin that said, "We're going to be all right". It made my heart race. I hadn't seen that playfulness in him since before Sarah was born.

As we were driving home in the cart, Thomas was brimming with excitement. He made me wait until we got back to Woodford as he said the road was too bumpy to discuss anything of import. I could hardly wait!

THOMAS — BAMAWM

Christmas Eve, 1913

It was a stroke of luck. But was it luck? I wonder now....that day Sarah decided that church was not for her. She was an active child of 15 months, walking and running and squirming whenever anyone picked her up. She wanted to be on the go. Church was not her idea of a good way to spend a Sunday.

We were at St Leonard's for Sunday Service with my family. It was the christening of John and Georgina's new baby, Mary, and Father and John had killed a lamb for the occasion. The new girl they had taken in from Chipping Warden, Grace, was preparing lunch as we worshipped. Her father had been killed in an accident on the railways and her mother had died soon after of dysentery. The other children had been farmed out to relatives but Grace was old enough to work so my parents took her in in exchange for cooking and cleaning duties. Although they had done it out of charity, Grace turned out to be an excellent addition to the family and her cooking skills were first rate. We were all looking forward to the feast.

In church, Father was growing anxious about Sarah's behaviour but try as I might, I couldn't stop her from laughing, wriggling and dancing in the seat. At one stage she got under the pew in front of us and grabbed old Mr Bromley's foot. Luckily, he was a good natured fellow and didn't make a fuss, just smiling at Sarah. Father leaned across to me:

"Take the child outside, Thomas, before she starts to take over the whole service!"

We made our exit as quietly as possible much to the delight of Sarah. As I put her down, she ran like a dog let off a chain. She skirted the tombstones in the front of the church yard, many of them marking her relatives, and around the Lebanese Cedars. When she disappeared out of sight to the side of the church, I quickly followed and it was then that I noticed a poster on the side wall. My heart skipped a beat as I read it.

FAMILY COLONIZATION LOAN SOCIETY
CAROLINE CHISHOLM
EMIGRATION TO AUSTRALIA
A PUBLIC GROUP MEETING FOR FAMILIES
AND SINGLE WOMEN
FRIDAY EVENING NEXT. APRIL 19
NORTHAMPTON TOWN HALL AT FIVE O'CLOCK

I read the small print and discovered that not only was the Society recruiting families for Australia, but they were paying their passage on a loan basis, to be repaid once employment was found in the colony. They wanted skilled men, especially carpenters. I couldn't believe my eyes.

I was so absorbed in reading the poster and thinking what it could mean that I forgot about Sarah and when I heard her crying, I quickly ran to find out what the problem was. She was holding her wrist and wailing at the sight of the blood seeping from the scratch. I picked her up, brushed away the blood with my handkerchief and cuddled her. She had obviously been trying to jump from one grave to the next, missed her footing and landed between two jagged stones. As I comforted her and ran my fingers through her thick, dark hair, I thought of her future. Would going to Australia offer her more opportunities or was I just trying to convince myself?

I couldn't wait to tell Jane but at the same time was nervous about mentioning it. What if she was vehemently against it? Would I be able to forget about it? The thought of going to Australia was like a seed that had taken root in my soul.

When I joined the others outside of the church, Jane was surrounded by relatives and there was no opportunity to talk but I whispered to her that I had something important to discuss later. She gave me a puzzled smile before making a fuss of Sarah who had dirtied her best dress. There was no opportunity to talk until, on the way home, Jane begged me to tell her what had made me so excited.

"Wait till we get home, Jane, after we have settled Sarah."

Over a cup of tea and some of Mrs Fairbrother's delicious fruit cake, I told Jane about the poster outside the church, how Mrs Caroline Chisholm was holding a meeting and how excited I had become at the prospect of going to Australia.

"But of course, Jane, I understand if you don't want to even think about going. I would respect your wishes."

Surprisingly Jane did not dismiss the idea out of hand.

"I've heard of her Thomas, Caroline Chisholm. Some of the woman in the village talked about how she requisitioned ships to take young women to the colonies, making sure they had employment when they arrived. She's married to a Captain Chisholm but I think she's the strong one in the marriage which doesn't go down well with some of the women who think he should take her in hand!"

"I don't know about that," I said, not wanting to get side-tracked into gossip, "but now she is recruiting families, and especially carpenters, and what's more she lends you the money for the passage!"

I had never heard of Caroline Chisholm or the Family Colonization Loan Society. I supposed women gossiped about such things like we men bragged about finding gold. Jane had heard mothers talk of young women who had chosen to go to the colonies as domestic servants instead of working in the mills or the factories of the big English cities. Maybe the mothers secretly wished they could go too. There were romantic stories of the same young women marrying wealthy farmers and living in genteel society.

I took advantage of Jane's show of enthusiasm to suggest we attend the meeting. We could leave Sarah with her grandmother in Byfield, borrow Mr Fairbrother's horse and cart as it was better than ours, and be home by midnight. Jane agreed but I wondered if it were the thought of the outing together to Northampton rather than the meeting which swayed her.

Could I dare to believe that we were really going to go to Australia?

JANE – WOODFORD
March, 1852

O my goodness, it is only two weeks since little Mary's christening and the world has taken on a whole new colour. When I arrived at the butcher this morning, I hardly remembered getting there as my mind was full of what lay ahead of us. Alfred had been talking to me and I hardly heard him.

"Was it lamb shank you were after, Jane? You seem a little distracted this morning."

"Sorry Alfred, I was miles away."

After we left Thomas' parents' house that Sunday, I couldn't wait to hear what Thomas had to say. We carried a sleepy little girl into the house, rebandaged her bleeding wrist and put her to bed. As I sang her to sleep, I wondered what Thomas wanted to talk about. The excitement in him during the lunch at Priors Marston reminded me of the Thomas I first met. Whatever it was had to be something good.

After listening to the story about the poster in the churchyard and the meeting in Northampton, I allowed myself to grow excited. A new life. Not just for us but for little Sarah whom I couldn't bear to see as a factory worker, susceptible to all the illnesses and abuse young women are subjected to. And I wasn't sure we could afford for an apprenticeship for her. Life even in the villages is changing, and women are having to move to the city where they are swallowed up in its iniquity. I would do anything to give little Sarah a chance of a different life.

The meeting in Northampton was only six days away so we didn't have much time to think about it, no time to change our minds. We left Sarah with Mother and borrowed Father's buggy amidst instructions not to drive the horse too hard. I told Mother as little as possible about the meeting. I knew how she would feel about her daughter and granddaughter moving to Australia!

As we neared the parish hall, we were amazed at the crowd, at least 200 people. There were folk from all over Northamptonshire, some I knew from Woodford, Daventry and Byfield, others Thomas knew from Priors Hardwick. But most were strangers. I did notice, however, that they were people just like us, our age and our class.

We found a seat in the middle of the hall and watched the people filing in. Soon there was standing room only. Thomas looked nervous. Was he rethinking the whole idea now that it was becoming a possibility?

Mrs Chisholm came onto the stage and positioned herself at the front. She knew how to address an audience with full effectiveness as she stood silent until the buzz of the room had subsided and then began, in a soft but projected voice. Every word she said could be heard clearly. Yes! I thought, she is a woman to be reckoned with.

She began by welcoming everyone, especially those who had travelled a great distance. She commented on the dry weather and the beauty of the Northampton countryside in early Spring. It was, she said, where she had grown up and after having been in Australia for many years, had been yearning to return. We were amazed at how she travelled between the two countries as if it were nothing. We couldn't conceive of the 'other side of the world' and were anxious to hear more.

I cast my mind back to the conversation I had had with the village women who talked of Mrs Chisholm's journey home some years earlier when she had given birth on the ship.

"She and the baby got sick and but for the goat's milk from the ship's goat, the little boy would have died. Her husband said he hadn't known what to do and it was one of the women on board who came up with the idea."

The topic for the meeting was the workings of the Australian Colonial Loan Society and what to expect upon arriving in Australia. When a lady handed us a booklet printed to help prospective migrants I leant over to Thomas and said. "Sounds too good to be true, an interest free loan for two years!"

"Yes," he replied excitedly, " and until the ship sails, the Society sets up a banking system for people to put aside part of their wages. Whatever the shortfall is by the time the ship sails, the Society makes up."

I knew Thomas would like this scheme as he would never have accepted charity or a totally free passage. People like him needed to feel that he was contributing something with the promise of paying the balance back when he could afford it. This was smart thinking on Mrs Chisholm's part.

I was excited and looking around at the people seated in the hall, and in turn, they were all looking at us. Mrs Chisholm cared for people, not just profit. She described the types they wanted to fill their ships.

"We want people of industrious and good character."

"That's us," I whispered in Thomas' ear. He shushed me good naturedly.

I found myself liking Mrs Chisholm as she spoke of everybody's being equal. No matter what religion or class people were, once they were on board, they were all equal. She even had teachers employed on the ships to teach people to read and write before they reached Australia. The man behind us interrupted Mrs Chisholm

"Is the journey to Australia risky? We've all heard about the shipwrecks and deaths on board."

"I do not wish any of my people to get sick or die on board, sir," said Mrs Chisholm. "We have succeeded in coercing the British Government to make conditions better, especially for women and children. Our ships carry fewer passengers and they are subjected to stringent hygienic conditions. The food we supply is better than most people have in their homes and so far we have not lost one person from a preventable illness, and none of my ships has been wrecked."

This seemed to answer the questions of most in the audience. It was true that many were struggling to provide good food for their families and life could not be much worse in Australia.

Another man asked a question about religion and whether because she was a Catholic herself, she gave preference to Catholics.

"I am no stranger to religious bigotry, sir, and I want none of that on my ships. People of any religion are welcome as long as they are of good character and have a skill to contribute to the growth of the new country."

Although her voice was quiet and measured, she certainly got her point across. We had seen this religious bigotry in Luton. People blamed the Irish for everything when most of the time they were just people who had fled famine and wanted a life for their families.

After Mrs Chisholm finished speaking, she urged people to go home and think about committing to joining one of her voyages. She placed on the blackboard a list of the ships to leave in the next few months and the number of vacancies left on each. She wished us a safe journey home and said she would be on the stage for another hour if anyone wanted to ask any more questions. There were no refreshments so people started to drift away.

One of the ship's names caught my eye. The Ballengeich.

It was sailing in July.

THOMAS — BAMAWM

Christmas Eve, 1913

The boy finished his beer as it was getting dark and a little chilly sitting on the veranda. Surprisingly, sharing Jane with him has made me feel light and cheerful. Or maybe it is the wine! Although it is summer, the evenings are unpredictable and tonight is cool. The rabbit stew is ready and Marriott is calling us for dinner.

'I'm game if you are, boy.'

The boy grinned and unfolded his gangly legs. A Marriott rabbit stew would be as unpredictable as the weather.

After a surprisingly edible meal, the boy and I retired to the living room where we both got settled with a book. It wasn't long before he asked me what happened after the meeting. It was as if he couldn't bear the suspense and I felt a warmth towards him as I continued with the story.

We left the Northampton Town Hall, walking into the streets with many other excited people. One man asked Jane and me to join him for a pint and a chat but we said we had to get back to Woodford. He was surprised we had come so far.

"I hope you've got a good horse," he said. "These roads can be tricky in the dark."

We assured him that we had excellent transport even though we were a little nervous ourselves. As Jane got into the buggy she said. "If a drive of 30 miles has us scared, Thomas, we had better think again about going to Australia!"

The first part of the trip was silent as we negotiated our way through the city and onto the Woodford Road. Once we had relaxed, we enjoyed the clearness of the Spring evening and talked about how different the trees and buildings looked in the moonlight. Neither of us could bring ourselves to ask what the other thought. After what seemed like ages, I decided to break the ice.

"Mrs Chisholm presented very well, Jane. What a confident speaker. She made the trip to Australia sound so easy."

Jane took a while to reply but as usual, when she spoke, she cut straight to the core.

"Thomas, I won't lie about the fact that I feel frightened to get on a ship and go to the other side of the world and the likelihood of it becoming a possibility is even more frightening. But from what Mrs Chisholm said, little Sarah would have more of a chance to be someone in Australia than she would staying here. And our other children as well."

I stopped the buggy and kissed my beloved wife, a long and lingering kiss. At that moment I thought Jane the bravest and most wonderful wife a man could ever have. At the same time I wondered what I would have done if she had refused to go!!

It was well past midnight before we arrived home, cold and hungry. Sarah was asleep at her grandparent's house. The house seemed empty without the sounds of a toddler and we commented that we couldn't remember a time without her. She completed us as a couple.

The leaflet Mrs Chisholm had given us was on the table.

Australia – the land of Sunshine.

JANE — BALLENGEICH
December – 1852

O Diary. I have neglected you. I start to write something and then I can't be bothered going on. It's this wretched mal de mer! I will put today's date as I am determined to finish a whole entry. Nine months since the last date — as long as it takes to bear a child! It is not that I have nothing to write, but rather I have too much and words don't do the actions justice. All my energy is taken with keeping balance in the crazy circumstances in which we have found ourselves.

We are almost in Australia having boarded the ship five months ago. It has not been a pleasant journey and I don't think I would ever be a sailor. I yearn for land. But first let me fill you in with the last nine months.

Following the meeting with Mrs Chisholm, we put our names down for the Ballengeich, and after an extensive interview on our character and ambitions, we were accepted. We had less than four months to prepare to leave England and sail to Australia.

Telling family was horrible, especially as not long after we told Mother and Father, Father died. We were all terribly upset, even though he had not been well. At the funeral, I couldn't stop crying, thinking that I was leaving Mother, possibly forever! Mother was brave but I knew her heart was breaking.

The four months went quickly. There was much to do. We tried to find out as much as we could about Australia but there were so many conflicting stories we decided to listen only to Mrs Chisholm. People were only too willing to describe the horrors that could befall us: cannibalism, murder, starvation, snakes and many more. Thomas just laughs but I must admit the stories scare me.

The endless farewells and tears before we boarded the train to Southampton were gruelling, especially as we knew we might never see our families again. Young Robert and James swore they would follow us as soon as they were old enough, much to the horror of Richard and Mary.

"Don't worry," I re-assured Mary, "they will probably forget all about it as they grow up and meet local girls. Anyway, if they do decide to come to Australia, they will have us to look after them."

My heart was heavy leaving Mother. I hated leaving her in her grief.

Elizabeth, the sweet soul she is, gave up her apprenticeship and returned from Leamington to dedicate herself to Mother.

"Do you think I should stay in England and join you later, Thomas? I know it would mean a lot to Mother." Was I clutching at straws and having last minute doubts?

Thomas looked panicked, "I wouldn't go without you, Jane."

I wonder did he mean that or whether he knew I would not let him go alone. Elizabeth was insistent, however, that she could manage.

"Aren't you sad to leave Leamington, Elizabeth?" I asked, wondering how she was going to cope with the quietness of Byfield after the excitement of Leamington.

"No, I was homesick all the time I was there and now that I am home I can work in the village making clothes, I don't ever want to leave again."

"But won't living here with mother and the boys irk you, after all the independence you have had?"

"Goodness, Jane, I didn't have much independence. We worked 12 hours a day and the landlady in the boarding house made sure we didn't do anything so much as sneeze without her approval. Mother is so much easier to be with than old Mrs Peabody!"

I don't know whether Elizabeth was just making me feel better about leaving but I was grateful to her. Elizabeth is everything I am not, and it is possible that she will be happier at home than living in a boarding house with other women. I have to remember, also, that Thomas and Sarah are my family now.

Sarah and my mother will miss each other terribly. They have developed a strong bond. Sarah has a mischievous spirit that endears her to all, especially Mother who has been her constant companion for almost two years. I think Mother will miss Sarah more than she will miss me.

Many of our friends thought we were mad, unable to understand why we would go to a land peopled by savages and ex-convicts. "Australia is just a dumping ground for the people England no longer wants," they said. I replied that the convict trade has largely ceased and anyway many of those convicts have repented and made a good life for themselves. In my heart of hearts, however, I harbour doubts of my own.

The Ballengeich was sailing from Southampton. This involved a train to London where we changed for the journey south. Sarah loved the trains. She giggled with delight watching the trees speeding by and made friends with everyone in the carriage. She is such a social little girl. Thomas took her down to the dining car and bought her some bread and butter and she thought she was the luckiest girl in the world.

When we arrived in Southampton and saw the Ballengeich waiting for us, we were overwhelmed at its size. A shiver of panic ran through me as I thought of sailing to the other side of the world on her but Sarah couldn't contain her excitement. From the moment she saw the ship, to climbing the many stairs, to seeing her strange bed – it was all one big adventure. The cabins were small, about six feet by eight and the beds took up most of that space. My heart sank as I thought of our comfortable bed back in Woodford but Sarah loved her cot when I put her in it. She jumped up and down laughing until she landed on her bottom with a thud. The mattress was hard. Seeing her excitement helped me to dispel my anxieties somewhat and I joined in her laughter as she bounced with delight.

As the ship was leaving, people were waving with great enthusiasm.

Even though we had no-one to wave us off, I thought it important that we join them. "See all the people waving at you Sarah, why don't you pick a person out and wave to them?"

Sarah pointed at a little boy in a green suit and started waving to him. Whether he saw her or not, he started to wave and Sarah giggled with delight and waved so hard her arm began to hurt. She was happy. For the last 3 days, she had had both parents to herself. As I watched her little body brimming with joy, I had to cuddle her yet another time.

She was the future. She was the reason we were doing this mad thing.

I could see Mrs Chisholm down below with the newspaper people. "See those men down there " I pointed them out to Sarah, "They are going to write about us in the newspaper because they think we are very brave." Sarah didn't really understand what I was saying. Perhaps I was talking to myself!

After the Ballengeich left the calm waters of Southampton, the journey became rather unpleasant. Most of us suffered from seasickness and couldn't bear the thought of eating. We lost weight and our stomachs felt as if they would never be right again. I remember one morning, leaning over the ship's rails towards the churning sea and thinking how inviting it was!.

One of the other passengers gave me some good advice: "Eat, even if you don't feel like it. It's better for the stomach to have something to bring up rather than dry retching." It seemed to work and after a few weeks we had our 'sea legs' making life far more pleasant.

So here we are, floating on the ocean in the middle of the unknown. The days and weeks go by, and by now we can hardly remember our previous lives. It's as if we have been in this state forever.

But I am so sick of water!

The Ballengeich has been our sole existence for five months. Thank God it is almost over.

Thomas is down below talking business with his new friends. What a brilliant idea of Mrs Chisholm's to put us together in likeminded groups.

Compatible Family Groups she called them. We have been grouped with James and Anne Russell, Helen and Joseph Little and Lucy and Arthur Pickersgill. The men are all builders and we all have small children.

We are as close to a family as we can get. I like Anne and Helen very much. Lucy is amusing but we are very different. She struts around as if she is better than everyone else and I can see that it is important to her to assert her superiority. Anne and Helen and I indulge her because underneath I think she is the most fragile of all of us.

The food is the same every day: biscuits, preserved meat and fruit, coffee, tea and sugar. The captain is a strict disciplinarian and takes seriously the mission of delivering all of us safely to our destination. With so many people living for five months in cramped conditions, illness is a major threat. Every morning, we have to roll up our beds and sweep underneath, throwing the dirt overboard. There is a curfew at 10pm and gambling, swearing and fighting are outlawed.

I suppose I should be grateful as we have heard stories about ships smashing on rocks in storms and others flying the typhoid flag on entering the harbour after having thrown many victims overboard. Luckily, we have had an uneventful trip in that no-one has died and the ship is intact. I believe we can thank both the captain and Mrs Chisholm for that.

I have taken every opportunity to sit on the deck and watch the endless rolling of the sea, positioning myself on one of the benches where I can look forward, not back. This is what I must do – look forward. I am often joined by other women and we all laugh as we attempt to keep our skirts dry from the endless floods of water on deck.

As all of the passengers have been chosen by Mrs Chisholm for their character, the discipline does not worry any of us. We can see the sense in it. We are all anxious to arrive healthy so that we can start our new lives unencumbered with illness and fatigue. From everything we have heard, the Ballengeich is one of the better ships.

One particular passenger, a single woman, Harriet, from Leamington, has been a godsend to us. She is just twenty but has made the brave decision to leave England and come to Australia. She has trained as a nurse and takes a keen interest in Sarah. When the rest of us are busy with children or bedridden with sea sickness, she reads stories to Sarah and the other children as well. She will make the most marvellous mother.

But Sarah isn't Harriet's only fan. Elijah, a young lad from Lancashire, is travelling with his two older brothers and has realised that if he takes an interest in Sarah, he can impress Harriet with whom he is clearly besotted. Sarah likes Elijah and thinks he is funny, especially when he makes faces at her and she runs away, leaving him to be alone with Harriet! I enjoy watching them. It makes me think of those days in Luton when I met Thomas and we took every opportunity to be alone.

Helen, Anne and Lucy and I have eight children under seven between us. When Sarah isn't with Harriet and Elijah, she is with William Little. They have become good friends and it is quite funny to see them walking around the ship holding hands. William is a few months older than Sarah and quite a bit taller and I think, even at two, he feels quite protective of her. I watch as Sarah and Willie chase each other round the deck, Willie's freckles and fair hair a sharp contrast to Sarah's dark hair and gypsy complexion. She is well known amongst the passengers for her cuddles which she distributes generously.

Thomas and I sometimes sit on the deck and watch the sun set. The warm evenings are beautiful and we swap stories about the people we have met on the ship and the plans we have. It's like we are courting all over again. I will be sad when we arrive and get into a routine and such moments will be just a memory. I expressed my hope to Thomas that when we get to Melbourne, we will be living close to the Littles and the Russells as I considered them family.

"Not the Pickersgills?"

I told him I like Lucy, but she makes me feel like a peasant with her airs and graces. She wants me to make her a hat so she can enter Melbourne society. We both laughed at the idea of Melbourne 'society' being anything like London society.

"I'm not too keen on Arthur either. He is so bloody religious! He has big plans for the future but I think he's one of those people who sets himself up for failure. James and Joseph are champion chaps though and they have great ideas. The colony needs builders." Thomas then told me of their plans to set up a contracting business in Melbourne. To see him so excited and animated did my heart good and made me feel we had made the right decision.

It's a strange sensation to watch the sun going down over the sea. When it is gone, you feel as if you have left the world entirely and are floating in space. Thomas and I sat in silence for a while longer, as the light faded. As I fought my way into the lumpy cabin bed, I wondered what sort of hats they did wear in Melbourne.

There are so many questions that I want to ask that are not answered in Mrs Chisholm's leaflets. Will there be markets? Will I be able to grow English flowers? Will it be safe enough to roam the countryside? Will I be able to understand what people are saying? Will the natives be a threat to us? Will we have more children?

Mrs Chisholm assured us there were good doctors and adequate hospitals but the thought of having children so far from my mother is one that frightens me

THOMAS — BAMAWM

Christmas Day, 1913

I am 88 years old. I wonder if people live too long

Jane was terribly sick on the Ballengiech. She lost weight and I was worried about her. I spoke to the Captain and he assured me she would be all right and sure enough, once the first few weeks had passed, she improved and started to eat although the sickness would return whenever we sailed through bad weather. I was not sick at all but I was one of the exceptions. There must be some sailor blood in me somewhere.

We didn't know what we were coming to and whereas I was optimistic, Jane worried about what sort of life it would be for Sarah. I know she was missing her mother as well.

The country we came to in 1852 has gone from a squalid, lawless melting pot to being a nation. I think it will be a great nation though and, In many ways I am sorry I will not be around to see it.

But increasingly, I miss the England of my youth, or is it just my youth I am missing? What would my life be like if I had never left? Would I still be a carpenter in Priors Marston? Or would I be dead?

It's Christmas Day and the weather promises to be quite mild, no more than eighty five degrees. I have slept late. Marriott has just brought me breakfast with a glass of the wine that I produced for the Elmore Show five years ago. I won a prize for it, then, so it should have matured well and truly by now. When did I start drinking wine with breakfast?

He asked me if I wanted to go in the buggy with him to see Agnes in Rochester but I told him I need to be alone. I don't need to see

Agnes and confront my guilt about Sarah all over again. I feel sorry for Marriott. He is trying to take away the melancholy he detects in me but is powerless to do so.

We have given the boy the day off, but he is around somewhere. I am surprised how much I miss him sitting here with me. He has given me a great gift, the gift of listening.

My room is cluttered with objects I have collected over the years. Letters, so many letters. After my sister, Mary, died, my nephew Robert sent me the letters I had written to her from Australia. He thought I might like them. There were so many of them. I had no idea I was such a letter writer. I have tipped them onto the floor and resolve to read them all. Then I will burn them.

This one looks like one I wrote on the ship before we arrived. God, that seems like an eternity ago.

Ballengeich
December 1852

Dear Mary
I hope this letter finds you well
After five months we have almost arrived.
As I said in my last letter, the journey has been better than expected. I hope you received it as I sent it from the Cape of Good Hope where we were docked for a few days. Also when we were there, we heard reports about a ship from England being wrecked not far from here and from all accounts most of the passengers drowned. Another one just a few weeks ago was labelled a "typhoid" ship and dozens of victims were thrown overboard.
These accounts make us grateful for Mrs Chisholm's insistence on fresh air, good food and fewer passengers. Also, our captain is a

strong disciplinarian and makes sure we don't get into bad habits even though some of the other men think he is a bit too puritan!

I am so happy Jane has enjoyed the company of new friends as she is missing you and her other friends so much. Everyone on board has been handpicked by Mrs Chisholm and it might sound arrogant of me, but they are all people like us. I am hoping when we reach Melbourne that Jane will become involved in some of the charities that Mrs Chisholm outlined at our meetings and also that she might set up a business making hats for the colonials. As you know, she is really quite gifted at it.

For myself, the journey has been a most beneficial time as Arthur, James and Joseph (I told you about them in my last letter) and I have made plans about starting a business in Melbourne. People have been flocking into the city in thousands, most in hope of becoming rich on the goldfields. I am not foolish enough to think that becoming wealthy through mining is even slightly likely but people will be needing places to live and who better than four builders to provide them with that facility. And for those who do make it rich, our prices may just be that little bit higher!

When we get into the port, we have to gather to register our details and be shown suitable accommodation. We won't be the only ship arriving so we may have to stay on board until such time as the authorities can get organised. That will be a challenge as all I want to do is get there, get off the ship and begin our new life.

Hopefully my next letter will have details of our great success.

Regards to Richard and all the children, especially my godson, Robert.

Your loving brother

Thomas

That sense of excitement! How I wish I could rekindle it!

The boy has made his way to my room with a bottle of beer. He said Marriott had said as it was his day off, he could help himself to the ice chest and do whatever he wanted. It seems he wants to spend it with me! He asked me to tell him what Melbourne looked like when we arrived, at the height of the Gold Rush. He has heard all about the Gold Rush but all he knows of it is the raped countryside around Bendigo. He can't imagine anyone finding gold there.

What did Melbourne look like in 1852? I do remember that arriving at the Port of Melbourne was a shock. We were greeted with absolute squalor. The streets had overflowing cesspits, polluted creeks and open sewers. The talk amongst the passengers was that this place was not called Melbourne but "Smellbourne."

There were riots in the streets, people fighting each other with troopers helpless to stop it. When we asked someone what it was all about we were told it was a battle between the 'Orange' and the 'Green'. It looked nasty and it was a reminder that Australia was not going to be the 'Land of Sunshine' of Mrs Chisholm's pamphlets. I remember looking at the women recoiling from the violent scene and wondering what we had done.

The boy asked me where we went when we first got off the ship. He said he wouldn't have known what to do.

I remember the chaos. There didn't seem to be anyone who knew what to do so we decided it would be up to us to look after ourselves. We were lucky we could stay on the ship until we found accommodation, otherwise it would be sheltering under canvas. Mrs Chisholm's ships were a godsend in that way.

It sounds ironic but arriving was the low point of our journey. Staying on the ship as it rocked in the harbour was more than some people could bear. So near yet so far. James, Arthur, Joseph and I left the women and children aboard and went on a search for somewhere to live. On the third day, we were lucky. We felt as if we had struck gold.

There were three iron cottages for rent, side by side, in a less than auspicious part of the city. We enquired and found that they were available. Fortunately the Pickersgills were moving further inland so we only needed three.

The boy was interested in the makeshift iron cottages which they brought out on ships from England and erected on site so I tried to describe them to him. They weren't too bad really. The windows were cast iron casement, the panels were corrugated iron and the front door was always brightly painted in blue, red, green or yellow. They were very similar to the cottages erected by the railways in Woodford.

When we returned to the ship, it was not before time as the passengers were driving each other crazy. Left on the ship with the children, running out of food and water, surrounded by other miserable passengers, some quite ill, they were calling on all their reserves to keep their spirits up.

Fortunately it was summer so we had until 8pm before darkness set in. We hired a cart to bring our luggage to the iron huts and ended our first evening in this southern land by eating bread, cheese and sausage seated at the roughhewn table of the biggest of the three houses which the Russells had claimed.

We were too weary to be excited but when we saw the accommodation other families were in, canvas tents, we allowed ourselves a sliver of gratitude. It was strange though, it felt unreal, like a game in which we were participating and which would finish soon.

"Our first meal in Australia," said Joseph Little as we clinked our glasses with the last of the ship's water. "I wish we had a drink to toast our venture. Aren't you going to make wine here Thomas? Pity you haven't got some with you now." Joseph was always the optimist and we loved him for it.

We settled the children on bedding of clothes and blankets for their first night in this new land. By the time Jane and I drifted off to sleep, I believe I was quite numb. If there'd been an opportunity, I think all of us would have turned round and gone straight back to England.

The Gold Rush had sent people into a frenzy. Pouring off the ships were thousands of hopefuls who had no idea what to expect and who were completely daunted by the process of setting themselves up with equipment before heading off to the goldfields. The trip to Bendigo or Forest Creek could take days, sometimes weeks, and all this in searing hot temperatures.

We heard stories of women giving birth in the dirt of their miserable home only to see the child die. In a little place called Moonlight Flat, there was a 'children's cemetery' which had been seized because of its uselessness as a gold mining site. Jane was horrified by these stories and could only imagine what the women were going through. She had no desire to go to the Goldfields.

The boy asked me if they walked or went in coaches. He was amazed that people would make the journey on foot but this was all most people could afford. Of course, now, all the talk is about motor cars. Wouldn't the diggers have liked them?

The conditions took their toll on people's health and also on their enthusiasm. The dream turned to a nightmare very quickly and many turned back from the goldfields, or never even arrived, trying to survive in Melbourne. The city was rough, dirty and violent crime was an obvious problem. I felt sorry for the poor blighters. I don't know what they expected and they couldn't return to England as they had spent every last penny getting here.

"Joseph, I don't think this city knows where it is going. It's grown up like Topsy!"

"Yes, Thomas, I must say I'm a bit nervous about the future."

I looked at my friend and saw his concern. Even he was worried about his wife and the children. It was my turn to do the reassuring.

Joseph was such a good man. The last thing I wanted was for him to give up hope.

"We knew it wouldn't be easy, Joseph, and as for the women, I think they're made of stronger stuff than us. It'll take time but we'll get there. And we've got each other."

Just then I saw Jane around the corner. She had been listening. I hoped she believed me.

JANE – MELBOURNE
August, 1853

I wonder what Jane Austen or Currer Bell would make of my life now! (I have just found out that Currer Bell, the writer of Jane Eyre is a woman called Charlotte Bronte! a woman! O how pleased I am. Who else but a woman could write such a beautiful romance?) She lived all her life in Yorkshire and did nothing so adventurous as Jane Fairbrother who travelled to the other side of the world with her husband, to a god forsaken land of savages and convicts!

It's eight months since I have written anything. It's a wonder I haven't gone mad. What a time it has been. None of us expected anything like what greeted us in December last year.

"Smellbourne!"- that's what they called this place when we arrived. And it certainly did smell. I thought the streets of Luton were bad enough but I was not prepared for what greeted us as the ship pulled into the docks. Oh the squalor. And the disgruntled people who hoped to arrive to gold lined streets. If it weren't for my concern for Sarah, I think I would have just sat down and cried. Even Thomas looked dismayed.

Anne, Lucy and Helen joined with me in a cry of despair which we tried to hide from our menfolk and our children. We were frightened witnessing the violence in the streets. Someone said it was an Irish altercation between the Catholics and the Protestants but I'm not sure if that was right.

"The heat, O I think I shall die" said the hapless Lucy Pickersgill. Helen Little, herself looking dreadful, let Lucy know that complaining wasn't helping. "Pull yourself together," she said with an anger that betrayed her inner frustration. "You're not the only one who feels hot!"

I really like Helen. She is one of those people who is good to be around. I feel if ever I need someone's shoulder to cry on, hers will be my choice.

The ship was now inhabited by exhausted, hungry, hot women and children and we couldn't wait to get off. We trusted the men to find us shelter and we concerned ourselves with the children who were wilting in our care. We kept them cool with rags soaked in water tied round their necks and on their heads. They thought this was amusing and little Willie pretended he was a pirate.

Sarah is a little champion. She never complains. I look at her and think that she will do something special with her life. If it weren't for Sarah, I think I would try to get a passage on the next ship back to England.

After three days of searching, the men returned quite animated. They had managed to find three iron cottages, side by side. Arthur found a more elaborate house further south.

The Pickersgills are a source of amusement; she with her dreams of grandeur and illusion of to her own importance, and he with his strict moral code and pomposity. I can't say I am sorry that they are moving some miles away, to what they consider to be the "better" part of the city, as I find his austerity quite off putting. He will still be a partner in the new business and we shall still see Lucy from time to time — our five months together on the Ballengeich will bond us together always – but I feel we will have different worlds once we settle into the colony.

When I describe just how difficult those first few days were, I am not exaggerating, and it was compounded by the heat. What was reassuring to all of us, however, was the strength we had that we never knew existed in us.

The heat, mosquitoes, flies, snakes. Melbourne had them all. The first time I saw a snake, I nearly died. It was an evil looking thing. Thomas killed it and hung it on the fence. He said it was to remind the neighbours of the dangers but I really think it was a bit of a trophy for him. The children would pretend it was alive and run away into the lane. Joseph delighted telling the children that the natives cooked and ate snakes and laughed as they screwed up their noses.

"Urrrgghhh, that's horrible," they all yelled and pretended to be sick.

But we did survive, not just the scorching summer but also the bitterly cold winter with winds coming from Van Diemens Land. Without each other, the Littles and the Russells, I doubt we would have made it. We were pioneers and soon we started to forget about England and imagine a future here. We began to see the potential.

We have moved from those first iron cottages and are quite comfortable. Mrs Chisholm did us a huge favour when she paired us with the Russells, not only because they are lovely people but also because they have money!

James bought land here in Errol Street, and he, Joseph and Thomas built the cottages we are in today. We rent the smaller one and the Russells live in the bigger one, the front room of which is an office for the business. North Melbourne is a much nicer area than where we were, the streets are wide and there are people everywhere, coming and going to the goldfields, starting up businesses, playing music and chattering incessantly. It's alive. It has a great spirit. Sarah enjoys being outside, playing, without the biting winds and constant rain of home and so far we have all avoided the sickness which is ever present around us.

I have kept the best news till last. I am with child again and I am so happy. Thomas is hoping for a boy. Yesterday I told Sarah that she would have a brother or a sister and she said: "Will it come on a boat from England like we did?"

I laughed and cuddled her for ages. She is such a joy to us both. In some ways I hope that it is a little sister for her although, for Thomas' sake, I will be just as happy if it is a boy.

I wrote to Mother with the news and suggested she might like to come to live with us. Wouldn't that be wonderful? If Mother were here I think

I would be completely happy to stay in this country. I miss her so much. I know what her answer will be, however. She will never leave England.

It will be a summer baby. In England that would be wonderful. I yearn for an English summer where the sun warms without frizzling every living thing. But here? I don't think I will ever forget the heat that greeted us on our arrival from England. How will we keep the baby cool? At least the stone walls of this cottage will keep the worst of the heat out and I will spend most of my time within their protection.

I love our little cottage. We have a substantial fireplace and the men collect wood from the nearby bush to keep it going. Sarah loves going with Thomas and the other children into the 'bush' as they call it here. She met some 'abowidginees' the other day and can't stop talking about them.

"Why don't they wear clothes, Mama?" I had to think for a while because I didn't really know the answer. It was Thomas who picked her up and said: "because they like to feel the wind on their skin." I knew what the next question would be. "Can we take our clothes off too, so we can feel the wind on our skin." "No Sarah. You're English and English people wear clothes."

I could see that that didn't satisfy her but she had had enough questions for the time being and climbed into my lap for a cuddle.

Since our cottages were built, dwellings have shot up like mushrooms. It is quite a community now and I am not short of people to talk to. At first I was wary about who I spoke to, confining myself to tea with Anne and Helen, but now I see that no matter where we are from, we are all the same, all trying to survive life here. The old ways of waiting for introductions and polite society don't exist here.

And I'm glad.

Kathleen Egan across the way is Irish and is having a child, her sixth! The other five are wild and unkempt but friendly enough. It took me a while to relax with her as she is a papist after all. But now we have become friends and I look forward to our conversations. We are no different really but back home our paths would never have crossed.

"Your little Sarah is a pet," she said to me one day, "not wild like my brood."

"She can be naughty sometimes,"

"Naughty? Your Sarah? Why my Patrick was looking sheepish the other day and when I asked him what he had in his pocket, he turned out two raisin buns. I marched him straight back down to the bakery and made him apologise for nicking them. He said he was hungry! I said, I'll hungry you!

I was a bit shocked. But then I realised that Mr Egan has not had work for some time and the children are probably hungry.

I asked Kathleen how she keeps her babies cool in summer

"I strip 'em down to nothing and get the older ones to take it in turns to fan 'em down and put wet rags all around the cot."

Her way of talking and raw confidence has me laughing and I come away wishing I were more like her. Whatever life throws her way, she is ready for the challenge.

Thomas is happy, happier than I've seen him in ages. James is an astute businessman and Russell & Co. managed to get work on the new City Hospital, an enormous undertaking, meaning we are assured of an income for quite some time.

"There are people from all over the world, Jane," he told me excitedly. "Some have returned from the goldfields, unsuccessfully, and are labouring on building sites. Others have made money and returned to Melbourne to invest in property here, anxious not to fritter away their profit on drink and gambling like so many others. Labourers, builders, carpenters, Catholics, Methodists, Presbyterians, Italians, Germans, even some Chinese, all mixed together. Every day is different and I am learning so much."

I have not told Thomas how sick I feel. I don't want to worry him. It's only for another few months then it will all be over. When I get miserable, I look at Sarah and I know it is all worth it. What would I do without her?

"When will my little sister come?" she keeps asking.

"Soon, Sarah, but it might not be a sister. It might be a brother."

"I want a sister," she yelled, stamping her feet so I put my arms around her tummy and tickled her till she started giggling.

Every Tuesday the Chinese peddler comes around. His name is Ah Foo and Sarah loves him. He is gentle and kind, always with something cheery to say. Sometimes I buy his wares but mostly I just look forward to meeting him and talking about our families. He has a wife and three children and they live down by the river. People round here speak badly of the Chinese and call them all sorts of names. Sarah looks forward to Tuesdays and keeps her best smile for Ah Foo who picks her up and allows her to choose a sweet from his cart. Some of the women are disgusted I let him touch Sarah but I think they are wrong. He is just a person like us.

Sarah and Willie still enjoy a special friendship. Helen and I laugh and think that they may one day marry and we will all be related! They sit out in the lane and just chatter baby talk. They know all the people in the street and everyone knows them. I don't think they will remember much of England.

"I would love to take Sarah home sometime soon, Helen, maybe when the baby is strong enough to travel."

" I don't fancy another trip like that, Jane, and it is so expensive. We are still repaying Mrs Chisholm's loan."

"I know. It's probably just a dream. I do miss Mother and Elizabeth though, and even the boys."

"Our children won't remember anything about England and they'll get sick of us talking about it." Helen is so sensible. She has life worked out. I wish I had her strength.

Thomas is trying to encourage his sister Mary and her husband Richard to come out but we don't think he will have much luck. Mary would never leave her parents and although she and Thomas shared childhood dreams of travelling, I suspect she is more a stay at home type.

Last week I received a letter from the young girl on the ship, Harriet. She and Elijah have married and moved to Forest Creek. She asked after Sarah and said they hoped to have a child just like her. Elijah is one of those hopefuls who thinks he is going to become rich on the goldfields.

I must write back and tell them of my news.

THOMAS — BAMAWM
Christmas Day, 1913

The boy couldn't believe that I didn't go to the goldfields after we arrived. But deciding not to chase the gold was the best decision I ever made.

Instead, we lost no time in setting ourselves up in more comfortable homes in the better part of North Melbourne. We purchased land and materials and set about erecting three stone cottages. James Russell had the money and we worked for him. He would own the houses and we would rent them from him. It was a good arrangement. The Pickersgills had purchased a readymade house some miles away. I thought they were foolish as where they chose to live was subject to floods but there was no persuading them. I can't say I was disappointed. I will be working with Arthur Pickersgill but I'm not sure I wish to spend more time with him as I find his sermonising a bit hard to take. He really is quite a humourless man.

We also brought Henry Swindale into the partnership. He had been in the colony for some time and had local knowledge. He was unmarried and older and apart from working with us, he kept to himself. I wonder what happened to him.

The day that we unveiled the plaque outside the Office was one of the proudest moments of my life. "Well what do you think?" said James as he stood back on the road.

Russell & Co.
Builders & Contractors

James Russell
Arthur Pickersgill
Joseph Little
Thomas Bradshaw
Henry Swindale

When I saw my name on that plaque, all I wanted was for my father to see it but of course he couldn't and writing about it in a letter would not be the same. I knew, however, that he would have been proud.

The buzz around Melbourne was intoxicating. So many new arrivals. We couldn't keep up with the work. We accepted small and large commissions. From a set of laughing lions welcoming visitors to a mansion in Camberwell, *Shrublands,* where Joseph and I almost died in the construction, to much grander works. The new Lieutenant-Governor, Charles La Trobe, seemed hell bent on making Melbourne a city to be proud of and with the money rolling in from the gold fields, it was as if the magnificent bluestone buildings were a sign of his own personal pride.

The scorching summer gave way to the sunny autumn days and the mild winter. Life was good, even better when Jane told me her news! Sarah was to have a little brother, and he would be born here in Australia.

JANE – NORTH MELBOURNE
Christmas night – 1853

The festivities have finished and so ends our second Christmas in Melbourne. I am feeling quite whimsical. Maybe it was that wine that Thomas found somewhere! I enjoyed myself. Good food, good company and the weather wasn't too hot.

I am growing bigger every day. Sarah won't stop talking about her little sister. She is convinced it is a girl. I feel stronger than I did with Sarah and not quite so ill tempered. I think the sunshine and fresh food has contributed to my good health. Thomas is more considerate also. In fact he has been spoiling me, bringing me tea in the mornings before he leaves for work.

It was hot today but not unbearably so. Can you believe that in this climate, we had a hot, English Christmas dinner? Yesterday I visited Kathleen Egan and took some mince tarts for her children. I was hardly in the door when they disappeared into the grubby hands of the little ones. I merely laughed when she apologised for her children's behaviour. They are a loving family and I have become very fond of her rough children. Sarah likes them too. Kathleen's husband, Con, has no work at present, and they are surviving on handouts from the Church and whatever she can earn laundering.

Her baby arrived a few weeks ago. A little girl she named Sheila. Cradling the child, I felt a surge of maternal feeling. Soon, I thought, I will be nursing my own baby, a baby born in this country. Kathleen must have read my thoughts: "Jane, how long have you to go now?"

"The midwife thought only a few weeks and I agree. This baby seems to be desperate to be born. Sometimes I think I will explode."

"Ah, but you are such a good mother and a great neighbour as well. I wish you all the best and let me know if I can be of any help at all."

As I left the Egan's ramshackle house, I had a strange feeling. I can't explain it but it wasn't a good feeling. I shivered and told myself not to be so silly. All women who are about to have a baby have these feelings of anxiety, I am sure I had them before Sarah was born.

I am very tired tonight but content. It did my heart good today to see everyone enjoying the hospitality of James and Anne and I thank God for their friendship. The children bring us much joy as we watch them playing together. Today they couldn't wait to finish their meal and go out to play in the laneway. Five months on a ship together has bonded them so they are like brothers and sisters. Sarah and Willie try to keep up with the older ones as much as possible, but when they can't they are content to find something else to do. Willie always takes the lead and is a bit bossy but Sarah doesn't seem to mind that. She just loves being with him.

Richard and Joseph are concerned about the outbreak of dysentery in the western part of the city. "It might be a good idea to keep the children away from anyone who has it," Richard said and Thomas agreed. " We need rain to flush the drains. The water supply is stagnant and filthy. Thank God we are able to get clean drinking water from the city near work. We try to discourage Sarah from drinking the local stuff."

All this talk of dysentery and bad water has made me homesick. I received letters from Mother and Elizabeth last week. They especially want news of Sarah and whereas they are pleased about the approaching birth, they would love us to return, even for a visit. Mother's letters always make me cry and I wish I could make her see how happy I am here .

Will I ever see Mother again, or Elizabeth or the boys? Will I ever see the green countryside again? Green has become an obsession for me. When I am choosing material to make clothes for Sarah, I always choose green. When I close my eyes at night I see green. I think, sometimes, that I even dream in green.

Only a few weeks to go – the baby will be born and my back will stop hurting. I am growing impatient for him, to meet his sister, his mother and his father. What shall we call him? Thomas wants to call him Marriott after his mother's family. I would prefer William after my father but we will see. Maybe it will be another girl!

Sarah thinks so.

THOMAS — BAMAWM
Christmas Day, 1913

Another Christmas Day!

The boy and I and Marriott are celebrating. They are drinking beer. I have my wine. We talk about nothing and everything. I don't like to talk about Jane while Marriott is here as somehow it seems disloyal to his own mother but I was so happy to hear Jane describe her own happiness at that Christmas of 1853, the Christmas that would be her last.

It's a funny time, Christmas. Everyone tries to be happy but it's really just the same as every other day. As a child, I loved Christmas. We gathered round the Green and sang carols while we decorated the huge chestnut tree with our home made decorations. There was a foot race with a penny prize to the school and back. I won it once but my brother, John, won it several times.

The boy said that in the orphanage, Christmas meant that the local charity women would bring them plum pudding and sweets. There was usually fighting as the bigger boys bullied the smaller boys out of their share. Most times, the boy missed out and used to look out the window as the charity women left with big smiles on their faces. He wanted to tell them not to bother next year!

The second Christmas we had in Victoria, 1853, was the happiest I remember. We had done something truly adventurous and had made it work. It had not been easy and there had been times when we could have given up and returned to England but we persevered and were well on the way to success. We were proud of ourselves. The building business was booming, Jane was glowing with health as the baby neared its coming and we were happy. Sarah was growing into a healthy and bright little girl who gave us so much joy. She was learning to talk and used to call sausages, *yosh* so we adopted the term and sometimes I would find myself asking for *yosh* much to the butcher's amusement!

That Christmas of 1853, Jane and I gathered in Errol Street with our friends and decorated the branch of a gum tree. It wasn't a chestnut tree but its branches were such that the children enjoyed climbing it and placing their home made decorations. Sarah's joy in the festivities with her friends, William, Joseph, Josephine, Catherine, Margaret, and John, reminded me of my childhood on the Green in Priors Marston.

Thank God for the Australian weather so we could leave the children outside while we prepared the meal. Then, when we called them in for the meal, the noise in the Russell household was deafening as our laughter filled the stone house. It wasn't the hottest day we had had that month, (the dreadful heat came a week later) but hot enough that we questioned the wisdom of having a baked English meal with the stove heating the whole house. We all agreed, however, that Christmas wouldn't be Christmas without roast turkey. Joseph and I ventured to a poultry farm a few miles from where we lived and chose the biggest turkey we could find.

"This one?" said the Italian whose business skills I couldn't help but admire.

When we nodded, the axe came down swiftly. Joseph flinched and I thought he was going to faint. Obviously he had not grown up on a farm!

The Italian turkey farmer was smart. He knew the British migrants would be longing for a meal to remind them of home and bred enough turkeys to fill the demand. Joseph and I laughed as we threw the turkey in the back of the cart and set off for home. We were two friends with the world at our feet.

I still see that scene as if it were yesterday. My good friends, business partners, gathered around the makeshift table. Money coming in and our wives and children all pioneers in a new country, our children happy and healthy spending most of their time in the sunshine. I wrote to Mary that night and told her how happy I was, how class and religion weren't as important as in England and how I numbered amongst my friends, Catholics, Italians and even Irish.

Life was better than I could have expected. What could possibly go wrong? Since then, whenever I was tempted to feel truly happy about something, I would share the feeling with sadness, for it was less than four weeks later that my world came crashing down. The future that Jane and I had planned together. All gone.

JANE – NORTH MELBOURNE
JANUARY 14th, 1854

The heat has started.

Yesterday I felt dizzy after hanging out the washing. I had to sit down for some minutes before feeling right again. Thomas has insisted I drink only the water he brings me as the water from the town supply is contaminated and there have been many cases of dysentery. I don't know where he gets the water from but he is determined that I not get sick.

He has been very sweet as I have grown in size. I have felt good up until now. Christmas Day was only three weeks ago and I felt so well. But this heat!

I hate it.

I have run out of water. Can I wait till Thomas gets home? I am very thirsty.

It is a New Year – 1854, almost two years since we first heard Mrs Chisholm speaking about moving to the new colony. She made it sound so easy and exciting but it has been anything but. We have survived and until this heat wave, I would have said things were going very well. It's amazing how your attitude can change with a change of temperature.

Sarah has grown into a beautiful little three year old. She is talking and asking questions and bringing us so much joy. She idolises her father and waits for him to turn the corner before running up and throwing herself into his arms. The smile on his face when he sees her is quite wonderful.

She and Willie still play together but she has many other friends as well. There is a school starting up not far from our house so she will be able to attend that when she is a little older. I think she will like school as she seems very curious about everything. In this country, women have more freedom than back in England. The owner of the pub on the corner of our street is a woman and many of them have shops, especially as so many of the men have deserted to the goldfields.

What will this year bring? We have seen so many changes in the city since we arrived. I truly believe Melbourne will be a great city. The buildings that are being constructed with the proceeds from the goldfields are simply magnificent. Thomas loves working on them and watching them grow. He looks forward to when he can say to Sarah and the new little one: "See that building? Your father built that."

One of the Egan children came down with dysentery last week. It was pitiful to see him so sick. The doctor thinks, because of his toughness, he may survive but time will tell. Kathleen and all her Catholic friends have set up a rosary vigil, praying for his recovery. I have kept away as I am so close to the birth but my thoughts and prayers are with her. Mr Egan doesn't seem to know how to help so he spends most of his time at the pub.

I can't imagine what I would do if Sarah should become ill. My love for her is sometimes frightening and I can't imagine a world without her. She is part of my very soul.

Helen and Anne are coming to visit me this afternoon, bringing their latest cooking experiment. They have been gleaning recipes from the people in the street and I swear we've all put on weight. At least I have an excuse! I thank God for their friendship and know that if ever I was in trouble, they would be there to support me. I wonder what country the recipe will be from today? They have tried Italian and German cooking quite successfully but I can't wait till they try Chinese!

Life is good but I can't shake this feeling of anxiety. It just won't go away. Don't be silly, I tell myself. All expecting mothers feel like this.

THOMAS – BAMAWM

Christmas Night, 1913

I have to hand it to Marriott. He has prepared two good meals in a row. Christmas Dinner was delicious. Maybe I have underestimated his cooking skills. We didn't have turkey, but the beef was a good substitute. And he even made Yorkshire Pudding. I was glad that we had plum pudding and the boy got his fair share!

After that last reading, just before our Christmas feast, I felt slightly ill. The boy knew it was Jane's last entry and I could tell he felt it too. Just hearing of her anxieties and 'strange feelings' made me wonder, did she know? Did she have some premonition that she would die?

I was glad of the distraction of Marriott's story telling to lighten the atmosphere. All through dinner he entertained us with his experience of trying to work out how to start a motor car a friend of his owned. He wanted to 'whip it' but after realising it was not a horse, gave up. We were joined at dinner by one of Marriott's pub friends who had no family and who was happy to be invited to our table. I enjoyed the meal much more than I thought I would but was keenly aware of the boy sitting opposite. Something had changed in our relationship since I had introduced him to Jane, and hence to the younger me.

He helped me into my room as I had had a little too much red wine. As he was easing me into my chair, he noticed all the letters tipped on the floor and looked at me quizzically. I didn't speak until I had eased myself onto the bed and rested my aching legs.

I told him I was going to read them all and then burn them, but I had to sort them according to their dates. He couldn't believe how many there were. I don't think he has ever written a letter in his life. I reached down and grabbed one. It was the letter I wrote to my sister some months after my world fell apart. The boy knew what happened to Jane. I wasn't intending to go into detail to him about it but I decided he might as well know what it was like for me then.

I asked him to read to me the one on my pillow. He looked intently, as if to say, are you sure? I waved him on.

North Melbourne, 19th May, 1854

"My dear Mary

You will have heard from Mother and Father the sad news about Jane. I have wanted to write to you many times since then but I have not been well. It is four months now and yet it seems like no time that my world fell apart. I wrote to Mother and Father and Jane's mother the details of her death and the arrangements I was forced to make for her burial but I withheld from them so much. How could I tell them that I had to borrow enough money for the burial in the new cemetery here and then, only in a common grave where I am forbidden to put any plaque of commemoration. When I remember the burial of Jane's father just before we left Australia, I am beset with guilt as a Fairbrother is used to lying in the choicest ground.

Mary, I am recovering slowly and considering my future, thanks to my very good friends and partners James and Anne Russell, and Joseph and Helen Little who have been solicitous for my wellbeing. I know that Mother and Father are anxious to hear from me but I could not write earlier as my letters would have filled them with a concern that they could do nothing about. Their letters to me have been read and drenched with tears and left in a pile beside my bed.

Oh that I could turn back time and be back in "The Butcher House" among you all.

I do have a need to unburden myself to you, my sister and friend. There are so many things I have spoken to no-body about and it is time for me to relive the events of that day and to face them. Jane is not coming back. I know that now and I know that what happened to her has happened to so many around us. I must see it for what it is and look to the future.

But how painful it is to revisit the 19th January when our little cottage was the scene of such sorrow.

Four days before that fateful day, Jane gave birth to a sweet little girl with jet black hair and fine features like her mother, and her sister. Sarah was so excited and adored her little sister. It's true I wanted a boy but I was happy for Jane to have two little girls. I thought there would be time for a boy later.

We had many moments of joy and all was well. Jane didn't suffer too badly giving birth and we talked about our future. She was exhausted of course and that night we all fell asleep restlessly as the January heat seeped through the stone walls and made for much discomfort. As I sit writing this letter In beautiful autumn weather, it is hard to imagine how oppressive January was.

North Melbourne is very different from Priors Marston, Mary. The conditions here are primitive and they were especially bad during that summer. Because of the heat, we were forever thirsty and the clean water supplies were dwindling. We prayed daily for rain to flush the drains as people were getting sick by the thousands. The population has risen to half a million in the last 12 months and the city is not able to support the new arrivals swarming here, all hoping to make it rich on the goldfields. Oh Mary, they will have their hopes dashed, one by one but each person has that optimism that somehow they will be one of the lucky ones.

Jane was happy and was regaining her strength hour by hour. She talked about a trip home to show the little one to you all and even though I said that would be some years away, she kindled her excitement by telling Sarah about England and places like Leamington Spa where you could swim in "magic" waters. She described the green valleys and fields with different kinds of trees that lost their leaves in winter but produced coloured leaves in autumn. Sarah sat with her mother, listening and playing with the baby's fingers and toes. I'm sure she thought she was a doll. She learnt how to say "Leamington" and thought herself very smart although I do not think she can remember anything of England.

It was lovely to see them so happy together, Mary, and I spoke to the midwife about what food Jane would need while she was feeding the baby, I planned to visit the Chinese gardener and procure fresh fruit and vegetables . We discussed names and I mean to tell you that I was in favour of Mary, after you and also Mother. That night, as we settled down to rest, I was glad we had come. The future looked brighter than it had for months. I had work, enough money to live and plans to acquire land when we saved enough money.

Imagine my shock, however, when in the next few days after the birth, Jane showed signs of the dysentery which affected so many people in Melbourne. On the third day, she also developed dreadful pains in her stomach making her scream for relief. It was like she had been poisoned. I have seen many people suffer from dysentery since we left England, but her pain was different and she was so hot to touch I was concerned. She was saying the strangest things also, about her mother and father and at times I doubted whether she knew where she was. This was no ordinary dysentery.

I didn't know what to do. I felt quite hopeless. The midwife had gone and I had no-one to turn to. I fed her tea and even gave her some of the local beer that I heard can help women after childbirth, but Jane became sicker and sicker, resulting in her inability to feed the baby who, not surprisingly, deteriorated quite rapidly.

I sent Sarah to stay with Helen Little as I didn't want her to see her mother so distressed. She didn't want to go and begged to stay with her mother. As she was pulled away by Helen, she looked back with such a look that I think she knew she would never see her mother again. Her cries unnerved me as they reached me from the lane next to the house.

The 19th January was the hottest day of the whole summer. Mary, it is heat like you cannot imagine, dry but scorching. It saps your energy and you feel quite dizzy. Birds fall from the sky while in flight, dead before reaching the earth. Remember, as children, how we used to talk about going to a land with lots of sunshine and we imagined a filtered warmth emanating from the sun? This heat, Mary, bears no resemblance to such benign weather. It is an enemy for it brings with it the enervating languidness that drains your very soul.

On the third day, I went for the doctor. Dr Arnold is a pleasant enough fellow although I do not have much trust in him. He told me not to be too hopeful but as Jane was young and strong, she just might survive. What kind of solace was that? I couldn't believe what he was saying. Might survive! Anne Russell was occupied with the baby and trying to get some water into her.

On the fourth day I woke at 4am, aware of a discomfort in my spirit, and that's when I saw that Jane was no longer with us. She, sweet Jane, had slipped away into another world.

It's strange, Mary, I couldn't cry or feel anything. It's as if it was all happening to someone else and I couldn't wait to tell Jane about it later. When the doctor came and pronounced Jane dead, he ordered me to get a wet nurse urgently for the baby who was scarcely breathing and showed early signs of dysentery. I must admit I had not given her much attention and thought it better that she die as well. Why not? She had taken my Jane! I thought it justice that she die also. Mary, can you condemn me for that thought? Anne Russell came as soon as she heard and was shocked at the state of the baby as she had thought she was on the improve the night before and had only just located a suitable wet nurse.

Because of the new Health Regulations introduced a few months ago, any household containing a person with dysentery, cholera or typhoid has to notify the authorities. The doctor was not sure whether the dysentery was the cause of death but it certainly was a factor so Jane had to be buried by nightfall. By then the baby had died as well. Mary I don't think it would have lived anyway but I confess to you and to no-one else, that I was relieved. Do you condemn me for this?

Helen Little brought Sarah in to say goodbye to her mother, just before they took her away. She moved close to me wanting me to pick her up like I always did, but I couldn't. I told Helen to take her away and I asked Anne Russell to leave as well. Helen gave me a disappointed look as she put her arm around Sarah, and announced, as she closed the door, that Sarah would stay with them until I had worked out what to do.

I can still hear Sarah crying, "I want Mama, I want Mama," as she was reluctantly taken away.

Mary, my dear sister, I so wish you were here. I left England with much hope and optimism but now I find myself in the darkest place. Work has not been going well as it was in January and more people are defaulting on their bills. My partners are concerned and feel inclined to follow the myriads heading to the goldfields of Forest Creek, Bendigo and Ballarat. We are thinking of selling the Business within the next few months and that will leave me with no work and no family but enough money to clear my debts and buy land.

I have considered returning home but I do not want to go back to my old life and how could I face Jane's family? Even though this country has taken everything from me, I do have a love of its rugged landscape and its promise of so much possibility. It has captured my soul. I wish you could visit, Mary, and I could show you what I mean.

Some weeks ago I met a man called Peter Lyon. He came into the shop to ask about building regulations and in conversation, we discovered that we had arrived in Melbourne in the same week on different ships. He does not know my story and thinks of me as a single man with no ties. He knew that we were thinking of selling the business in North Melbourne and asked me what I intended to do. When I told him I had no real plans, he became quite interested. He has eleven children! Can you imagine? They are from Kildare in Ireland and he has an optimism like few I have ever met. How do you think you and Richard would handle eleven children, Mary?

Peter has applied for land in a place called Laanecoorie. There is, as yet, no settlement there, and he will be the pioneer of the district. It is on the Loddon River about 80 miles from Melbourne and gold has been discovered nearby. He has asked me to join him, although it could take years for all the permits and surveys to be done. I have agreed. What do I have to lose? Until then I will stay in Melbourne although I don't quite know where, maybe St Kilda which I believe is much nicer than North Melbourne, maybe even build my own house there. Buying and selling can bring tidy profits as so many returning from the goldfields are looking for accommodation.

Joseph and Helen Little are also moving to St Kilda and they have agreed to look after Sarah. She has become attached to them and I do not think Laanecoorie is any place for a little girl to grow up, especially without a mother. Peter mentioned that there had been trouble with the natives there and some settlers have been murdered. Hardly the place for a little girl. Besides, Peter knows nothing of Sarah. I am ashamed to admit that I allowed him to think I am a single man. You may judge me for this decision Mary, as I cannot imagine your Richard ever doing the same should something happen to you, but I am not like Richard. Maybe I am cruel or just weak, but I simply cannot be a father to Sarah in my present state. She is far better off with the Littles whom she knows and loves.

Pray for me, Mary. Pray for me to feel again and to be able to look at this wide, blue sky and thank God I am still alive because at the moment I cannot thank God for anything.

Give my regards to Richard and also John. He wrote recently and it is no surprise to hear that he is carrying on Father's butcher business successfully and now he is experimenting with bees and honey. I know he will make a success of that as well., with his keen mind and dogged determination. Tell everyone I am fine and I will write soon.

Your ever loving brother
Thomas

The boy hung onto the letter and looked at me. Was it pity, Judgement, or surprise that I saw on his face? He said nothing for a long time and then carefully folded the letter and placed it back in the box. He poured a glass of water and brought it over to me. That is when I saw the tear in his eye. He would want to hear the rest of the story so I thought it would be a late night.

I did build a house in St Kilda, in Pakington street, not too far from the bay. It was a much better area than North Melbourne and the people seemed gentler but I couldn't seem to get any enjoyment out of life. My spirits were low. Had Jane lived, we may have settled permanently in St Kilda. I know she would have loved it but I was anxious to go onto the land and do what I had always wanted to do, grow vines and make wine.

I watched Sarah growing with the Littles and she seemed content. I knew she wanted to come and live with me but I didn't feel that I could handle her even though the Littles were putting pressure on me to take her. I worked on the Catholic church in St Kilda with Joseph and waited impatiently for when I could make the break to Laanecoorie.

By the time the lease on the land at Laanecoorie came through, Sarah was eight years old and just presumed she would be coming with me. "Papa, why can't I come with you?"

I spun some story about the natives but that wasn't the real reason. I just didn't know how to be a father to her.

The boy knows that I married again, to Marriott's mother. I think he was disappointed because he had grown quite fond of Jane and felt that I had betrayed her. He softened a little, however, when I told him that my second wife, Catherine, was Irish! Sitting here in my room, fifty years later, I struggle to remember much about Catherine at all.

When she died, barely nine years after our marriage, I did not go to that dark place that I went to when Jane left me. I was sad, yes, but it was a different sadness from when Jane died. In many ways, it was as if my heart had hardened and nothing could break it again.

Was marrying Catherine a mistake? I can't say that as I needed her and she gave me back something which I had lost, a zest for life. She was the oldest girl of eleven children and her father was one of that breed of hard Irish men who believed the older daughters had a duty to work in the home like a servant. I'm sure she saw marriage to me as her way out of the almost slave conditions her parents kept her in. I think we both saw the marriage as a way of escaping different things, she of servitude and me of despair.

The boy looks at me. I know he likes me but the more I talk, the more he sees the darker side of me. By asking him to read my letters I have opened my soul to him, something I have done to no-one else since Mary died.

When my new wife, Catherine, found she was with child, I admit that I panicked. I did not want to go through what I did with Jane so I took her to the Tarnagulla Lying In Hospital rather than leave her in the hands of the local midwife. She had a difficult labour, due in fact to her age, and after Marriott was born, she never really recovered her health. We had a few good years but it was becoming apparent that her illness was serious and the treatment she needed was expensive, facilitating long trips to Melbourne to a specialist.

The pain that racked her body also rendered her moody and difficult. It wasn't an easy marriage. The ghost of Jane was always present and when she found out about the existence of Sarah, the daughter whom she never met, trust had been broken.

The boy knew Laanecoorie. He had come with me to buy some cattle there. I showed him the land I had owned and he shook his head, saying I must have been mad. There's nothing there now except a giant weir and a beautiful bridge. Bamawm is Paradise in comparison.

The travel from Laanecoorie to Melbourne was becoming too much. Catherine couldn't take it. We needed to move. It was easy for me to get a job on the railways and I wasn't sorry to be back in Melbourne. Although I was not using my skills as a carpenter, I was earning enough to pay the medical bills.

"Why don't you leave the boy with us?" Peter Lyon had said when we told them of our move to Melbourne but I was adamant. Marriott was to stay with us. I did not want the guilt of abandoning another child.

Returning to Melbourne, something quickened in me. The thought of our arrival, fifteen years before, dominated my thoughts.

Jane and little Sarah — wondering what sort of world I had brought them to, but trusting, trusting in me.

Fourteen years on, Melbourne had changed so much. It was 1866 and It looked like a real city, cleaner, with roads, buildings, police stations, and people making their way in an orderly fashion. We passed the City Hospital which I had had some hand in building. It looked magnificent.

I looked forward to visiting Sarah, excited about seeing her after so long. She was now sixteen. Joseph had kept me abreast of what was happening and it appeared there were no problems although he hinted that she was rather headstrong.

As Catherine's doctor was located in Sandridge, my old house in Packington street, St Kilda was perfect. Setting up in the house I built when my heart was broken, the memories came flooding back, threatening to drown me. But I had to be strong. Catherine was my priority now. I could not dwell on the past. It was not difficult to procure cheap labour, and like my parents back home, I hired a girl to live with us in exchange for work. Her name was Brigid. She was like a little mouse at first but didn't take long to come out of her shell. She came from an Irish family with 13 children, the older ones having to work and send their wages home. Her accent was so strong, I understood less than half of what she said.

Marriott was almost five and he loved Brigid and understood her. They would chatter away for hours. He was a welcome distraction for us with his funny antics and affectionate disposition. Many times, he kept me from going mad with despair and worry. Catherine loved Brigid also and felt protective of her. At times, when she felt a little better, she would help her with her embroidery. It was good for both of them.

I was humbled by the support I received from my friends in Melbourne and felt guilty that I had been so remiss in my communication. One such friend was Frederik Taubner who had been a friend from when we first arrived in the colony. I had helped him with plans for his house in North Melbourne and when we discovered a mutual interest in wine making, we shared our ideas and dreams. Since going to Laanecoorie, I had lost contact with him but one day I ran into him at the *Wine Makers Association* meeting and we spent hours talking, mostly about grapes and vines.

He had become a successful businessman and with his new found wealth had purchased *Shrublands* in Camberwell, a newly built, magnificent house with several acres under vines. I told him about Catherine's illness and I was moved by his concern. He was, I thought, a thoroughly decent man. He often visited after that, bringing fresh produce from his garden for all of us and of course a bottle of wine for him and me to share. One summer evening, as we sat out the front of the house, after Catherine had retired and Brigid was reading Marriott a story, we watched the comings and goings of St Kilda, reflecting on the growth of the city and critiquing his latest vintage.

"Thomas when are you going to make your own wine?"

"When I get some decent land. Laanecoorie has been something of a disappointment."

"Heard they're opening up land near Echuca, on the Murray. That could be a possibility."

We talked until the sun went down over the bay. Catherine was ill and I felt guilty that I was happy. The thought of leaving Laanecoorie and growing grapes somewhere and making my own wine had my spirits soaring.

"How's that young girl of yours Thomas. Where is she now? Sarah, isn't it?"

I told him about the arrangement I had with Joseph and Helen Little and that I planned to visit her the very next day. I didn't tell him that it had been six years since I had seen her. I kept that to myself.

"I've been looking for a bright young girl to train as a housekeeper, Thomas. Can't seem to find anyone. They're all either dumb or lazy. What about Sarah? Would she be interested?" The opportunity seemed too good to be true. Over a third glass of wine, we discussed the details and I told him I would bring Sarah to *Shrublands* myself.

When Frederik left, I wondered had I done the right thing. I had been in Melbourne for weeks and still had not gone to see Sarah. Was I nervous about the reception she would give me after so long in Laanecoorie with practically no contact? Would she want to work as a housekeeper at *Shrublands*? I convinced myself that my decision was in everyone's best interests as I made Catherine a milk drink to help her sleep.

The next day, walking up the path to the Little's St Kilda home, I was full of doubt. Six years had seen the garden grow and give the front a shield from the street. There were signs everywhere of a happy family that lived within and I was glad Sarah was part of that family. I expected a cool reception and this is what I received, although tempered with Joseph and Helen's Christian charity. I knew they were disappointed in me as I had not been in contact with Sarah since I had married Catherine.

The boy asked me if Sarah even remembered me. I think he was disgusted with me, too. I can see his sympathy for Sarah growing the more he learns about me.

She did remember me and I think she was pleased to see me though she was now a young lady. I hardly recognised her. She was quite beautiful and so like her mother, the way she used to put her head on the side and peer at you in a way that melted your heart. I got quite a jolt when she began speaking to me.

There were some tense moments when Joseph challenged me about my absence from Sarah's life and my marriage to Catherine. He was hurt and angry that I hadn't ever brought my new wife and son to meet Sarah or that I hadn't organised to bring Sarah back to live with me. But when I explained how ill Catherine was and that she probably wouldn't ever recover, his attitude softened.

Helen fussed around the kitchen making tea while Joseph and I spoke about the building opportunities in Melbourne. The atmosphere became slightly less icy but it was not like old times. Sarah helped Helen with the tea but I noticed she kept looking at me with a quizzical look on her face, almost as if she was trying to work out where I fitted in her life. As we all sat around the table, I told them about Marriott and what a delightful little chap he was but I quickly realised that maybe this was insensitive of me and changed the subject.

When I finally told them of my conversation with Frederik about taking Sarah into service, Joseph and Helen were amenable to the idea. Joseph remembered Frederik Taubner from North Melbourne days and knew Shrublands well as he and I had constructed a fountain there, nearly killing ourselves in the process. Helen wanted more reassurance, however. "Is he of good moral character Thomas? We need to know that Sarah is going into a safe environment." I took offence at her tone as she was hinting that I, her father, would send my daughter into a compromising situation. I was rather short in my response. "He is a respected member of the community, Helen, prominent in the Church and about to stand for Parliament. I can assure you, Frederik Taubner is of the highest moral character."

Immediately I felt guilty. Helen had been Sarah's mother for over ten years, had housed and educated her, comforted her and most importantly kept Jane alive by talking about her. I had done none of these things. I knew she was just anxious that Sarah would be happy, like she would for her own children.

When I said that I would take Sarah with me that very day to start at *Shrublands*, Helen almost dropped her cup. "What, so sudden!" She looked across at Sarah who looked quite pale. I explained that with doctor's appointments and Mr Taubner's schedule, it had to be that day.

The boy asked me what Sarah thought about the idea of me turning up and taking her away. I confessed to him that I hadn't taken much notice of how she felt. It was a good solution and in time she would understand that. She didn't say much but was polite in expressing her gratitude to me for finding the position and asked me to wait while she changed into her good clothes for the journey. Helen went with her.

While she was gone, Joseph asked about Catherine, offered sympathy, and asked if there was anything they could do. The conversation was forced, with both of us regretting the strain that existed between us. We had been such good friends.

I helped Sarah into the carriage and as the horses pulled away, she waved goodbye to the house that had been her home for thirteen years. I must admit I didn't think enough about what a wrench that would have been for her, so intent was I on delivering her to *Shrublands*. As we approached Chapel street, she turned and smiled at me and I was surprised at how happy that made me.

At first we were shy with each other and the conversation was stilted but as we drove towards Camberwell and I pointed out projects that I had worked in, we both relaxed. She told me about school, her attempts at becoming a pianist and of course, her friendship with Willie. I told her about my life in Laanecoorie, Catherine and Marriott. She wanted to know if Marriott knew about her and if they would meet soon. I assured her I would arrange it. I asked her if she was nervous at the thought of working at *Shrublands* and she surprised me with her quiet excitement. She is like her mother, I thought, strong willed and optimistic. Looking back, I realise that that was the first real conversation I had ever had with my daughter and I also realised how much I had enjoyed it.

As the carriage turned into the driveway of *Shrublands,* she was overwhelmed by its magnificence. I pointed out the fountain with the two lions that Joseph and I had constructed and we both laughed as I told her that one of them almost fell on top of us as we tried to mount it. "Not many people are killed by lions in Camberwell," she said.

In that moment, we were father and daughter and the past did not exist.

Frederik gave us a warm welcome and talked to Sarah about Jane which she seemed to appreciate, asking lots of questions. I was surprised at her confidence. When a young servant girl arrived to take Sarah under her wing, Frederik turned to me and said: "You must be proud, Thomas, she is a fine girl." If only he knew. I had no right to feel pride.

I had told Sarah that I would come and find her before I departed but instead I left without a goodbye. I regret that decision because Frederik told me later that she was most upset. I don't even know why I did it, I just thought it would be easier.

The boy shook his head when I said that. He knew how it would affect Sarah for me to leave without saying goodbye. He thinks me very cold and uncaring and I'm sure is reappraising his view of me.

The next three years were difficult for me as Catherine grew worse. From work on the railways to caring for Catherine, spending time with Marriott who grew increasingly concerned for his mother and wondering about my own future, I had little time to think about Sarah, although occasionally I visited *Shrublands.* I trusted Frederik to be a man of his word and look after Sarah and when I did visit, she seemed quite happy. She had yet to meet Marriott who, despite what I told Sarah, did not know of her existence.

Brigid was not much of a housekeeper but I didn't care. She was like a big sister to Marriott and that was all that mattered. Catherine found great solace in her company and Brigid was smart enough to get help if anything happened.

The end came suddenly. The surgeon, Mr Curtis, a competent but arrogant man with a comical lisp, told us he needed to operate to give Catherine some relief from the pain. I think she knew it was the beginning of that journey that all of us dread, the one I am on now.

As Mr Curtis stood telling us this, as nonchalantly as if he were suggesting a stroll by the bay, Catherine reached for my hand. I took it and thought, it's happening all over again, the woman I love is leaving me. I was beginning to wonder what I had done to deserve it. I was not totally surprised that she died during the operation. I was partly prepared for such an outcome. The cause of death was ovarian dropsy. When they opened her up, there was little they could do.

The boy muttered something about 'rotten luck' and I couldn't disagree. But it was different this time. The worst part was explaining to Marriott that his mother would not be coming home. He grew very quiet. At seven, he was old enough to understand but he didn't cry in front of me. His tears were kept for Brigid and when she returned to her family, he was inconsolable.

It was hard for the boy to imagine the larger than life Marriott that he knows, as an inconsolable seven year old, but I think it gave him a sympathy for him nethertheless. I knew what he was wondering, however. Did I keep Marriott with me or give him to another family like I did with Sarah?

Mr Lyon wanted his daughter buried in Eddington, with the other Lyons, but I didn't want that. I paid for a plot in the Melbourne General Cemetery where I had buried Jane 15 years earlier. But this time, I did it properly. Catherine was buried in the Anglican section in her own plot. Her resting place is on the edge of the cemetery so she can look across the road to the houses opposite where people are laughing, crying and growing, where people are alive.

Strangely enough I had never been to the Melbourne General Cemetery. When Jane died, Richard and Joseph took care of everything. I never visited the 'common grave' where Jane and the baby were buried. But now I wanted to find them. What part of the cemetery were they in? I became disoriented. The complex was enormous and there were no markings on common graves.

I never found her.

As I took my leaden heart down Royal Parade, I knew I was saying goodbye forever to the two women who had been such a big part of my life and who had left me with two children. I walked all the way into the city. I wanted to be part of it, part of life in Melbourne in this year of 1869. I watched the horse drawn trams carting people here and there and thought of the futility of life. People laughed and shouted but I couldn't ever imagine doing that again.

I had a strong urge to visit Sarah. Before I knew it, I was hailing a cab and ordering the driver to *Shrublands*. As luck would have it, Sarah was sweeping the front steps and I think I almost collapsed into her arms. She must have got a terrible shock. She took me into the kitchen where she made me a cup of tea and listened as I talked about Catherine and Marriott. At one stage, I swear I thought I was talking to Jane. As I stood up, shakily, I felt better and Sarah walked me back to my carriage. "Take care," she said. "Soon I would like to meet my half-brother."

I returned to Laanecoorie but as soon as I arrived there, I couldn't wait to leave. I hated the place. The Lyon family were broken hearted at the death of their oldest daughter and in a way their grief only compounded mine. The aunts fussed over Marriott and spoiled him. I wasn't going to stand for that. I needed to get away and thought of the land near Echuca that Frederik had told me about. I made enquiries.

Carpenters were needed in Bamawm, a growing town half way between Echuca and Rochester on the Campaspe River.

The Restdown Estate was to be subdivided and there was talk of irrigation schemes. I packed up my meagre belongings, left my land for Peter to sell at his leisure and put my house in St Kilda up for sale. The money from the sale would enable me to buy some decent land suitable for growing vines. I returned Catherine's belongings to her family, keeping only her books which I knew Marriott would appreciate in later years.

With an excited Marriott, I caught the coach to Bamawm and as it drew away from Laanecoorie, I felt like I did when we boarded the train to Southampton in 1852, leaving the past behind and blindly going into the unknown. I felt free.

The boy has no family. He knows what it feels like to have no-one and understands what it is to make a new beginning. That is how he felt about coming here, I am sure. It's late and I suggest that he go to bed. I like his company but I am tired and want to be alone. He says goodnight, his eyes knowing that the next few hours will be difficult for me but also knowing he can't help. I know he is disappointed in me but I also know he has a great affection for me. It means a lot to me.

Too many memories. Too many regrets. Does it matter where you die? Does it have to be in a place you love? Bamawm is my place. I'm happy to die here. I feel at home amongst the houses and shops, some of which I have built with my own hands, the vegetables and vines I have grown, the neighbours who respect me and of course, my daughter. Even the parched earth. I wonder sometimes how the grave diggers can penetrate the hardened clay earth enough to bury anyone.

Jane why aren't you here to see what I have achieved? Would you be proud of me? Would you be proud of Sarah and the seven grandchildren she has given you or would you be disappointed in her? Would you have been the rock in her life that she needed?

Since I have become an old man, I cry more easily, weeping because my daughter died before I could say to her what I needed to say, to ask for forgiveness, but also selfishly because she is no longer here to mourn for me.

I don't want to go to Torrumbarry with Marriott. Looking around the room, however, with letters strewn all over the floor as a witness to the ghosts of my past, I'm not sure I want to stay here either.

Mon. 16 March 1914
Bendigo Advertiser
The death occurred in the Echuca Hospital on Thursday of one of the oldest identities of the Rochester District, in the person of Thomas Bradshaw. The deceased gentleman came to Rochester in the early seventies and was employed on the old Restdown Station. He also worked as a carpenter and builder, and erected some of the first houses in the district.
For many years he occupied a farm and vineyard at Bamawm, now in the possession of Messrs. Wright Bros., and later moved to Torrumbarry where he had lived ever since.
He leaves one son, Marriott, who is well known among sportsmen.
(The burial will take place in Echuca)

PART TWO

SARAH

England: 1850 – 1852
Australia: 1852 – 1913

Chapter One

Shrublands – Camberwell
1866

The carriage rattled down the flattened, dirt drive to *Shrublands*. As the magnificence of the building became visible to Sarah, she was overcome with the scale of it. Did this all belong to one person? Who could possibly afford to own a place like this?

She looked at her father sitting beside her and felt a warm glow flowing through her. How she had longed for his company over the last thirteen years. How she had wished he would come to her and say, "Sarah, I want you to come home." And now, here he was, suddenly appearing in her life after an absence of six years but bitter sweet, he was taking her to another home where he would leave her, friendless and alone, just as he had thirteen years before.

"What do you think Sarah? Is this place grand enough for you?"

"Papa, Does Mr Taubner own it all?"

She thought of Jane Eyre arriving at the home of Mr Rochester. The battered Bronte book was the one thing she had of her mother's, and she had read it so many times, the pages were coming adrift from the binding.

"Mr Taubner is a very wealthy man, Sarah and a good friend. It's very decent of him to give you this chance and I know you won't let me down."

"Did Mama know him too?"

Thomas didn't speak for some seconds. Why, thought Sarah, was he so reluctant to speak about her mother?

"She did know him, and she liked him." There followed a slight smile, "She used to imitate his accent."

Sarah wanted more, more talk of her mother, the mother she could hardly remember. Her picture of her was like a silhouette against a black background and she was forever trying to bring it to life.

But her father was not offering anymore. As the horses rounded the bend, he asked the driver to stop beside a fountain. Water was streaming out of the mouths of two lions who were majestically perusing the glorious gardens.

"You see that fountain, Sarah? It was your uncle Joseph and I who built that. The lions were sculptured and brought over from England and we had a devil of a job to position them like that."

Sarah glanced sideways at her father. He was proud, she could see that and why not? it was quite a structure, but there was something else, a sadness almost as if the fountain reminded him of better days.

The horses continued to the front of the house and for the first time Sarah had a chance to see it as a whole. There were steps at the front but also at the side so you could ascend from three directions. Once onto the veranda, (or was it called a balcony), you were encircled by the walls of the two storey mansion.

Was this really going to be her home? She and her father alighted from the carriage and stood at the base of the steps. The driver was lifting her trunk from the back of the carriage.

"Your trunk is light, Missy, for a girl your age. Not that I'm complaining mind you."

Sarah felt slighted. It wasn't her fault she didn't own much. She didn't reply. A servant appeared and took the trunk from the driver.

"Welcome to *Shrublands*," he said with a grin which spread right across his freckled face. As he lifted the trunk, he said: "Not too much gold in here, then"

Another reference to the fact that Sarah's worldly possessions added to not much. She should have been annoyed but somehow, it didn't sound as demeaning coming from this friendly face. She didn't know whether to speak or not but found herself saying, "My Aunty Helen packed it for me so I don't even know what's in it."

He put the trunk onto the ground and held out his hand. "The name's Seamus. If you need to know anything, don't be frightened to ask. We're all a friendly lot really."

Sarah didn't know what she didn't know so she just thanked him and moved towards her father on the steps. Her tummy rumbled. Was it nerves or the fact that she hadn't eaten since Aunty Helen's delicious porridge early that morning?

She felt strange, hollow, as if she wasn't really there but an ephemeral object devoid of any solidity. When she reached her father, he put his arm around her. After the shock of such an intimate gesture, she relaxed. It felt nice. For just a brief moment, she could imagine an intimacy between them such as Uncle Joseph had with his daughters, where she could talk to him and he would see her as a person.

What would she tell him now if they could talk, really talk? That she was scared. That she felt like a little girl instead of a sixteen year old woman going into her first place of employment, that try as she might, she didn't feel the sense of excitement that others said she would feel on embarking on a new venture?

Why was her father being so affectionate all of a sudden? The thought that he was trying to impress crossed her mind but she didn't want to entertain it.

They were ushered into a room which Sarah guessed was the 'parlour'. She had read about such places in Jane Eyre. There was so much to look at, her eyes darted all around. The chandelier, the ceiling rosettes, the timber doors, the stained glass and the magnificent rug covering the timber floors.

Standing to welcome them was Mr Taubner, her father's friend, a man who had known her mother and the owner of all this. He wasn't as big as her father but well-built with a beard which was not meticulously maintained. He wasn't what she expected and didn't look rich at all. She was anxious to hear him speak as she liked to think of her mother imitating him.

"So Thomas, this is the girl. My, My, she is nothing like you. Takes after her mother eh?" He turned to Sarah. "The last time I saw you, my girl, you were little more than a baby. I remember you were always with your friend, Willie."

"William Little," offered Thomas, "and yes she has Jane's looks, thank God." Her father had spoken her mother's name and his tone was different.

"Your mother was a beauty, Sarah," said Mr Taubner with an affectionate tone, and what's more while he spoke he looked directly at her, as if he saw her. His accent was quite funny but for some reason it relaxed her.

"Did you know my mother, Mr Taubner?" She surprised herself by asking the question she already knew the answer to. Was it just to prolong the conversation about her mother? She felt herself blushing. Oh how she wished she wouldn't betray herself like that.

Mr Taubner said what Thomas had already told her. It wasn't much, that Jane was a lovely person and a 'beauty,' but she wanted more. Everything she knew, she had learnt from Aunty Helen who had been her mother's friend, who had travelled to Australia with her and who had been with her in her illness. But even Aunty Helen seemed reluctant to go into too many details.

"Awful business that Thomas. Such a pity." He paused as he came closer to Thomas putting an arm on his shoulder." But well done man, you've married again. Best idea. A man can't go through life alone eh?"

No, thought Sarah, but a little girl can!

Seamus re-appeared at the door and said he had taken Sarah's trunk to the room she would be sharing with another housemaid. Mr Taubner thanked him and whispered another instruction to him which Sarah couldn't hear. She noticed his kindness and felt her heart lighten.

"A good lad," he directed at Thomas. "Came from the orphanage and is as keen as mustard. I have great plans for him. His mother and father both died during the typhoid epidemic on Richmond Flat about the same time as your Jane died."

'Died.' Mr Taubner used the word, 'died,' thought Sarah. Nobody ever used that word about her mother. It was more like she had just ceased to exist.

Thomas and Frederik Taubner settled into an easy conversation about wine making while Sarah sat self-consciously rearranging her pinafore and looking around at the art works on the wall. Most were landscapes of country she wasn't familiar with and guessed they were of England or Germany. She wondered why anyone would want to leave such a pleasant place. The mention of Willie's name had ignited her loneliness and she longed for his company.

After what seemed like ages, a girl not much older than Sarah appeared at the door. Mr Taubner acknowledged her straight away and called her into the room.

"Kitty, come and meet Sarah, the new maid. She will be sharing your room."

Sarah looked at her and felt a sliver of distaste. Kitty was a tough looking individual and didn't seem the sort of girl she could become friendly with.

"Kitty will take you to your lodgings, Sarah, and then show you around the property. I have released her from any work for the rest of the day so you can use the time to get to know each other. Your father will come and find you before he leaves but it won't be for some time as we have quite a bit of catching up to do." He looked at Thomas. "And I can't wait to show you my new vineyard."

Sarah stood and looked at Thomas. Was this it? She knew in her mind that he was only delivering her to *Shrublands* and the would go back to his new wife and son but somehow she had blocked that thought and hoped that he would stay in her life. The conversation on the way here, the hand around the shoulder, the story about her mother, all of it had lulled her into the hope that it was how things would be. I haven't seen him for six years, she thought, he appears, takes me away from the family that has housed me for thirteen years, reorganises my life and then disappears again. Sarah's heart was heavy. It was that feeling of abandonment, again.

"Pappa?" she said, not knowing what else to say, and she threw her arms around his neck.

"Go on Sarah," the tone was dismissive as he prised her arms away and gently pushed her. It was as if he had exhausted his good will towards her. "I'll find you after you've settled in."

The push brought back one of Sarah's few memories about her mother's death when she had sought out her father and he had roughly pushed her away. As she screamed, "I want Mama, I want Mama," a crying Aunty Helen had dragged her away.

She stood humiliated that she had done such a childish thing and realised that not only did she love her father; she also hated him. Kitty didn't look overly keen about this girl coming to share her room either. She looked at her impatiently, the look judging Sarah as not one of her sort at all.

They walked in silence across the landscaped stones to the servants' quarters. The room she was to share with Kiitty was nothing like what she was used to at the Littles which was filled with knick-knacks and soft toys and colour. Here it was drab and basic. Sarah took one look and thought she might as well be in prison. A pang of loneliness tugged at her heart. In one day, her whole life had changed.

Aunty Helen and Uncle Joseph weren't her parents but they had looked after her with affection and Christian charity. She had wanted for nothing. Here, however, she was on her own. No-body knew her, her story, her likes and dislikes and no-body cared. She thought of Willie, and wished she could climb a tree with him and just sit and watch the world below. But those days were gone. Kitty, seeing her face, did her best to cheer her up but when Sarah asked her if she wouldn't mind leaving her for a bit so she could unpack in private, she shrugged her shoulders and said brusquely, "suit yourself," and left the room.

Sarah sat on the bed, releasing the tears that had sat behind her eyelids since her father waved her away. Here, now, more than any other time, she ached for her mother. But what did she know of her? Scraps of information. She thanked God for Aunty Helen for without her she would know nothing.

She unlocked the clasp on her trunk. Seamus was right. There was no gold in here. A few items of clothing, a brush and comb set, Jane Eyre and at the bottom, Emily, the doll Aunty Helen had given her. She thought she had outgrown Emily but Aunty Helen had packed her, knowing that she just might need her.

"O Emily," she said out aloud, "here we are in the most beautiful house you have ever seen and I feel so lonely. What will become of us?"

She decided to test out the mattress and lay down looking at the bleak ceiling. Being wrenched out of the security of the Little household had brought up all the bad feelings she thought she had laid to rest. She had taken for granted the warmth of the Littles,

Uncle Joseph singing while Aunty Helen played the piano and she and Willie getting up to mischief when they were supposed to be listening.

But she wasn't a Little. She was a Bradshaw and should have been living with her father and mother who had brought her from England for a better life. Ha! The irony of it!

She heard Kitty outside talking to Seamus and tried to block out their voices and take herself into her past, trying to make sense of it.

Chapter Two

She had been told her mother died of infection, probably caused by the midwife, Doris Crosby, who had come straight from a neighbour's confinement to attend to Jane without washing her hands. The utensils she used, she wiped down with a rag, itself a source of infection. Because Jane had diarrhoea, the doctor who completed the death certificate thought she may have had dysentery, a notifiable disease and ordered she be buried before nightfall. He declared that the cause of death was 'childbirth' and 'dysentery' although he was confused that she had seemed so well in the hours after the birth.

Sarah remembered people talking and arguing and she remembered being frightened and confused. She recalled her Aunty Helen and her father arguing about 'milk.'

She wondered why milk was so important as for her it was a luxury and she hardly ever drank it. Would she die too? These were questions she wanted to ask her father but she couldn't or he might push her away again. The days went by and her mother was never mentioned again, seemingly forgotten, gone with no reminder that she had ever walked this earth.

Sarah had always thought of her life as a 'before' and 'after'. Before was her happy time when she and her mother and father laughed and played. If she wasn't with her mother in the kitchen or going to the market, she was with her father visiting friends or with her playmates in the laneways of North Melbourne. She couldn't remember much but enough to create a paradise in her mind of life before her mother and her little sister were taken away.

The 'after' was now. She was living it. Immediately after her mother's death, before she went to live with Aunty Helen and Uncle Joseph, she remembered being smacked by her father when she misbehaved. It seemed he never smiled anymore and didn't find her childish pranks amusing at all. She remembered throwing herself to the floor and screaming, sometimes for ages and feeling exhausted afterwards.

Maybe if she had behaved better, her father would not have abandoned her.

Aunty Helen and Uncle Joseph had taken her in and were kind. She didn't remember misbehaving after that but she did remember feeling sad. The Littles lived around the corner from her father and every day, she would walk along Errol Street to see if her mother had returned and this is when her father would get angry and tell her to go away.

It seemed he wanted nothing to do with her and her whole world was crumbling. She thanked God for Willie and her friendship with him. They had been thrown together on the *Ballengeich* and she couldn't remember a time when Willie wasn't there. She would talk to him and tell him that she hated her father and wished he would die too!

Every afternoon she would swing on the picket gate and watch as Thomas turned the corner and went into his house, their house. He sometimes waved but not always and she waited desperately for him to beckon her to come back and live with him. The days turned to months until Sarah gave up hope. The village of North Melbourne, which had been a delightful source of adventure for the little girl and her friends, now looked dreary and miserable.

Aunty Helen made her a rag doll out of scraps of wool, rags and buttons. It had two blue eyes, red hair and a blue woollen dress.

"Sarah, I made this for you because you have been such a brave girl." She couldn't remember being brave but she fell in love with the rag doll and decided to call her 'Emily.'

She still played with Willie and the other children, usually in the lane beside their house. The lane was protected from the traffic in Errol street and the children knew all the hiding places. They could imagine that they were bushrangers and troopers. Sarah wanted to be a bushranger but the older children always made the decisions and she was invariably a trooper and destined to lose the battle while the bushrangers rode off with the gold. Sometimes one of the men who owned the adjacent businesses would chase them away but they would always return. This was their playground.

As the years passed, Sarah settled into her new surroundings and came to think of herself as part of the Little family. She sometimes overheard Aunty Helen and uncle Joseph talking about her father but didn't understand most of it although she remembered one conversation when they were talking about moving to St Kilda.

"What about Sarah?" It was Helen's voice

"We'll have to talk to Thomas but I suppose she could come with us if he doesn't want to deal with her at the moment. It would be our Christian duty, I think."

Sarah did know the meaning of the words: 'if he doesn't want to deal with her' and she felt unwanted. What was wrong with her that her father did not want 'to deal' with her? What had she done wrong?

She became withdrawn trying to think of ways to make her father love her. She liked Uncle Joseph and Aunty Helen but they were not 'hers'. She had no-one left but her father and he didn't want her. She harboured hope that one day soon, things would change and every night when she climbed into bed with her doll, Emily, she would talk to her as if she were her little sister. She had to do it quietly so the others didn't hear her. She and Emily were family and no-one else could belong.

These were childhood memories but the Sarah who lay on a bed at *Shrublands* was no longer a child. She was sixteen and over the years had pieced together the circumstances that had removed her father from her life. One day she asked Uncle Joseph about why they had left North Melbourne and moved to St Kilda.

"Running your own business is hard work, Sarah, and depends on everything going right. People don't pay bills so you can't pay your workers. We had a good thing going for a while but it was time to move on and there was more money to be made working for Government and Church authorities. At least they pay you for work you do."

Sarah suspected her mother's death had something to do with it as well. From things that were said, she gathered her father had lost interest in everything after her mother died and was not pulling his weight in the business.

"I got a job building St Mary's Catholic church in St Kilda." Uncle Joseph continued. " I was keen to work with William Wardell whose architecture I admire very much. He also designed St Patrick's Cathedral. After being persecuted in their own country, the Irish were keen to build the best churches they could afford and money flowed in from the goldfields to make that possible."

Uncle Joseph was so matter of fact. He always answered her questions honestly but without any of the emotion she craved. She knew he was a good friend to her father and always loyal to him. Through his eyes, her father was a wonderful man who always did the right thing by her. She felt guilty for hating him.

They moved to St Kilda, into a rambling, big house with an enormous back yard. Aunty Helen was having another baby and was not very well. Uncle Joseph declared that the children would have to do more around the house as he would be very busy working on St Mary's church and would not be at home as much as he once was.

St Kilda was very different from North Melbourne. There was more space and the people dressed better. There were no open drains and the streets were wider. Willie and Sarah and the other children missed their lane but they soon found other places to play at bushrangers and troopers, sometimes even at the new St Kilda cemetery although they were wary of the strange types that were working there. Willie said they might have been 'ghosts.'

As the seasons came and went, Sarah's life developed a routine. A new baby arrived in the house and new rules were made. The newcomer was a boy and he cried so much that Uncle Joseph and Aunty Helen didn't have much time for any of their other children, let alone Sarah. This did not bother her as she preferred to be invisible anyway. She had Emily, and Willie and her hopes. She was starting to live much of her life in her own head.

One day, out of the blue, after her fifth birthday, Thomas arrived to speak to Uncle Joseph. She had thought he had come to wish her a happy birthday but it seemed he had forgotten. She greeted him at the door and waited for him to give her a packet of boiled sweets or a toy but he just said:

"Hello Sarah, you look well. Is Uncle Joseph here?" She heard them talking. Her father was coming to work on the church with Uncle Joseph. She heard Uncle Joseph say: "We'd put you up here Thomas but with a new baby and Sarah, we just don't have the room." Her father answered: "Thanks, Joseph, but I'll be staying at a hotel nearby, but not for long as I've bought land in Pakington Street."

"Next to the canal? Yes I saw that advertised. It's a good buy, I believe."

"I'm going to build a house, designed along the lines of the portable iron cottages, but in timber."

Sarah could hardly believe what she was hearing. Her father was building a house, a home. Soon she and Emily would be tucked up in their new bedroom with Father smoking his pipe in the kitchen. She couldn't wait and told Emily that night how happy she was.

"Emily, you and I are going to have a room to ourselves with no-one else to annoy us. You'll like that won't you?"

The next eighteen months were happy for Sarah. No-one told her officially that she would be leaving the Little household but that didn't matter. She knew it to be true as soon as the Pakington Street house was finished.

During this time, her father was a constant visitor to the Little house, often having an evening meal with them. Aunty Helen had recovered her health and simply said. 'One more mouth to feed when you have so many, is nothing.'

But best of all was sometimes on a Sunday, Thomas would take Sarah and Willie to the beach for a play in the sand. Sarah loved these days and snuggled between Willie and her father in the phaeton as they traversed Chapel Street on their way home via her father's new block of land in Pakington street, a place she hoped to live very soon when the house was built. Thomas was happy on those days and so was Sarah. She couldn't wait until she and her father were a family again. She confided in Emily every night and almost imagined that Emily was joining in the one way conversation.

Her seventh birthday approached as the house neared completion so it was a surprise to her when she heard talk of Willie and her going to the new school at St Mary's after Christmas. Wasn't that her father's decision? After all she would be living with him. Why would she be going with Willie? His house and her new house were in opposite directions from the school.

"We're going to school, Sarah," said Willie as they climbed the giant gum in the backyard. Sarah was a better climber than Willie but she would never think to tease him about it. It would never have occurred to her. Instead she climbed and waited for him to catch up.

"I won't be going with you, Willie, 'cos I'll be at Papa's house."

"I don't want you to go, Sarah, I want you to stay here with us. Anyway Papa said that we are very lucky to be able to go to a school."

"I don't want to go to school," said Sarah as she lowered herself onto the overhanging branch. "The teachers might hit us."

"If they try to hit you Sarah, I will tell them not to." He took her hand and allowed her to help him onto the branch.

"When I get married and have a boy, I'm going to call him William after you because you are my best friend, but I have to go and live with Papa because he always looks so sad."

"Sad?" said Willie, "I think your Dad is grumpy!"

"He misses my mother. That's why he's sad, and that's why I'm sad too."

"Why did she die?" said Willie as he quickly regained his balance after a near fall.

"I think the baby made her sick," said Sarah

"My mother has had lots of babies and they didn't make her sick," said Willie

And with that, they had climbed to the extremity of the overhanging branch and could go no further.

On Sarah's eighth birthday, her father remembered. When he arrived, he brought a packet of boiled sweets. She suspected he stopped at the shop on the corner and bought them. Usually they were gone before Sarah got any as the Little children hardly ever got sweets and devoured them greedily. Thomas talked a lot about his house but he also talked about buying land somewhere. He had met a 'lovely' family, Irish, The Lyons, and he had been spending a great deal of time with Peter Lyon.

She didn't want to hear about any 'lovely' family. She just wanted him to listen to her stories about school and how Aunty Helen was teaching her to play the piano.

"She has a real talent, Thomas, "said Aunty Helen. One day I found her just picking out the notes and before long she had made a tune. Why don't you show your father what you can play, Sarah." What followed was a wonderful musical evening that Sarah remembered fondly. As she began *My Bonnie Lassie,* her father sat beside her picking up the tune, playing a duet. The whole family joined in, singing, playing and laughing. Sarah's heart was filled with gladness as she watched her father and Uncle Joseph, arms around each other, filling the house with baritone sounds. She never knew her father had such a good voice.

That night she was happy and could almost forget that her mother was dead. She could dream again and not feel like an 'orphan.' She had a father. The children were sent to bed, leaving Uncle Joseph and Aunty Helen and her father in the kitchen. She heard them talking downstairs and decided to creep across the hall and listen to what they were saying, hoping against hope that they were making arrangements for her to move in with her father.

Helen sounded nervous, "I suppose, Thomas, now that you've finished the house, you will be taking Sarah to live with you?"

"I can't!" said Thomas in a way that betrayed his feelings of guilt. "I've bought land in Laanecoorie and just as soon as the lease is approved, I'll be moving there. Anyway, Helen, Sarah is so much happier here with you than she would be with me. Look how close she and Willie are. They're like brother and sister."

"She is your responsibility, you know, Thomas. She has been with us now for five years and our family is growing. Of course we are happy to have her but don't you think she should be with her father? Couldn't you see how much she enjoyed being with you tonight? I don't think I've seen her so happy since Jane died."

Sarah then heard Father's voice saying the fateful words.

"Of course, Joseph, you are right. She is my responsibility and I wouldn't expect you to look after her without some remuneration.

Here is all the money I can spare at the moment and I will get some more to you by next month."

Sarah collapsed against the wall and brought her knees up to her chin. The tears rolled down her cheek. So she was to be bought and sold, like a prized lamb. The happiness she felt a few hours earlier dissipated. She was to stay with the Littles and her father had made it quite clear that she was a nuisance to him while he got on with his life. He left not long after, but Sarah stayed in her hiding place, not because she wanted to hear more but she felt an inability to move.

"He doesn't want Sarah back, Joseph. I can't believe it?" It was a disappointed Helen.

" He thinks she is happy here and should stay."

"Is she happy here, Joseph?"

"I think she is, Helen and I must say I am very fond of her. She and Willie are such good friends."

"She needs her father. Oh, if only Jane had lived. What would she think of Thomas ignoring his responsibilities?"

Joseph's voice was slightly defensive, defensive of a friend whom he was struggling to support.

"He's doing his best, Helen. It's difficult for him."

"And for us, Joseph. Sarah is not our responsibility and yet Thomas seems to think he can just walk away . He could afford to get a housekeeper and Sarah is already at school." There was anger in her voice. Joseph needed to finish the conversation for the sake of peace.

"Helen," he said kindly, "we are Christians and Sarah needs us. We must do what is right. Hopefully Thomas will see fit to change his mind one day soon."

Sarah crept into her bed and hugged Emily close to her, the tears wetting the already bedraggled dress of the doll whom she pulled ever closer.

Chapter Three

She and Willie walked the mile journey to St Mary's school, near where both their fathers were working. The church was almost finished and the first time they walked past it, they gasped.

"It's gigantic!" said Willie

"Huge!" said Sarah

"Monstrous!"

"Enormous!"

And both giggled as they ran out of words.

The brick school building beside the church was designed for Catholic children but because Thomas and Joseph worked on the church, the parish priest allowed them to attend.

In the years that followed, Sarah was glad she had Willie beside her as she learnt what school was about. Word had got around that she was an 'orphan' taken in by the Littles and some of the children teased her and called her names. Willie always stood up for her and although he was not a boy who would ever threaten to fight, his support meant a lot to Sarah. The teachers weren't as bad as she feared but you couldn't relax around them or you would receive a whack across the ears for being in the wrong place or doing the wrong thing, whatever that was. Sarah never really found out.

She liked the learning and before her ninth birthday, both she and Willie could read, count, and write. She learnt about a country called Ireland and how they had lots of fights with England. She knew she was English and was confused about which side she was on. Her biggest confusion, however, was about this thing called religion. Her father had stressed to her that she was an 'Anglican' but she knew the Littles were strict 'Wesleyans' and here she was at a 'Catholic' school. When her classmates were learning about the Catholic religion, so was she and when Willie and the other children went to Sunday school to learn about their religion, so did she. Somewhere in her nine year old mind, she decided that she would do what she was told and not think about it too much.

The one thing she wanted to do was to please her father, not God. She wasn't so sure about this God who had taken away her mother and little sister and that night in bed she told Emily that she didn't trust him!

After the church was completely finished, Thomas visited and Sarah was surprised that he brought her a present as it wasn't her birthday. It was a snow dome which, when you shook it, Westminster Abbey became shrouded with a white substance, supposedly snow. Her father had come to tell her that he was moving away from St Kilda to a place called Laanecoorie. She couldn't bear the thought of his leaving and asked him if she could go with him. She was 9 years old now, not a baby.

"Laanecoorie is no place for a young girl, Sarah" he said. "There are still savages there who don't want white people on the land. Some of the settlers have even been killed."

Sarah knew that remark should have scared her but it didn't. She imagined making friends with the "savages," and remembered the blacks in North Melbourne and how gentle they were when her mother took her to the market near the river. She remembered feeling sorry for them and wished she could play with the children, envying the fact that on hot summer days they could wear no clothes.

"I can look after myself, Father and I could help to look after you as well."

But Thomas was not a man to be persuaded. There was a time when she could persuade him to do anything she wanted but that was a long time ago and she hardly remembered that man at all.

"Are you going to sell the house?" said Uncle Joseph.

"I will, Joseph, but not yet. I will lease it until I get settled in Laanecoorie."

Sarah watched as Uncle Joseph and her father excused themselves from the family. She knew they would be talking about her and what to do with her. She went to the bedroom and sat on the bed, the snow dome still in her hand. She looked at it, shook it and then threw it across the room.

One of the older Little children had watched Sarah as she struggled with this news and tried to cheer her up by getting a map from her school bag and showing Sarah where Laanecoorie was. It was not marked on the map but Bendigo was and she knew it was near there. She tried to distract Sarah by challenging her to try to spell Laanecoorie but Sarah couldn't think past the fact that she had been cast aside yet again.

She discovered thaat her father purchased 125 acres in Laanecoorie next door to land owned by the pioneer of the district, Peter Lyon. She remembered the name, Peter Lyon, but couldn't remember where she had heard it. That night she told Emily that when her father's new place was made safe from the natives, she would be going to live there. Willie thought that she was getting too old to talk to a doll but for Sarah, Emily wasn't just a doll.

Occasionally, during winter, when the sun was shining, Uncle Joseph and Aunty Helen would take the children to the beach at St Kilda and allow them to paddle in the water, squealing as the cold water reached their toes. None of them could swim but Sarah loved the feeling of the salty water on her feet and watching the tiny crabs scuttling away from the shore.

"Do you think those crabs have any feelings?" she asked Willie.

"Don't know," said Willie as he splashed her, evoking a squeal and a laugh at the same time. Of late, Willie had become different with her and seemed to love teasing her. She laughed along with him but sometimes it hurt.

On one such occasion, not long after Sarah turned ten, Aunty Helen asked Sarah to come and sit beside her. Sarah looked at her aunt and somehow knew, yet again, her fragile heart was to be broken. She had sand between her toes and focused her eyes on how funny they looked.

"Sarah," said Helen with a voice that was vibrating with either sorrow or anger, she couldn't tell which, "we are very fond of you and see you as one of our family. I hope you know that?"

Sarah muttered an appropriate sentiment and wondered what was coming. She was nervous.

"Your father was going to tell you this himself, but he has asked me to tell you," she paused and ran her fingers through the sand. "He is getting married again."

She wasn't expecting that! Her feelings were mixed. Did that mean she could go to live with them both and have a stepmother? But how could my mother be replaced by someone else? Aunty Helen continued:

"Your father is marrying Catherine Lyon. She is the daughter of his good friend, Peter and he has known her a while."

She had to ask: "Will I be going to live with them?"

Helen answered as if she had been dreading that question.

"No, Sarah, Catherine Lyon doesn't know about you and your father thinks it best that we all keep it that way. He will break it to her gradually and we'll see what happens then."

She thought Aunty Helen was going to hug her but it was aborted at the last moment. She just wasn't the hugging type. But Sarah saw her bite her lip in distaste at the fact that she had to deliver such unwelcome news. A miserable, little girl, she said nothing, the tears dropping on the sand making a dark wet patch which dried up almost as soon as it hit. She looked at the ocean and knew that the waves would just keep rolling in, oblivious to the fact that she was drowning.

"Doesn't know about me! She doesn't even know about me!" Sarah sobbed these words to Emily in bed that night, wetting the already smelly, woollen dress.

In the weeks that followed, Sarah sought solitude. On Sunday, after the family dinner which was sacred to the Littles, everyone would drift apart to read, sew or just relax. If Willie had gone with his friends to play cricket, Sarah would often just walk. One time she found herself at the new cemetery, not far from the school. She pushed open the huge, iron gates and walked away from the busy road until she could hear no traffic. The workers were not there as it was Sunday. It was eerie but she didn't feel frightened as she looked at the mounds of dirt all around. She thought of Mama buried beneath the ground and wondered what she looked like now. The thought sent a shudder through her.

A gravestone caught her eye. There weren't many as the cemetery was only a few years old but this one had a statue of a cherub looking wistfully towards the sky. Sarah moved closer and saw the inscription:

In loving memory of Charlotte Green
1845 — 1855
Beloved youngest daughter of Daniel and Frances
'when he comes, he'll her awake
And soul and body, happy make.'

She was the same age as me, thought Sarah, but she was beloved of both her parents. She gazed around at the acres of space making ready for the people of St Kilda to be buried there in the years to come. The air was growing chilly in the late Melbourne winter afternoon and Sarah didn't want to leave. She knew she would be missed if she didn't make her way home but there was a new sadness in her soul. Aunty Helen had told her that her father's new wife didn't even know of her existence.

Maybe, thought Sarah, she didn't exist!

Chapter Four

Something died in Sarah that day on the beach, something she had been keeping alive since her mother died, something called hope. She withdrew and no longer confided in Willie who was growing up and had good, male friends of his own. So when she heard that Catherine Lyon, her father's new wife, had had a son, Marriott, her half-brother, she hardly reacted. She didn't want to meet him or hear anything about him.

"My father has a son, now. He'll be so happy," she said bitterly to Willie who just shrugged and walked away. He was finding Sarah's unhappiness difficult to deal with and was spending less and less time with her.

Sarah never went to Laanecoorie. To her, it was just a big word on the map. She had no concept what it looked like and she told herself she didn't care. Gradually she found a measure of happiness, having left school and doing what she could to help Aunty Helen with the smaller children. She had made friends at school and enjoyed spending time with them, sometimes walking to the seaside and other times catching a cable tram into the city. Her father was becoming a distant figure and she never heard from him.

How surprised she was, when, on her 16th birthday, in 1866, her father turned up on the Little's doorstep. She had not seen him for six years. Apparently, he and his new wife and son had just moved back to Melbourne, to St Kilda. Sarah thought he had changed, looking older and quite worn. He talked mostly about Marriott.

"The little fellow is five now," said Thomas, "and a real mischief. He has learned to sit on a horse and loves collecting the eggs from the chickens."

Sarah was aware of the fact that Aunty Helen was looking at her, feeling sympathy towards her as her father talked about his son. Five! Two years older than she was when her father walked away from her. She heard Uncle Joseph raising his voice in an uncharacteristic way.

"And Catherine?" asked Uncle Joseph. "We haven't even met her and we are supposed to be your best friends. Your daughter here has not even met her half-brother." He was angry and found it hard to disguise his disgust. Sarah felt her father's embarrassment as he looked at her. She was aware of the fact that she had transformed from a little girl to a young woman since he had seen her last and they were both self-conscious with each other.

"I've told Catherine all about you," said Thomas softly to Sarah. "She wants to meet you and hopes you can come to Laanecoorie for a holiday. But sadly her health will have to improve first." He told them about Catherine's illness and how she had been ill for a very long time. Sarah saw Uncle Joseph look sadly at his friend, a man he had admired, helped and been guided by ever since they left England. She knew he felt bad about the harsh words he had spoken to him. His sympathy towards his friend was genuine.

"We're sorry to hear that Thomas. Of course, if there is anything we can do to help, please let us know."

"We are managing, thank you. We have a little girl helping and the doctors have been good but I will let you know if there is anything else. The reason for my visit, however, is not about Catherine. It's about Sarah. I have managed to get her a position in service, in Camberwell. You remember Frederik Taubner, don't you Joseph? He's done very well for himself and has purchased *Shrublands* in Camberwell. He has planted vines there and is now the president of the Australian wine growers' association. He needs a young girl he can train to become a housekeeper and assistant. I told him that Sarah is a capable and reliable worker and would be a perfect fit for the work. He is happy to take her on my recommendation."

Sarah was stunned. Was he saying what she thought he was saying? A position? Was she to leave this home and go somewhere else? Aunty Helen and she had talked about her finding a position somewhere, but this was all too sudden. She grabbed the chair as a dizziness descended upon her and she was in danger of fainting. Why didn't her father tell her this news himself, alone, without Uncle Joseph and Aunty Helen there? Did he not even think of asking her what she thought? Did he not even think of her as a person? Did it matter what she thought?

She wondered how he knew that she was reliable and capable when he hardly knew her at all. Was she reliable and capable? She wasn't sure. After their initial shock, she could sense that Uncle Joseph and Aunty Helen welcomed this news as they knew she was ready to move on to a life of her own. Living with them had been a haphazard arrangement for thirteen years and although they had done their best for her, she needed to find a place where she truly belonged.

"It's a bit sudden, Thomas," said Joseph turning to Sarah. "But I can see that it could be a good thing for you, Sarah."

Aunty Helen could see how this news affected Sarah. She had seen her grow from a baby to a young lady, the daughter of her good friend, Jane, whom she had done her best for. She knew her father's actions had hurt her and that the scars would never heal so when she spoke, it was in a forthright fashion, like a mother paving the way for a daughter.

"Is it a suitable position, Thomas? She has been quite protected here you know."

She heard her father reassuring them, not her, that Frederik Taubner was a good man with impeccable credentials in the church and society and that she would be well looked after. He was here to take Sarah to *Shrublands* – that day! She felt sick.

"I'll go and change," she said weakly and made for her room thinking, my life has been decided and I have no say. I wasn't even asked how I felt about it. Although she was angry at how this had all come to pass, and scared, there was also a tinge of excitement. Maybe this was a chance to find a new life, one where she might feel as if she belonged.

Aunty Helen had left Thomas and had come to help her pack. Sarah realised she was saying goodbye to the only mother she had ever really known. She looked at her and for the first time she could remember, Aunty Helen reached for her and hugged her. Both were in tears. "Mind you make your mother proud of you, Sarah."

Just as she was thinking of what to say, Willie appeared at the door. He was now a strong sixteen year old, taller than his father and, Sarah thought, very good looking. As he said goodbye, she thought she could see a tear in his eye. He would always be her Willie and she would love him for the friend he had been to her. He touched her hand as she turned away from him to catch up with Thomas and whispered in her ear:

"Don't forget, you said you would name your first son after me!"

For the first time that afternoon, Sarah smiled.

Chapter Five

A bell was sounding in the distance and Kitty came stumbling through the door looking flushed. It took a while for Sarah to realise where she was as she had been so lost in her memories. She saw Seamus disappearing near the doorway and suspected what he and Kitty had been doing outside while she was lying there, lost in her memories.

"The dinner bell has gone Sarah. Best not be late on your first day," she grabbed Sarah and pulled her into the garden towards the big house.

They arrived at the staff quarters where the staff ate and Sarah was surprised at the number of people needed to run a place like *Shrublands*. She felt overwhelmed and when Kitty found her a chair and told her to sit down she obeyed.

Looking down the table she noticed a man with a shock of red curly hair.

"Who's that?" she asked Kitty wondering why he stood out so much. Was it just that he was a bit strange looking?

"That's Alexander Hamilton," said Kitty. "He's OK but doesn't say much for himself, hard to get a word out of him. He spends his time with the plants in the garden, doesn't mix much with the rest of us. I heard one of the other girls say he has a history! " She said the word 'history' as if it were a delicious scandal. "The one next to him is Seamus."

"I've met Seamus," said Sarah. "He brought my things in."

"He's so nice," said Kitty with an air of possession, "always so funny."

Maybe Kitty wasn't so bad, thought Sarah, and she made a mental note that If she were to get on with Kitty, she would need to be a loyal friend. She wondered what Alexander's story was, though. There was something lost about him. Maybe he just reminded her of herself.

The meal finished and Sarah looked around for her father. She saw Mr Taubner in the distance. He smiled when she approached him. In a matter of fact voice, he said:

"Oh Sarah, settling in I hope? Your father has gone. He needed to get back to his wife and he asked me to say goodbye for him.

When would it end, this ache of disappointment? She had so wanted to see her father again before he left. He had been so different when he was with Mr Taubner, affectionate almost. Her spirits sank and she wanted to find a place away from everyone and just cry.

Just then she felt a dig in the ribs from Kitty who was behind her asking if she wanted to continue her 'tour' around the 'property,' this said in a posh accent. She agreed, wiping the tears from her eyes, grateful for the rough generosity of her room-mate who had sensed Sarah's mood perfectly.

After the initial loneliness and feeling of displacement, Sarah actually enjoyed being in service and loved *Shrublands*. The palace, as she called it, had so many rooms that for the first few weeks she was constantly in need of rescuing, so many times did she get lost. The grounds were majestic and when she had time off, she could roam the perimeter and pretend that she was a princess surveying her realm. It took her fifteen minutes to walk the gravel path to the wrought iron gates, past the two lions, the fountain and the numerous beds of flowers, scattered in themed brilliance.

The vineyard was in the opposite direction from the front entrance and she didn't go there often. She much preferred the route which had brought her there, up the gravel path and past the fountain which her father and Uncle Joseph had built.

Also surprisingly for Sarah who always tried to get out of the many chores she had to do at the Littles, she loved the work. Being extraordinarily busy was the best antidote she knew for not feeling sorry for herself. Whereas other girls complained about the drudgery, she found it stimulating, enjoying learning the skills of lighting and maintaining the copper, dissolving blue bags and washing and starching Mr Taubner's shirts, heating the irons on the hot coals and pressing the shirts to perfection. Her favourite job was replacing and lighting the candles in the chandelier. Normally this would be a job for one of the male staff but she begged them to let her do it as she loved to be a small part of bringing light into the room that she remembered from her first day there.

Mr Taubner was a decent man and the staff respected him. He had travelled a great deal and sometimes he would wander into the staff quarters and strike up a conversation about the countries he had been to, especially Italy and Spain. It was here he had learnt the art of wine making. Sarah warmed to him quickly and had lost her fear of being in the presence of such a wealthy man.

One day she plucked up enough courage to ask him about the rugs he brought back with him. "They're Persian, each one different," he said, "and I like to replace them often. You have one in your room don't you?"

Sarah did, and she loved it. It was one of the rugs that had fallen out of favour when a new one arrived. It warmed the room and every morning as she was getting dressed, she would see something new in the pattern. She could imagine how many hours it took for some poor woman to make and felt she needed to respect it.

Kitty, she found out, couldn't read or write but was fast becoming a friend. Whereas her rough ways had annoyed Sarah at first, once she heard the stories of the conditions in the benevolent home she had come from, she had nothing but sympathy for her. But for the grace of God, thought Sarah, that could have been me.

Their room was in the servants' quarters at the back of the house, away from the main driveway. It was quiet except for the kookaburras that perched on the branches, their laughter piercing through the bush. Kitty had a pet kookaburra which she used to feed scraps of meat and, Sarah thought, if the bird could find a way, it would be in the room with them.

Sometimes, when they had time off, Sarah and Kitty would sit on the ends of their beds and talk about their dreams. Kitty's future always included Seamus and it was clear to Sarah that she was very much a girl in love. She wasn't sure Seamus felt the same way, however. He seemed to be friends with everyone and Sarah wondered if he saw Kitty in his future. She hoped her friend would not have her heart broken.

"Kitty," said Sarah one evening before they went to sleep, "would you like me to teach you to read?" Sarah couldn't imagine not being able to read.

"No, love, ain't got no use for readin' but thanks anyway."

Even though she was at the bottom of the pecking order as far as staffing was concerned, Sarah never felt demeaned or 'put in her place.' She remembered the annoying Mrs Pickersgill talking in North Melbourne about how, in England, the 'Lord of the Manor' stood on ceremony and was constantly reminding his staff where their 'place' was. Mrs Pickersgill always imagined herself at the top of the tree and mourned the lack of class distinction in Australia.

Here, however, you couldn't tell who was old money and who had struck gold, literally, since their arrival in the colony. She didn't think Mr Taubner was a gold digger who had made good, but she doubted whether he was old money either. He had a certain class about him but he treated everyone as if they were equal. Maybe he was of the same faith as Aunty Helen and Uncle Joseph as that was their attitude towards people. 'We are all created in God's image,' she remembered from Sunday School, and 'we are all equal in the sight of the Lord.' Sarah wondered if this included the Aborigines and the Chinese, but as there were none working at *Shrublands*, she couldn't tell.

Most of the staff were easy to get on with as they were grateful to have found such a place to work. As she and Kitty were the youngest, they were afforded special privileges such as sleeping in longer and lighter duties. But Sarah was often up early and anxious to get started. She surprised herself with her own enthusiasm.

Chapter Six

After that first day in the dining room when Kitty had pointed out Alexander Hamilton, Sarah had found herself wanting to meet him. She wasn't sure why. Maybe it was just the challenge — that he was a man of few words and someone who didn't mix much. Maybe it was something else. She wasn't sure.

She guessed he was in his thirties as his shocking red hair was receding at his temples. She wondered if a comb could tame it. He had the look of a man who had 'knocked about' — not tall but strong looking with broad shoulders and thick arms. She guessed he had worked hard all his life. There was no doubt Mr Taubner thought a great deal of him as he was in charge of the front garden and it always looked magnificent. She loved walking in the garden and felt as if she had her own parklands. Every chance she got, she would bring a book into the garden, sometimes to the fountain, and read.

Her first meeting with Alexander was some weeks after she started working at *Shrublands*. She wanted to know the names of the flowers and plants and when she saw him tending a newly planted garden bed, she casually said. "What are those plants called?"

The directness with which she spoke surprised her. Was she losing her shyness or was there something about this man which drew her to him?

Alexander spun around and smiled shyly at her. He was surprised also as not many of the young women spoke to him at all.

"They're called acacias, a native plant and one that grows well in this soil."

"And the tree over there?"

"That's a plain old eucalyptus. Nothing will kill that."

There was an embarrassed silence while Alexander turned back to the soil and Sarah was left standing there. She decided that if he were a man of few words, she had to be the first to speak. "My name is Sarah Bradshaw, Mr Hamilton, I'm new here and I think your garden is magnificent."

"I know who you are," he said while standing up and facing her, "I've seen you out here often." The comment took her aback. Had he been watching her? And did he ask someone who she was? She found herself flattered. He talked of the qualities of acacias and their different flowers, all the while continuing to have his hands immersed in the soil.

"Next time you come down here, I'll test you on the names of those two plants," he said playfully.

"Please do," she said. "I want to learn all about them."

He smiled at her and she noticed his eyes, they were kind eyes, eyes that had seen suffering. It was just a conversation with a gardener, almost old enough to be her father but Sarah returned to her duties with a spring in her step. She mentioned it to Kitty that night:

"He seems really nice, Kitty. He wasn't shy at all."

"It's you, you old duffer, you're one of those people that everyone feels comfortable with. No wonder he wasn't shy with you. Maybe he likes you…ooooohhhhhh"

Sarah threw her pillow at Kitty and laughed. "He's too old for me, Kitty, but he was nice to talk to. How is Seamus these days? At the mention of Seamus, Kitty's face lit up. "I'm hoping he asks me to marry him before the year is out." Sarah didn't say anything but had a bad feeling about Kitty and Seamus.

She looked forward to her chats with Alexander very much. In some ways it was like the days when she and Willie were friends. There was a bond and they were special to each other, something Sarah realised she needed. With each meeting, he opened up more and Sarah laughed at the way he had been described as a 'man of few words.'

"How do you know so much?" she asked him one day.

"Because I'm curious," he said. "When you're curious about anything, you learn. If you're not curious, you will never learn."

"Did you always know about plants?"

"No, because I grew up in a land that was covered with snow or water most of the year. Have you ever been to Scotland?"

Sarah's face clouded over, "I don't think so, or Mama would have told me about it. The only places I remember are Leamington, Woodford and Priors Marston. But then again, I don't think I really remember them at all. Is Scotland beautiful?"

"Very, but not so beautiful that I didn't want to leave. Scenery can never be everything. Bad things happen even in the nicest of surroundings."

She wondered what memories he was experiencing.

"I joined the Navy to see the world when I was just a lad. It was a pretty brutal life but it toughened me up. Our ship arrived in Melbourne during the Gold Rush. The Captain gave us a warning and said if we deserted to the goldfields, the penalty, if we were caught was a flogging worse than death and no pay for the whole trip. That was meant to scare us."

"And didn't it?" asked Sarah, wide eyed to hear the rest of the story.

"It only strengthened our resolve. A few lads and I put a plan together to jump ship while on shore leave. We paid a digger to hide us in the back of a dray on the way to Mt Alexander. Once we got there, there was no hope that the police would find us, if, in fact they were looking for us. They had enough to do without worrying about us. Anyway they'd never catch us all as there were hundreds like us. Gold Fever. It was compelling."

"Aren't you scared they'll catch up with you?"

"No. A few years ago there was an amnesty so we have nothing to fear now. It's all just become a bit of a historical joke. So here I am, Sarah, a Scot who found absolutely no gold but who thoroughly enjoyed the search!"

Sarah laughed, "Did anyone find gold?"

"Sure they did but most of them, as soon as they found it, drank it at the local pub. Only a few wily diggers made it count towards their future. I realised pretty soon that it was a mug's game and put my energies into making money from people who'd made it rich. They built big houses and wanted English gardens. And I convinced them that I was their man."

Alexander told her how he had moved to Melbourne after the amnesty and worked for several wealthy landowners, the latest of whom was Mr Taubner. He had been there for over seven years when Sarah met him and although he was not the most social person in the world he was respected by all.

"This is a great country, Sarah," he said. "If you work hard you can make something of yourself. Back home I would still be a lowly labourer with no hope of ever bettering myself. Here I have the respect of my boss, the friendship of people like you and the money to enjoy myself on my day off."

"Do you miss Scotland though?"

"Of course I do. It's where I was born and grew up. I miss the music, the scenery and God forbid even the weather, especially during these hot Melbourne summers."

"My mother died during one of those hot Melbourne summers" said Sarah and then proceeded to tell Alexander her story or at least, what she knew of it.

"So your father took off without you, did he? Probably for the best. If you'd gone with him you would have become his slave, cooking and cleaning, whereas with your other family you had some sort of childhood."

Sarah had never thought of it that way. She had resented that she couldn't live with him but all the time she thought if she did, it would be like old times but as Alexander pointed out, it couldn't have been.

The seasons changed, the months and years passed and Sarah began to think of *Shrublands* as her home. The happiness she felt was mainly due to her growing friendship with Alexander. She had never known anyone like him. She could tell him anything but most of all, when she left him, she felt as if she were a better person. She wondered why he wasn't married and determined to ask him next time they talked.

Chapter Seven

"almost married once", said Alexander as he picked a particularly delicious apricot for her to eat. It was Sunday. Many of the staff returned to their homes or went with friends to St Kilda beach which was the place to be seen. Sarah, however, decided to stay at the house and catch up with her mending and reading. She had her mother's copy of Jane Eyre which she absolutely loved and was onto her third reading of it. In fact she had almost worn it out altogether! She wondered why her mother had loved it so much as she couldn't imagine that her father, Thomas, was anything like Mr Rochester. Maybe he was once, before he had turned into the man she knew.

Sarah bit into the apricot and made slurping noises. They both laughed. "What happened?" she managed to say between gulping the delicious fruit and trying to stop the juice from running down her pinafore.

"It was in Mt Alexander, on the goldfields. She was the daughter of the chap who had the patch next to me. She was smart, like you, and we used to talk about all sorts of things. She was interested in the flowers of the bush like you are and we used to go on 'expeditions'. I remember her smile, it used to start on the left side and then creep over her whole face. I teased her about it. Her father didn't seem to mind us being together and I never knew where her mother was. We became sweethearts and I asked her father for permission to marry. He was a man of few words and all he said was "Aye". That was it "Aye"! Not how will you support her? or make sure you look after her, but, "Aye". We were happy and looked forward to making a life together, even though we didn't have a bean to our names. "

Sarah was wondering what could possibly have happened to her. She was down to the stone of her apricot but didn't dare throw it on the ground, instead held it in her hand. "What was her name?" This was important, she had to have a name so she could become real in Sarah's mind.

"Hilary, her name was Hilary. She was quite tall with long, dark hair and for a woman, a sturdy build. Because she was so strong, people tended to give her lots of responsibilities, as if physical strength makes you more sensible. But she had that thing called common sense and the midwives used to call on her from time to time to assist at the births, even though she was only not much more than a girl herself. One night, she had just finished helping deliver a baby boy to one of the miner's wives and it was late. It had been a long confinement and she had arrived in broad daylight so had not brought her lamp. Trying to find the way back to her tent on the darkest of nights, with no light from the moon at all, she met with an accident. Mick Doyle hadn't covered his mine as he wanted to get started early the following morning. He didn't think anyone would be out so late. But Hilary was, and she didn't have a light. She missed the track by some yards and tumbled down the mine. Mick found her the next morning and there was nothing they could do.

"My whole future disappeared down that mine, Sarah, and I can tell you I was a mess. I kept imagining her lying there all night, suffering. A doctor on the goldfield told me that the fall would have killed her but I wasn't so sure. It tortured me for ages to think that I couldn't save her."

Sarah felt the urge to put her arms around Alexander but of course she couldn't. It would not have been proper. She didn't know what to say. This man had known so much sorrow and yet you would never know to meet him. Sadness had not stopped him from seeing the beauty in the world.

"I was pretty knocked about by what happened, but so was her father. I could see that he was devastated but he couldn't talk about it. I used to take him to the pub for a whisky and I think he liked that but I never heard him mention her name. Sometimes I'd hold up the glass and say: 'To Hilary!' and he'd say, 'Aye.'"

"When someone doesn't say your name, it's as if they never existed," said Sarah thinking about Thomas and her mother. "As if the earth wipes out their being. Alexander, you must never forget Hilary and I don't mind how many times you talk about her." Then she added. "At least she died knowing that someone loved her!"

Alexander was drained from telling this story, she could see that. He wasn't used to opening his heart to someone he had only known for a short time. It was up to her to make him feel that she appreciated his openness and would never betray it.

"Perhaps we could plant a tree and call it the Hilary tree," she said in an effort to lighten the atmosphere a little.

"You're a right good one, you are," said Alexander with a strained smile obviously still affected by the memory of the tragedy. "How old did you say you were?"

"Almost eighteen," boasted Sarah

"Well I've been around thirty five years, Sarah, and you have to be one of the nicest people I have ever met. I'd like to plant a Hilary tree. Think about where we could put it."

"Well, not close to a mine shaft, I wouldn't think," said Sarah to herself with a chuckle as she made her way back to her room. She couldn't stop thinking about Alexander's story. Not so much about Hilary but about him. He was unlike so many of the rough men around the place that she came in contact with, men who delivered items to the Manor. He was decent and kind. But there was something else and she couldn't quite put her finger on it, a nervousness in her stomach which wouldn't let her settle on anything.

Chapter Eight

Mr Taubner often met her father at the winegrowers' meetings and he would pass on messages to her but she had seen him only twice since the day he had brought her to *Shrublands*. She wished he would come more often but, after a while, her friendships with the other girls and especially Alexander, became all important to her and she thought of him less often.

Her nineteenth birthday was celebrated by Cook making her favourite caraway seed cake and Kitty giving her a handkerchief with the letter 'S' in the corner.

"It's a bit messy but I'm getting better." Sarah hugged Kitty and told her it was the best present she had ever received and its messiness made it even more special.

She felt part of the place, at home almost. Her routine was settled, her work was praised and her precious things were on the mantlepiece of the room she shared with her good friend who made her laugh with her unselfconscious actions and blunt turn of phrase. I wish I could be more like her, thought Sarah, and not worry so much about what people think of me.

Seamus had not proposed marriage. In fact he had left *Shrublands* in search of his fortune in Western Australia. Mr Taubner was disappointed as he had him earmarked for advancement but understood that the lad's many qualities would be the very thing that would see him leave. Kitty had been upset at first but not as much as Sarah would have thought. She quickly turned her attention to other eligible young men on the staff and presently was keeping company with one of the stable boys.

'We are different," thought Sarah. And immediately she thought of Alexander. Could they become more than friends? She dared hope so even though he was seventeen years her senior. But how did he see her? Was she just someone he liked talking to or did he like her in that other way? Occasionally he would seek opportunities to touch her and when he did, she felt the thrill through her whole body. Did he feel it too?

She smiled as she thought of one such occasion a few days earlier. He had climbed on the branch of their special apricot tree by the creek to retrieve a particularly juicy apricot and pretended he was stuck. She knew he wasn't and he knew she knew he wasn't but they were both happy to pretend.

"Sarah, can you give me a hand to get down, I seem to be stuck."

Willingly she reached up and took his hand. He held onto it while he manoeuvred his foot around the branch. Then he jumped – but still kept holding her hand. They looked at each other and she thought she saw – was it desire? But then he abruptly snatched his hand away and said something about needing to be somewhere else. She was confused but that touch stayed in her mind while she mopped floors, scrubbed baths and changed the candles in the chandelier.

The seasons came and went. Autumn was her favourite when the towering trees were dressed in orange, red and yellow, shouting their colour at the dull eucalypts. But as winter approached, those leaves would drop and the bare trees would be humbled in the shade of those same eucalypts whose greenery had not changed.

One of her morning jobs was to sweep the magnificent front steps leading to the entrance of *Shrublands*. One day, Sarah had almost finished when she looked up to see a carriage approaching. A man got our slowly. He looked like her father but it couldn't be. He was stooped, with head on the side, walking slowly, impeded by the limp which he had sustained from an accident but which he usually managed to hide so well. Her heart raced. Something was wrong.

The carriage remained, making no effort to drive away.

"Father?" She walked quickly towards him, broom in hand.

Her father reached for her and embraced her. Sarah was caught unaware at this uncharacteristic show of affection. But was it affection or something else? She felt embarrassed that the hug was prolonged and longed for him to release her.

"Catherine is dead. She died yesterday." He said it without tears but Sarah could feel the heaviness in him. She didn't quite know how to react. It was a shock. They had only been married a few years, hadn't they? How could she feel grief when she had never even met Catherine. How could she be sorry when she blamed her for taking away her father? Did she even feel sorry for him? She knew she had to say something to this broken man before her who evoked a deep compassion within her.

"I am sorry Father. It just doesn't seem fair." Maybe this was the wrong thing to say. Didn't people talk about God at a time like this?

"She suffered a lot," said Thomas in a dreamy way, "and I couldn't do anything to take away her suffering. Something was wrong inside her. The pain was always there and she was never going to be cured. People say it's for the best but I don't know. She so wanted to watch her boy grow up. You're right Sarah, it just doesn't seem fair. Poor Marriott. How is he going to survive without his mother?"

Sarah was surprised that her father confided so much to her, or was he talking to himself?

"How old is Marriott now, Father?" An edge was in her voice. She knew she was being selfish but she couldn't help it. Did her father worry about her like this when her mother died?

"He is seven and a mummy's boy. She protected him and molly-coddled him. He's not dealing with it very well. I thought, Sarah, maybe you could come to meet him and try to help him."

"What, and tell him how to survive the death of a mother?" It was out before she could withdraw it and Thomas was shocked at the venom in her voice. He jerked his head in such a way that he was looking straight at her with such sadness in his eyes. Neither spoke until the angry words had dissipated in the air.

"I'm sorry Father, that was cruel."

His voice was pleading and pathetic.

"Sarah, I have always tried to do the best for you. I paid the Littles to look after you and then managed to obtain this employment for you. I think I have done my duty"

The mention of money did not help! Nor duty!

"Father, you never told Catherine about me before you married her."

"And I regret that, Sarah, but you had to know Catherine. She was delicate, a little unstable, not like your mother. She wouldn't have married me if she knew about you."

Sarah realised there was no point in nurturing the bitterness that existed in her heart. She had a confidence now that she had never known before and could see that her father was suffering. Angry as she was, she did not want to add to that suffering. She took his arm and led him into the kitchen where she made a cup of tea and gave him a freshly made scone with homemade apricot jam and cream. The apricots were from the same tree that Alexander had given to her some years ago when they first became firm friends.

"Does Marriott know about me, father?" She had always suspected he didn't.

"I told him a few weeks ago. It seemed to buck him up a bit and he is keen to meet you. He asked me why he didn't know about you before."

Sarah wondered what answer her father gave but did not pursue it. She wondered if he looked like her.

"What's he like?" she asked

Thomas smiled for the first time since they started talking. "He's a story teller and really quite funny. You'd like him."

"When will I meet him?"

"He is going back to Laanecoorie with his grandparents tomorrow. They thought it best that he be back with them while I attend to business matters," then he added quickly. " But I could bring him here tomorrow morning to meet you."

"He's lucky to have grandparents," said Sarah, not bitterly but airily. "But Papa I don't think it a good idea for me to meet him at this time. Perhaps sometime soon, when everything has settled down." Sarah became aware that she was taking the initiative with her father. Had the roles reversed?

"Yes, perhaps you're right." He stood up suddenly without finishing his tea, "I have to go Sarah. Would you be so kind as to tell Frederik the news when he returns. I am sure he would want to know. I will be down in Melbourne quite a bit in the future as I am selling the land at Laanecoorie. I can't stay there and cope with the grief of the Lyons. I need to start a new life."

As she closed the door of the carriage, she asked, "Will you come back to Melbourne?"

"No, there's a land sale in a place called Bamawm and I intend to move there. The new channel system means that I can finally grow some vines."

Her father's plans surprised Sarah. It was almost as if he was excited about the prospect of being single again. She wondered if he loved Catherine as much as he had loved her mother. She wanted to say something to her father about always running away but instead she said: "I hope it all works out well for you Papa."

As she watched the carriage disappearing down the drive, she realised she was beginning to see her father as a person. He had been through the deaths of two young wives, each leaving him with a small child. She hoped he would be kinder to Marriott than he was to her. At least he came to tell her the news in person. That was something.

She needed to talk to Alexander.

Leaving the broom standing against the column of the steps she had been sweeping, and the pile of dirt on the bottom step, she hurried into the orchard. She knew Alexander was always there in the mornings. As she approached him, he saw the look of concern on her face. He could tell something was amiss.

They sat, perfectly at ease with each other and almost touching, on a low lying branch of the most prolific apricot tree and she told him everything.

Alexander, in his usual positive way, helped her to see her father's point of view.

"It can't be easy for him, poor bugger. What's the boy's name? Marriott…that's a strange name isn't it?"

"My grandmother's maiden name is Mary Marriott and I think Papa wanted to honour her with the name. She is still alive in England and would probably be thrilled that her grandson is named after her."

"Do you ever hear from her?"

"She used to write but I haven't received a letter for ages and I haven't written either. I was only a baby when I last saw her and don't remember her, although in a strange way, I miss her. Can you miss what you've never known?"

They talked for ages. She wasn't worried about leaving her work as she always did extra anyway. She told Alexander that she felt guilty that she didn't feel sad about Catherine's death.

"But you never met her did you?"

"No, But she was family wasn't she?"

"Depends what you mean by family," said Alexander bitterly

Sarah realised she didn't know much about Alexander's family. He never seemed to want to talk about them. She needed to change the subject.

"I gave Papa some of your apricot jam. It's quite magnificent. I could eat it by the jarful."

"And then, my dear Sarah, you would be the shape of an apricot."

When they bantered like this, Sarah always wanted to move closer to Alexander and touch him. It seemed natural. Sometimes she would see in his eyes that he wanted it too. It was becoming harder and harder. Her feelings were tearing her apart because she couldn't express them, not even to herself. Was she being silly? She couldn't bear thinking of a life without him. He had told her about wanting to have his own farm, a market garden, where he could grow food and sell it to the markets. He felt he had enough knowledge and enough business sense to make a go of it and she agreed. She found herself wanting to do it with him. Once she would have allowed her father's situation to affect her mood but it seemed nothing could take away the happiness she felt.

That night as she related to Kitty the events of the day, she decided to tell Kitty a little of how she felt about Alexander.

"Kitty, I think I love him."

She expected Kitty to laugh at her and tell her that she could do better. Alexander was such a shy, boring person. But that's not what happened.

"Cor Sarah, we've all known that for ages. Good on ya. Just hope he's got enough guts to ask the question."

Sarah hugged Kitty and thanked God for her friendship.

Chapter Nine

The city of Melbourne continued to prosper and had been transformed from 'Smellbourne,' to become known as 'Marvellous Melbourne.' The new Treasury Building and Parliament House in Spring Street stood as a majestic testimony to a city that, in thirty five years had evolved into a sophisticated, genteel society.

Closer to home, the vines of *Shrublands* had produced their finest crop of grapes, Kitty was in love yet again and it was common knowledge amongst the staff that Alexander Hamilton and Sarah Bradshaw would soon become husband and wife.

One day, in that season when the last of the autumn leaves can be seen floating towards the densely covered ground and the winter clothes are brought out, Mr Taubner gathered the staff in the drawing room to tell them of a foreign visitor who was staying for a month at *Shrublands*. He impressed upon them all how important he was, an owner of some of the finest vineyards in Spain and Italy, at whose home he had enjoyed generous hospitality. Mr Taubner wished to return the favour so the staff were to make sure his stay was comfortable and that he had everything he needed and wanted.

"Can't wait to see him," said the cook. "Must be pretty special to word us all up like this."

"I wonder if he's good looking," said Kitty.

Alexander and Sarah talked about what sort of man is invited to another country for a month, all expenses paid.

"He's just another person," said Alexander. "Might have more money but in the end he's no better than you or me. I am curious to talk to him about his vineyards though. That Italian wine is pretty damn good."

He arrived in two carriages! One for him and one for his luggage and his valet. The staff were gobsmacked. He was quite slim and very good looking, with his dark features offset by the magnificent clothes he wore. A kerchief tucked into a silk shirt, striped pants and the most highly polished boots Sarah had ever seen. Sarah wondered how long he took to dress but then she saw his entourage and supposed he did very little for himself. Mr Taubner also wore expensive clothes but he always looked ill at ease in them. This man didn't wear clothes, he inhabited them.

"He can put those polished boots under my bed anytime," said the cook and they all laughed at the thought of the cook and this handsome stranger.

After the initial greeting, the staff went about their work chatting about the foreign visitor and hoping that their efforts to make him comfortable wouldn't fall short in his eyes. He made a point of speaking to each of them and asking them questions about their lives, endearing himself to them, even those who had tried not to like him simply because he was a 'foreigner.'

Sarah remembered vividly the first time he spoke to her. How could she forget?

His dark eyes seemed to pierce her soul. He smiled and kissed her hand and told her she was beautiful. No-one had ever told her that before and she wanted so much to believe that it was true but something told her that he was what was known as 'a lady's man' and he probably said the same thing to all the female staff. She couldn't help but be flattered, though, when he paid her special attention and she responded by flirting with him in a sincere kind of way, as she did with many of the other men on staff.

She thought it was an innocent game until one day he surprised her in the laundry and kissed her, full on the lips pushing her back against the copper. This was the first time she had been kissed, except by Willie in childhood games, and she was taken aback, quickly retreating, apologising about having something to do, careful not to be rude.

That night she felt her lips. He had pressed hard. She had spent so many hours imagining Alexander's lips against hers and what it would feel like. But not like this!

Feeling uncomfortable, she kept out of the visitor's way as much as she could but it wasn't easy. She knew she would be in trouble if he complained that he wasn't getting the service he had been promised. He was forever asking for a new pillow, or sheets, even for a new chamber pot.

It was a Sunday. Normally she would have spent it with Alexander or even with some of the other girls but the foreign visitor had made a request to Mr Taubner for Sarah to help him to sort out some paperwork before a meeting at the Melbourne winemakers association the following day. She was uneasy because she knew there were others on the staff who could do such a job far better than she could.

She went into his room and asked him to tell her what he wanted her to do. He mumbled something about sitting at the table, which she did. As she waited further instructions, he came up behind her and started fondling her breasts. She was panicked. What to do? He whispered in her ear that she was beautiful and he found it hard to keep his hands off her. He said other things too but she was so overwhelmed that she couldn't think. When his hands strayed further she knew what was happening and tried to extricate herself but he was too strong. She wanted it to end.

But she couldn't hurt his feelings. He was a guest and didn't he have a right to do what he was doing? After all she was just the hired help, a woman of no import. Added to that she knew that he could have any woman he wanted and he had chosen her. Maybe this was meant to happen. Maybe it was a compliment. If so, why did she feel so sick.

Too many thoughts went through her head until he lowered her onto his bed and she knew then she just had to surrender to the awfulness of what was happening. It hurt. She lay on the bed sobbing. He whispered softly to her that next time it wouldn't hurt at all. Next time? O God! Was this really happening?

The mid-winter afternoon dragged on as she lay on his bed growing colder. Her sobs had abated giving way to a melancholy. He stoked up the fire and put a blanket over her and lay down beside her whispering all the right things, how he wanted to take her back home with him, how she was the most wonderful woman he had ever been with and how he couldn't stop thinking about her. She listened to his words but she knew that this was wrong and it wasn't meant to be like this. Her head was spinning in the realisation of what had happened.

She left that room a different person. Never again would she be the innocent Sarah Bradshaw whose biggest problem was how to find a way to be with Alexander. Everything looked different. She couldn't stop thinking about the moment when he had thrust himself into her, claiming her as his prize. She stayed ages in the bathroom before she staggered to her room knowing that anyone who saw her would know!

Her tears flowed into the pillow. She had never cried like this before, even after all the times her father had let her down. It was as if she had lost something of her soul, something she could never recover. She had lost a mother and a little sister, but this was different.

Kitty was standing over her, perplexed.

"Sarah, you all right love?"

Sarah mumbled something about feeling sick and could Kitty tell them she needed a day in bed. Kitty agreed but as she left the room, she knew Sarah wasn't sick. She was surprised. She didn't think Alexander had it in him.

All the next day Sarah sobbed and slept. At least when she slept, she could forget. She was sore but knew that would heal. But would she? Kitty brought her food and a hot cup of tea. Sarah wanted so much to tell her what happened but she was ashamed, so ashamed.

The next day was business as usual for all the world except Sarah. She knew she had to get on with her life and pretend nothing had happened. Collecting the vegetables from Alexander, she couldn't look him in the eye. He sensed that something was wrong and asked her straight out.

"What's wrong Sarah? You seem to be distant today."

She put him off with words that didn't ring true and made her escape. She brushed him aside as if he were an annoying stranger, knowing how much he would be hurt by her actions. But what else could she do?

She wouldn't see the foreign visitor that day as he was still in the city at the meeting, the meeting he asked her to help him with, when his agenda was quite different. What would she do when he returned though. How could she face him? She tied herself in knots thinking about it.

Three times over the next two weeks, he trapped her in situations where she could not escape. He was like a man possessed and whereas he was right that it did not hurt as much as the first time, she did not enjoy or want it. Allowing him to do with her what he wanted, she felt like an inert vessel and just prayed that it would soon be over. She no longer listened to his words because she did not believe them but she knew that she couldn't report his behaviour as Mr Taubner would not believe her. It would be his word against hers.

She wondered if the foreign visitor thought that she liked him. She was not rude to him, as a protection of her own employment but did he misconstrue her behaviour? When he embraced her, she did not fight him as it was comforting to be held but she wished it ended there. What if she had told him she didn't like it, would he have stopped? Where was that new found confidence she thought she had acquired? Why did she feel such a fool? At what point could she have said stop?

When she heard the staff talking about how nice the foreign visitor was, she cringed. It actually hurt to hear him spoken about in such positive terms.

Kitty noticed the change in her friend. "You know you can talk to me, Sarah. Tell me what's wrong." Kitty wondered why Sarah was so unhappy when she knew how in love with Alexander she was. For the first time she began to doubt whether she had been right in her diagnosis.

The foreign visitor left, without even saying goodbye. One minute his presence and the conflicting emotions of it obsessed her and the next he was gone. Was she a little bit sad? She didn't know. Now that he was gone, she was not special to anyone. Alexander was lost to her. There was no-one to hold her. She had been discarded. Again!

Normality returned to the household and the sense of relief she felt outweighed any sense of loss. I am now a woman, thought Sarah, and hoped she could put the whole experience behind her.

The worst part, the part she mourned most of all, was that something had broken between her and Alexander. She did not have the easy going, innocent relationship she once had with him and found avoiding his company easier than the shamed feelings she experienced in his company. What would Alexander think of her giving herself to a man like that?

She knew Alexander was hurt. She could see it in his face and she could also see desire now that she knew what it looked like. It's not fair, she thought, just when everything could have been so good. If there is a God, he certainly doesn't like me.

The winter of 1872 was quite mild. The weak sunshine made for delightful Sunday strolls around the village of Camberwell. Sometimes, the girls would take the cable car into the city of Melbourne and stroll by the Yarra observing all the fashions and the society women of this outpost of London, trying to impress. Sarah spent more of her Sundays with the other girls as she no longer spent time with Alexander. The treat was to spend their savings at a tea house in one of the arcades where they sat with ladies and ordered tea and cake, keeping an eye out for any young men who looked as if they might be eligible.

By Spring, Sarah knew the truth of what she had dreaded. The sickness she had felt was not a result of something she had eaten or even the first signs of illness. She was carrying the child of the foreign visitor.

Chapter Ten

The realisation that she was with child crashed through Sarah like a cyclone. NO. she felt like screaming, It's not fair! She knew what happened to women like her. Whether it was her fault or not didn't matter. She was hanging by a thread, to life, to hope, to sanity.

Who could help her? She thought of Kitty but apart from sympathy she could offer nothing and it was not sympathy she needed. Soon she would not be able to hide what her body would reveal. Oh the scandal! What would people think? What would her father say?

She thought of Aunty Helen but imagining her look of disappointment expressed through the veil of her strong religious views, put that thought out of her mind. She thought of her father and wondered would he help when the cook came rushing through the swinging doors, interrupting her thoughts.

"Mr Taubner wants to see you, Sarah, and let me tell you he's in a right old mood."

She climbed the stairs to his office. On each step she paused, feeling sick, her stomach churning. She had to tell him. The problem was not going to go away. She didn't even wonder what he wanted to see her about. It was as if it was fate to be called to his office now. She sighed deeply trying to regulate her breathing. His door was closed. She'd never noticed how formidable a door it was.

She knocked.

And waited.

Another deep sigh and a feeling of faintness, dizziness.

"Come in!"

Sarah had entered this office many times and always felt welcome. The chair she usually sat in was waiting for her to relax into but she remained standing.

"Sarah, what's wrong? You look as pale as a ghost. For goodness sake sit down. I've just had to tell cook that she better pull her socks up or she will be out on her ear. I was looking forward to seeing you and giving you news of your father whom I saw last week. He is bringing Marriott to meet you very soon."

Sarah began to cry. Once she started, she couldn't get the words out. Mr Taubner gave her his handkerchief and managed to stem the flow with his kindness until...

She blurted out the whole story.

Between sniffles, sobs and pauses, Sarah told of the behaviour of the foreign visitor, the surprising and trapping. She told of his promises, his assurances and his position in the household. She wished it had never happened and didn't know what she was going to do. More than anything she wanted for Mr Taubner to embrace her and tell her that everything was going to be all right.

But this was not to be

She had never before seen Mr Taubner's fury. He stood to his full height, face reddening, eyes narrowing, hands pressed against the desk. He was yelling:

"Whore! I was so wrong about you Sarah. You're nothing but a liar and after all I have done for you"

His breathing was shallow

"What do you think people will say when they find out. That I allow my girls to prostitute themselves in their spare time?"

"YOU ARE DISMISSED."

"I want you out of here by next week."

He grabbed the desk for support.

Sarah was stunned. She had expected anger, maybe even to be 'let go,' but this vitriol from the mild mannered man who had been her guardian for the last four years made her unable to respond, either by way of movement or by words. From deep down in the pit of her stomach, she felt the internal cry, the cry of the scorned, the desperate and the helpless. When she looked up, he was still standing over her, a judge ready to condemn. She struggled towards the door, the reality of her situation becoming oh so clear, as it had for so many women before her. What would she do now?

She walked back to her room in a daze, glad that Kitty would not be there. She sat on the bed and picked up her mother's copy of Jane Eyre. Oh mother, she thought, why did you die?

Her eyes were red and her head was aching. Exhausted, she wanted to lie down and sleep forever. She felt her belly and thought about what was inside her. There was only one person she could turn to. She reached for the paper she kept on her desk, took a deep breath and began to write.

"Dear Father,

This is a letter which may cause you much grief but I have no-one else to turn to. I am with child and Mr Taubner has dismissed me. He wants me gone immediately.

I shall spare you the details but please believe me when I say that I was seduced and did not want for this to happen. The man who forced himself on me was a powerful foreign friend of Mr Taubner who cannot believe such behaviour of his friend and so has blamed me.

I beg of you that I may be allowed to come to live with you in Bamawm and have the child there.

Your loving daughter
Sarah"

Her friends among the staff sensed something was wrong but Sarah told them nothing. Only Kitty guessed. She was sure now that the culprit was not Alexander and was concerned for her friend. "Sarah, who was it?"

Sarah turned her head sharply and looked at Kitty. How did she know? Was it that obvious? She began to cry. "I can't say, but I have been dismissed."

"Oh," Kitty put her arms around Sarah and stroked her hair, her beautiful, long dark hair. They stayed like that, in silence, for a long time, both girls reflecting on how unfair life was for women.

How could she leave *Shrublands*, she thought. It was her home. She grew up here, made friends, learnt skills. How could she leave the person she had come to love, Alexander? She wanted to tell him everything but she suspected his reaction would be the same as Mr Taubner's.

The injustice of the situation! Her future was now determined. She was a fallen woman, a whore, and society deemed that she should feel shame.

But she didn't. There was a living person inside of her, a miracle which had been the consequence of such an unfortunate act. She talked to the unborn child and told him that she couldn't wait to meet him. (She felt sure it was a 'him.') She told him she would never abandon him even though she wasn't sure how she would manage to keep him out of an institution.

For the next few days, she did not speak to Mr Taubner. They avoided each other. She wasn't sure exactly when she would be turned out of the house so she just kept doing what she had always done, in her efficient and competent way.

The week passed, nothing happened, and her anxiety increased. One evening, after supper, three weeks after she had dropped the bombshell on him, he summoned her. This time, she sat in the velvet chair nervously picking at a scab on her hand. Mr Taubner was seated with his head over some papers and Sarah looked above his head at the picture of an English hunting scene. She felt like the fox with the hounds after her.

The man who had her future in his hands leaned back in his chair in a more affable pose than the last time she had seen him. She tore her gaze away from the hunting scene and looked into his eyes, waiting, not knowing what was to come.

"Sarah, I owe you an apology. I have had a letter from your father begging me to keep you on here. He has also led me to see that my actions in dismissing you were unjust as you were the unwilling victim of this man I called my friend. I must admit, much of my angry response to you was my disappointment in him, a man whom I thought had more character. Fortunately he has not yet returned to Europe and is staying in Healesville. I took it upon myself to visit him to find out the truth of the situation. After some denial, and several glasses of red wine, he admitted to me that he seduced you. He is sorry that you find yourself in this plight, and has provided me with a sum of money for the unborn child. However, he has made it clear, if you accept this money, you must obey the following conditions."

Sarah wondered at the cheek of the foreign visitor making conditions.

"You can stay here until such time as the baby is born. A credible and respectable story will circulate as to your condition. When the time comes for the birth you will be provided with a good midwife and enough time for you to be able to recuperate. You must not mention my friend's name on the birth certificate as he obviously does not want an illegitimate child claiming his fortune in years to come."

Mr Taubner then stood, but not in an intimidating way. He came round to the front of his desk, pushed aside the papers there and sat so that he was level with Sarah, close enough to touch her. His voice was firm but kind, more like the man she had known since she was sixteen.

"Then, Sarah, you have a choice to make. I will keep you on in my employ as long as you give the baby up. If you want to keep the baby, you must leave and I have no more responsibility for you. You cannot continue to do this job with a child and that is my last word. Do you understand what I have just said?"

Sarah understood and whereas she should have been pleased with his words, her heart was breaking. She had had visions of her father allowing her to keep the child and supporting both of them. Once again, others had mapped out her options, this time her father and her employer. Her father did not want an unwed daughter and her bastard child living with him in a community where he was trying to gain respect. He would want her to give up the child and stay in service. She had no choice really. Women like her didn't.

She politely and mechanically thanked Mr Taubner, said she understood perfectly, stood erect trying to feel her legs and stumbled out of the room.

She found herself in the garden, beside the fountain with no memory of how she got there.

There seemed no way out. She couldn't bear the thought of giving up her child, a child who would wonder all his life if his mother had ever loved him. Would the strangers who brought him up tell him his mother had died or would they tell him the truth? Which was worse?

Although the sun illuminated the flowers which were coming into bloom making the garden look fresh and vibrant, Sarah's world was dark, darker than she could ever remember. All sorts of thoughts raced through her mind, even the unthinkable! But she didn't want to die and she certainly couldn't bear the thought of the child dying.

She looked around her. This was a place where she had been happy, surrounded by giant eucalypts towering over the landscape dating back to before white man settled this land. The fountain was gushing with life giving water. The pair of lions stared at Sarah in solidity. She looked into their eyes. Does one person matter in this world? she thought. Do I matter? Would anyone grieve if I were to depart this world?

Just then, she felt a quickening inside her. She placed a hand upon her stomach and prayed that it not be a girl. She sat on the ridge of the fountain, shoulders slumped. The tears flowed.

She felt his presence. Had she hoped he would be here? Should she run away from the one person whom she yearned to hold her. Could she bear to receive his judgement and disapproval? As he came closer she knew she would not run. She wanted him to find her.

The voice was gentle. "Sarah, won't you tell me what's wrong?" She turned, looked into his eyes with her tear stained face and embraced him, sobbing into his shoulder.

"O Alexander, what am I going to do?" When she realised what she had done, she quickly withdrew her arms. "I'm sorry. I shouldn't have done that." For a few moments, neither one spoke.

"You are carrying a child."

Sarah was shocked. How did he know?

"I've been worried about you and saw you sitting there rubbing your stomach. Who was it Sarah? Was it that wretched stable boy?" Sarah blurted it all out, without any filter. She didn't try to make herself out a victim or even a temptress. She just told it as it was. He listened without judgement and then did something which seemed natural but would never have happened before. He put his arms around her and held her tight.

"That bastard!" Alexander paused long enough to be able to piece together the sequence of events. "I never liked the bloke. Seemed far too smarmy. I should have warned you. I've met men like him before – think they have a right to everything and everybody."

Sarah was about to defend the foreign visitor, why she didn't know, but instead she couldn't take her eyes off Alexander. It was the first time she had seen him angry and she loved that he was angry for her sake. She had been frightened that he would react like Mr Taubner but she couldn't have been more wrong.

"Do you want to keep this baby, Sarah?"

"I couldn't bear for him to go to an orphanage, Alexander, but I don't know that I have a choice."

His words came out hurriedly and awkwardly, but genuinely. "Sarah, if you marry me, I would bring the child up as if it were my own." Sarah could feel her heart beat. The words. Were they real? Did Alexander mean what he was saying?

"Alexander, I ….," she could not find the words, instead looked into his eyes and the word 'miracle' kept coming to her.

"Say yes, Sarah, that is if you like me, just a little? And I wouldn't just do it for you," he grinned, "it would not be completely selfless. I would like to have more children and I can't think of anyone I would want by my side more than you."

"But could you love another man's child?"

"The baby will be your child, Sarah, and yes I could love him, or her, just as long as he or she is as beautiful you. We needn't tell the child that I am not its father. This baby will not be illegitimate."

He kissed her. Instinctively she stiffened, remembering the foreign visitor, and Alexander, sensitive to the situation, stopped. But this was not the foreign visitor, Sarah told herself, it was a man she had loved since she was sixteen, a man who had asked her to marry him, a man who was willing to bring up another man's child. The kiss that followed started with Sarah. It was tender and beautiful filled with a love of friendship, unselfishness and mutual desire. Sarah would never forget it.

They decided to walk to the orchard and celebrate their betrothal with a splurge of new season's apricots, even though they were not quite ripe. They talked, planned and kissed some more and she doubted whether she had ever felt happier, just hours after she had considered the unthinkable!

She did not see Alexander for the next few days as he and the other gardeners were working in the vineyard. Her emotions were all over the place. She began to doubt what had happened and tortured herself with questions. Would Alexander decide that he didn't want to go through with being the father of her child? Would they find somewhere to live? Would the baby love her? Could such happiness last? Was it all just a cruel dream?

"It's about time he made a move," said Kitty whose opinion of Alexander had soared since she saw him through Sarah's eyes. "And to agree to bring up a child that's not his. Cor, Sarah, you've got a good one there."

When next she met Alexander, she knew they were meant to be together. It was as if everything had led to this moment. The shadow of the foreign visitor was gone and the unborn child was coming into a home where two parents would love him. Their conversation now was of the future.

"I suppose we better tell Mr Taubner our news?"

"He'll be happy. It's the perfect solution for him. He won't have to lie because everyone will think the baby is yours."

"I'll ask him for a reference. With his contacts I should be able to apply for the lease of a market garden. The city of Melbourne is crying out for more supplies of fruit and vegetables and I reckon I can make a go of it." Sarah cuddled into him and they both felt the kick. "He agrees," said Alexander as he pulled her closer.

Chapter Eleven

Hartwell
1873

Sarah looked towards the heavens, where she imagined God to be, and said a prayer. It was mid-summer and the heat was oppressive. Her headaches were sometimes so bad that she needed to lie down, easing her aching back at the same time.

The last few months had been the happiest of her life. Alexander had taken possession of a market garden in Hartwell on four acres with a house attached. Alan Pool, the owner, was a contact of Frederik Taubner's and was more than happy to follow his recommendation of Alexander as a dependable tenant. Everything was falling into place.

Leaving *Shrublands* was hard and as the cart had trundled away from the house, she had looked back with affection. Although her worst moments had happened there, so too had her best. She was especially sad to leave Kitty who had become like a sister to her.

"I'll miss you Sarah. I always thought it would be me leaving with a chap but you beat me to it."

Sarah felt for her friend. She had fallen in love so often but for some reason nothing ever eventuated. She wondered if she fell for the wrong sort of man.

"You must visit us in Hartwell, Kitty. It's not so far."

"I'd like that."

The two friends hugged, knowing that they would probably not meet again.

All her life, since she was three, she had felt on the outside looking in. She was never a real part of the Little family even though they treated her well. She was never part of *Shrublands* either, just a servant. But now she was part of Alexander and she was part of the child she was carrying.

If she died now, she would die happy, as Mrs Alexander Hamilton. She watched Alexander out the kitchen window. She could watch him forever. She had convinced him to allow her to cut his unruly hair and he looked so handsome now that it was tamed. At night, when he had come up from the garden, they would sit and talk about the future, about the coming child, and about how lucky they both were to meet each other. These moments Sarah treasured.

The market garden was run down and needed work but the soil was good and the creek was close for Alexander's makeshift irrigation system. They had not bothered to get married officially but called themselves Mr and Mrs Hamilton. What did it matter anyway?

One evening, as they were watching the light fade over the city, Alexander said to Sarah: "Penny for your thoughts Sarah. You seem a bit down in the dumps."

"I was just thinking about my mother and how she died giving birth."

"That won't happen to you, Sarah. Those days are gone. Your mother died because of the conditions in the city years ago. We have strict sanitation and health regulations now. Besides, to a girl like you who can lift heavy, wet sheets from the copper with a wooden pole, childbirth will be a walk in the park."

She smiled and reached for his hand. "I was just being silly," she said, but at the same time she knew that Alexander was not correct. Women still did die in childbirth, although not so many as in her mother's time. The thought of her mother giving birth and not living to enjoy the fruit of her labour haunted Sarah through those dark times. She wished she could remember more about her.

Life had made her more sympathetic to her father. Having their second child should have been a happy time for him and her mother. Instead he buried both of them. Her heart ached for him in a way it had not before. Loving someone like she loved Alexander made life seem fragile. The dread, the fear of losing him played havoc with her late night thoughts.

She knew he would love this child as if it were his own. A son. Yes, she would give Alexander a son. And he was to be a Hamilton.

It was mid-March, the leaves on the trees were beginning to change colour, the nights and mornings were crisp but the days were filled with sunshine. Sarah's cries rang through the cottage as Alexander paced in the kitchen. He had gone for the midwife early that morning and decided not to go down into the garden but to stay close. The hours ticked by and he wondered if everything was going normally. He too had had dark thoughts about losing Sarah, thoughts that he would never have admitted to her.

At three o'clock that afternoon, he heard a baby cry and felt an enormous relief. The midwife told him that it was one of the easiest first births she had experienced and that he had a healthy little boy. 'Goodness,' he thought, 'if that were easy, I would hate to experience a hard one.'

"What will we call him?" he blurted out when he came into the room and saw his wife with a scrunched up little bundle in her arms. "My father was Alexander and I have a brother called Robert."

"He is to be named William, William Hamilton," said Sarah looking lovingly at this little miracle and handing him to Alexander to nurse. She could see that he would be darker than either Alexander or herself but she hoped questions would not be asked. She told

Alexander the story about her childhood friend, Willie, and how she had pledged to call her first son after him.

"And will he call his firstborn girl Sarah?" said Alexander feeling a tinge of jealousy.

Sarah noticed his tone of voice. "Our next boy will be called Alexander," she said, reaching her hand out to him. Alexander sat on the bed holding William in one hand. His other hand was around Sarah who was experiencing the euphoria of all first time mothers. The pain had stopped, the baby had emerged and pride in having produced another human being flowed through her. Alexander looked down at William and thought. 'This is my son and I am his father.' William, on cue, whimpered in his sleep. The midwife took him and shooed Alexander from the room.

Sarah was to learn how to be a mother.

Chapter Twelve

She was glad to see her father when he visited. Until now, she had wanted him in her life because she needed him, but now that she had Alexander and William, she wanted him in her life in a different way, as a father and grand-father. He had lost Jane and Catherine and although he had Marriott, it was not the same as having a life partner. Sarah, Alexander and William were Thomas' family as much as he was hers.

Thomas liked Alexander. He had heard glowing reports of him from Frederik Taubner and couldn't have been happier for Sarah. As he nursed his little grandson he was careful not to make any comment about his dark appearance and as Sarah walked him to the gate, after a most enjoyable afternoon, he said to her. "You have done well, Sarah. Alexander is a very fine man and little William is perfect. Soon you must make the journey to Bamawm and show him where his grandfather lives."

The irony of the invitation was not lost on Sarah. Now I am welcome in his house, she thought but she just smiled and said yes, they would do that sometime, knowing full well they probably wouldn't. "Travel safely, Father."

She watched him limp towards the tram stop. He was looking much older and more vulnerable. She was glad she no longer felt anger towards him. What had changed? Maybe she was no longer a little girl with her arms reaching towards a father who pushed her away. Maybe. Instead, her arms were stretched invitingly towards him.

Sarah knew she had to register William at the City Office. She wanted to lie and put Alexander as the father on the official certificate but Alexander would not agree. "You can't tell a lie, Sarah, not on an official document."

So, with reluctance, she wrote 'father unknown' in the appropriate column and he was registered as William Bradshaw as she had promised. But to everyone, he would always be William Hamilton.

What's in a name? she thought as she cradled him to her breast thinking she had no idea she could ever feel this way for a child. Did her mother love her the way she loved William? Did her mother spend hours just watching every movement in her face and little body? Did her mother enjoy her baby smell just after a bath?

Sarah delighted in seeing Alexander take his place as head of the family and anyone watching him with William would never know that he was not the father. Everything she had ever wanted, a family, she now had.

The Hamiltons settled into the life of so many Melbourne families whose hard work and sacrifice would be the backbone of the young country. As she scrubbed the cottage, with its whitewashed walls, timber floors and wood stove, Sarah was content.

It was the winter of 1875. Sarah was helping Alexander to provide the insatiable Melbourne market with produce. She patted her extended stomach and spoke to the infant inside. Soon, my love, you will meet us all. Your father and mother and your big brother, William. The light was fading as Alexander came into the kitchen, kicked off his boots and sat in the wooden chair closest to the stove.

"Sarah, we've been invited to afternoon tea with Frederik Taubner at *Shrublands,* Should we go?" Sarah didn't answer straight away. "I'd love to see Kitty again."

"She's no longer there," said Alexander, " I don't know where she's gone, but would you believe Cook is still there."

"I'd be curious to go back," said Sarah. "Why not?"

"Then I'll accept the invitation and we shall dress in our finery and take William to see where his mother and father met." With that he put his arm around Sarah, and lifted William into their embrace.

Sarah was nervous about revisiting *Shrublands* but once they were in the parlour and being entertained by Frederik Taubner, her anxiety eased. His warmth towards her reminded her of the man she had known before there was any unpleasantness between them. She knew he felt guilty about what happened but all she had to do was look at William and her anger towards him dissipated.

"Do you like the wine, Sarah? I'm very proud of it. I sent a bottle to your father in Bamawm as he is soon to produce his first batch."

Sarah said she liked it but had not the foggiest whether it was good or not. She swallowed a sip with great difficulty and then placed her glass on the table and made to attend to William so she wouldn't have to drink any more. "I have heard good reports about the Market Garden, Alexander." he said

"Times are good, Mr Taubner, "but I've lived long enough to know that things can change at any time. I saw it on the gold fields. One minute, rich, the next skint."

"We miss you here, your replacement is not half the gardener you were. In fact, we have been running low on some things and wonder could we set up a contract with you to provide enough to top up the larder."

"Should be all right," said Alexander. "I've still got half an acre not yet under cultivation. William will help me, won't you lad?"

At being addressed, two year old William hid behind his father's coat, shyly peering at Mr Taubner who, Sarah wondered, was looking for a resemblance to the foreign visitor.

"He's a good looking lad, Sarah, takes after his mother I think!" Sarah shot a glance at him. Was he referring to William's parentage? No she was being too sensitive and William did have some of her features, just that he was more like his father.

After a pleasant afternoon, they left knowing that they would probably not ever return again. Sarah kissed Mr Taubner on the cheek in such a way that he knew she had forgiven him. "God be with you and the new child, Sarah. Let me know if you need any help won't you?"

He bent down to shake hands with William who was too quick and made sure his father was between them. Frederik Taubner was not so easily deterred, however, and grabbed him and tickled him. William laughed and then shook his hand.

"You've won the lad over" said Alexander, "not many can do that!"

Chapter Thirteen

Annie was born in the Spring of 1875 and named after Alexander's sister in Scotland. She had reddish hair like her father, who was overjoyed with his first child.

"This one won't be called after you, Alexander. Are you disappointed it isn't a boy?"

"I already have a son, Sarah, don't I, son?" he said as he put his arm around William who was watching his little sister wondering what kind of toy she was. Alec arrived two years later, named after his father and looking the spitting image of him, same shape of face and shock of unruly hair.

The Hamilton family welcomed 1880 as a new decade of prosperity and progress. People who had known poverty all their lives found that they had money to spend for the first time ever. The economy was booming. Alexander couldn't keep up with the orders on his produce. With three children to support, he was glad that he didn't have to see them go hungry. He remembered what that was like from his own childhood.

Sarah loved her three children but it was William who was her favourite. She saw something in him which marked him as different from the others, a sensitivity or was it an unusual intelligence? He spent his days shadowing his father, learning about plants, creeks and the natural surroundings. He could name the birds and recognise their calls and knew always to be on his guard for brown and tiger snakes. Sarah loved to see father and son together and was amazed at Alexander's patience with the small boy.

"Have you collected the eggs today, William?"

"Yes, Papa, we got three."

"And did you give them to your mother?"

"Yes, Papa. Mama said she would make a cake for us."

"Well aren't we the lucky ones?"

Sarah would put William on a stool round the table where he would crack the eggs into the basin in readiness to make a cake. She was patient with him but it was a balancing act and although he got annoyed when she tried to help him, they would somehow work it out. Nearby in his chair, Alexander was enjoying a rare moment reading the paper.

"Says here they're bringing Ned Kelly down to Melbourne from Wangaratta for the trial. Tomorrow morning, he arrives at Pentridge. Why don't we go William?"

William left the eggs in the bowl and ran to his father. "Yes please, Papa."

Sarah was taken aback at this idea of Alexander's. "Alexander! Ned Kelly is a violent criminal. Will it be safe for a six year old? What if there is a riot when he arrives? I heard a lot of people are unhappy about his arrest." The pictures of Ned Kelly had fascinated Sarah. There was something beguiling about him. He certainly did not look like the bloodthirsty bushranger he was made out to be. She thought he had sad eyes.

"There won't be a riot. Most people want him hanged. It's just the Irish who have sympathy for him."

"Not just the Irish, Alexander, I have some sympathy for him. His family were treated very badly by the police."

"Hmmm, not sure I agree."

"William will be excited, but you will look after him, won't you?"

The next morning, she watched them go out the door. Father and son. Both as excited as the other, off to see a murderer brought to trial. She wondered how it would go as she turned her attention to making stew from the meat bones Alexander had got from the market the day before. She hoped to finish early so she could take Annie and Alec for a walk in the Spring sunshine. If Alexander and William were having a day out, so she and the children would also. She loved to sit on the banks of the creek and stare into the flowing water. There was something about moving water which brought her peace.

Later that day, after a tiring but most enjoyable walk, Sarah was putting the bread in the oven when William ran in, full of the experience of sitting on his father's shoulders, waiting for Ned Kelly to arrive. She couldn't shut him up.

"He didn't turn up," said Alexander. "They tricked us all and took him somewhere else. Maybe you were right, Sarah. People had more sympathy than I thought."

"There were so many people there, Mama, and there was a man selling lemonade. It was so hot that he made a lot of money."

"I don't think it mattered that we didn't see him," chuckled Alexander later that night after they finally got the over-excited boy to bed, "William had a good day just watching all the people. You know Sarah, he's a bright boy. I think we should send him to school."

"But he's so frail, Alexander. He coughs and coughs at night and I'm not sure he could manage the long days at school."

"He told me today that he'd like to go with the Eddy kids next door. I think he feels as if he is missing out."

Fighting sleeplessness that night, Sarah thought about what Alexander had said. She wondered if she were being too protective. It was true she treated William differently from the other children. Annie complained that he was the favourite and got everything, which was probably because Annie was as strong as William was frail. She never worried about Annie.

The next evening, sitting round the fire, she told Alexander that she agreed with him. William should go to school. Alexander smiled, drew on his pipe and said, "I'll go down to the school tomorrow and enrol him for next year and I'll enrol Annie as well. They can go together."

It was Sarah's favourite time of the day, when the children were in bed. She and Alexander would talk about everything and anything, just like they had at *Shrublands* when they became friends. Yes, that was it, she thought, they were good friends, not just a married couple but good friends.

Sarah watched the seasons come and go. The market garden prospered and the children grow from babies to little children. The loneliness and sorrow that had been with her for so long had given way to a deep joy. She often thought of her mother and wondered if she had experienced that joy in the short time she had had on this earth.

Late in 1882, after the birth of Agnes, they all caught a tram into the city to see the new Exhibition Building which was the talk of Melbourne. It had been a year of unprecedented prosperity in the city and it seemed the growth would never stop. Sarah sat with baby Agnes on her knee looking at Alexander trying to control Annie and Alec who were so excited with such a rare outing that they couldn't contain themselves. William sat beside his father trying to impress him with his knowledge of the workings of the cable tram.

As the tram rattled towards the city, Sarah thought over the previous nine years — meeting Alexander, William's birth, the market garden and the birth of three more children. Her body was tired and longed for a rest from the constant demands of children and physical work, but her soul was at peace. She looked across at Alexander and prayed that this moment would last forever.

The tram stopped and Alexander marshalled them across busy Nicholson street. As they walked through the gardens towards the Exhibition building, they were all amazed at its scale. It towered over the gardens shouting its magnificence. Alexander, kneeling on the grass with his arm round William and Annie on his knee, pointed out the features of the architecture.

"Think you'll be a builder like your grandfather, William?"

"No, Papa, I want to be a gardener like you."

Chapter Fourteen

She never resented the work involved in the market garden, caring for baby Agnes and helping Alexander with the orders, organising the Saturday markets in Malvern and Hawthorn. William was a great help with the facts and figures and was doing well at school. She often watched her son, no longer seeing the foreign visitor, but rather a boy whose father was Alexander.

Her garden was struggling outside the back door and she wondered why some people could get things to grow and others couldn't. She was trying to grow English varieties of plants to add colour about the yard. "Now don't you die on me, little rose, I want you to grow big and strong."

"Are you talking to those plants again, Mama?" William had come up from working with his father. He was filthy. More washing. "Papa wants some more string."

She walked gingerly on the newly washed kitchen floor, got the string from the dresser drawer and gave it to William who ran back to his father. William took his role as the oldest with great seriousness, even becoming bossy at times but Annie was more than a match for him. Seeing them together made her mourn for her little sister and she remembered the doll she had christened 'Emily'. She still had it somewhere. Where was it?

When she closed her eyes now, she couldn't even remember her mother's face and of course, they had no photographs. She envied those people who had portraits of their parents commissioned so that they could visualise them. She wondered if Annie or Agnes looked like her mother.

With such a busy household and being so happy, Sarah didn't notice the change in Alexander at first. Maybe she didn't want to and it was gradual. She knew he was coughing more than he should but she told herself it was just a passing illness. She was no stranger to the illnesses which surrounded them, scarlet fever, dysentery, measles, diphtheria and consumption and was forever frightened that one of her children would be snatched away from her like her mother and little sister.

But Alexander? He was a strong man who worked from dawn till dusk and never got sick. Even the cough that he had developed had not stopped him.

But it didn't go away.

She noticed he was finishing work earlier and would just want to lie down when he reached the house. He slept later and seemed excessively tired. The cough persisted and Sarah noticed how thin he was becoming. She couldn't pretend any longer. She persuaded him to see a doctor.

She went with him to the surgery on Burke Road and waited outside, watching the incessant traffic. The volume had changed considerably in the ten years they had lived there. The village had gone from a friendly, small place to a bustling, rather chaotic part of the world. She didn't mind the busyness, it made her feel alive, but she mourned the passing of the friendliness.

Alexander wished to see the doctor alone. She understood that. When he hadn't come out after fifteen minutes, all sorts of negative thoughts started plaguing her and when she saw Alexander emerge from the consulting room, her fears were realised. His head was down and his shoulders dropped. In that instant, Sarah could see what the next few months would be like.

The diagnosis was consumption. And they all knew what that meant. She was a little girl again, frightened and overwhelmed.

Would she be strong enough to help Alexander through this? Would she be strong enough to get through it herself? The fragile walls of her security were crumbling.

The doctor had told Alexander of the research coming from overseas, especially America, which advised that people with consumption should retreat to the mountains and engage in exercise and wholesome diet. 'Sanitoriums' had been set up with the express purpose of treating people with consumption. Was there somewhere Alexander could go which would fit this criterion?

Alexander had dismissed the idea immediately. Only wealthy people could do such a thing as leave their family and pamper themselves. It was out of the question for him.

"Perhaps you could go and stay with Father," said Sarah. "William, Annie and I could keep things going here." She was clutching at straws.

Alexander managed a smile, "I don't think Bamawm is quite in the mountains, Sarah. All I'd be inhaling there would be dust and sheep shit!"

Sarah knew he was right and knew that he would work until it was no longer possible after which she would look after him at home, keeping in mind what the doctor had also told him about the spread of the disease. Alexander repeated the words to Sarah that night as they sat and tried to process the day's events. He tried to inject some humour into the conversation by imitating the posh voice of the doctor.

"Mr Hamilton, we used to think T.B was hereditary but now we know that it is contagious and that as you cough and sneeze, you can spread the disease to your wife and children. You must take precautions." The humour fell flat. Sarah wasn't laughing.

The children stopped going to school. William and Annie liked school and were disappointed but they knew they were needed at home. Alec was glad. School was not his cup of tea. All three children helped their father until he could no longer work and it was not long before he was unable, even, to leave the house.

In the mornings, Sarah would take William and Alec with her to work in the garden while Annie looked after Agnes and her father. After lunch, William and Annie would continue the work while Alec rested and she cared for Alexander. It was exhausting but she was determined to maintain the garden until such time as Alexander was better. She knew in her heart of hearts that there would be no cure but making believe was something which kept her going.

"Why do we have to stay away from Father?" asked Annie who loved to climb all over him and tickle him, or ride on his back pretending to be in a horse race.

"Because he's sick," said William, his angry tone coming from his own sorrow that the man he loved was lying in a room coughing his heart out.

Each day saw him deteriorating. She was losing him. To see him fading away was torturous. She disobeyed the doctor's instructions to be careful and lay beside him at night, talking to him, assuring him that he would get better. She knew it was hopeless but the thought of losing him was one she just could not entertain.

"Sarah," Alexander could hardly talk. "The rates are due tomorrow. Take the money in the tin and pay Mr Pool. That way we can keep the Market Garden for another year. I should be better by then."

"Are you sure, Alexander, that you want to renew the lease? We could use the money to move to Bamawm to live with Father until I can find us a place to live. The rent is so much cheaper there. And he could help with the children."

"Sarah, this is our home. We have to keep it. I have so many plans for when I am better." He paused for quite a while. "And If I don't get better, I want to die here. Twelve more months is all we need either way."

Sarah nestled into him noticing that her arms could almost encircle his thin frame. She knew that paying the lease for twelve more months was important to both of them and their make believe. "I'll go and see Mr Pool in the morning."

Alexander's illness dominated her life. She knew she was not giving the children enough attention and they were thrown together in their own confusion about what was happening to their family. She was short with them when they made too much noise and told them to be more considerate. She heard William and Annie talking together one morning about what would happen if they had to move from their house because their father could no longer keep the market garden going.

"Cats don't like moving, William. What would Ginger do?"

"I dunno," said William shrugging his shoulders helplessly, "I just want Papa to get better."

At the end of each day, she would pray: God give me one more day with him. And maybe she convinced herself that there would always be one more day.

When the end came, it was sudden. She and William were working in the garden with a young lad they had employed to help them. Annie was in the house with Agnes and Alec. The Spring weather had seen a surge in the plant growth and it took constant weeding and watering to maintain the vegetables. They had a huge order to fulfil for the coming Saturday in Hawthorn, plus the regular market runs. Alexander's condition had improved slightly and that morning when Sarah had left him, she had felt quite hopeful.

Alec appeared beside them. He was crying. As soon as Sarah saw him, she knew. She raced up to the house closely followed by William and a sobbing Alec. The young lad who had been helping, kept going with his work as he didn't know what else to do. Sarah entered the house and met Annie whose face told her everything.

"Was anyone with him, Annie?" she said sounding quite matter of fact and wondering how that could be.

"Alec was," said a distraught Annie. "I was trying to stop Agnes from crying and Alec called me to tell me that Father wouldn't wake. I know he shouldn't have been with Papa but he wouldn't listen to me. He had been trying to tell him a story and didn't know why he wasn't listening. When I went to the bedroom, I saw Papa lying there and tried to wake him. That's when I knew he had died. Mama I am sorry I wasn't with him."

Annie ran into her mother's arms and Sarah felt a surge of protectiveness of her strong willed, independent daughter. She looked around and saw Alec crying in the corner of the kitchen. She picked him up and felt the shudder of his sobs. She kissed him and told him he was a good boy but he was to stay with Annie. She put him down and went towards the bedroom. She knew that there were things she had to do.

Her cool demeanour disintegrated as soon as she saw Alexander. In that moment the dream she had been living came to an end and she let out a howl which frightened the children in the kitchen. She had loved Alexander so much.

William appeared beside her but looking in the direction of his father. It was his first death and he didn't like the feeling.

People often said they couldn't believe it when someone died, but Sarah could. She knew it was real.

For the next few days, the process of notifying officials, organising a burial, and telling the children what was happening occupied her. She was in a dream. People commented on how brave she was but she knew it wasn't bravery. She was numb. She couldn't feel a thing. She felt the sense of desolation she had felt as a girl. The last ten years seemed to have disappeared. Did they really happen?

Her father helped with burial costs but did not attend the funeral. She was disappointed as the children did not really know their grandfather and she thought it was time they did. She would need him in the next few years. There was no-one else.

What now? They had nine months of the lease to run but after that?

Sarah felt alone

She knew, for the sake of the children, she had to keep going.

Chapter Fifteen

Sarah received a condolence letter from her father:

My dear Sarah
Please accept my condolences on the death of Alexander. I was shocked and did not realise he had been so ill. He was a very good man. I am coming to Melbourne in February to stay with Frederik Taubner. I want to share with him the wine with him which won me a prize at the Echuca show this year. I will come to visit you on the 17th if that is convenient for you.
Your loving father,
Thomas.

When he came, the children were at school. Mr Taubner had generously sent Sarah two of his own workers to help with the Market Garden following Alexander's death which freed up William, Annie and also Alec to go back to school. Sarah and baby Agnes were in the garden talking to the new workers who were harvesting the produce.

After apologising for not coming to the burial, Thomas raised the question of Sarah's future. "What are you going to do, Sarah?"

"We can't stay here, Father. The work is too much for me and we can't afford to pay workers. I just don't know."

"Come to Rochester. I could help with the children and their schooling. Also, I have a few properties in Rochester. I could rent one of those to you at a cheap rate, just enough to cover maintenance and rates."

Sarah looked at her father. So much, she wanted to go to him and hug him but she knew that would not happen. "That would be very much appreciated, Father. But it will be some months before everything is finalised." Sarah didn't know whether to add the following but she was at her wit's end.

"I am also concerned about William. He is missing Alexander terribly and he has been very cranky with me. He is also not strong enough to be working in the garden the way he has been. Sometimes he can hardly breathe. I don't like keeping him home from school as he is such a bright boy but sometimes he is not well enough to go."

Both were silent for some time. Sarah had thought long and hard about William and knew he needed attention, both for his health and for his attitude. She hoped her father would be able to help. She looked at him and saw that he was weighing up what she had said. At last, he spoke, slowly as if he was measuring every word.

"Then William will come to live with me, until you have moved. He can finish his schooling in Bamawm and by that time he will almost be old enough to earn his own living." After a pause he added, " Marriott will relish the idea of his nephew living with us."

"It would only be for six months at the most, Father. I would be grateful. I will miss William but sometimes he looks at me almost as if he blames me for Alexander's death. I found him in the garden the other night, late, sitting in the dark, crying."

"I am staying with Frederik tonight," said Thomas, "I will come by tomorrow and collect William to take him home with me. Perhaps I can teach him to make wine!"

That night as she faced another lonely evening without the man she had thought would be by her side forever, she thought about William. Was she abandoning him just as her father had abandoned her? Did he think he was doing the right thing just as she thought moving to Bamawm was the best for William? Would William see it that way or would he resent the decision she had made for his benefit? Suddenly she was a three year old again screaming for her mother.

But then she thought of William and how country air and good food was what he needed most. It didn't matter how she felt. All that mattered was that her little boy would grow strong and healthy. And happy as well. She knew his father's death had affected him terribly and she also knew he needed a man to guide him on the path to manhood. Thomas and Marriott could do what she could not. She hoped that William would understand.

If this was the right decision, why then did she feel so desolate?

Death left behind an emptiness, Sarah knew that. It was a slow draining of your insides. Unless you could forget and put it behind you, there was no return. Unless you could say, I accept it. I didn't want it but I accept it, it was very difficult to move on with your own life. With Alexander, there were no regrets. She did all she could for him and loved him with her whole being. It still racked her insides but that was different from what William was feeling. William didn't think his father would ever die and he hadn't accepted it.

Her father returned the next day about midday. He appeared at the door of the cottage and smiled conspiratorially at Sarah. She had kept the children home from school so they could say goodbye to William but she hadn't told them what was happening, not even William. She hadn't trusted herself to have the right words. She knew this was a mistake.

The younger children didn't know who he was and just stared at him. William remembered him from when he was a child, vaguely. Sarah saw the puzzled look on his face and when she told him what was happening, he looked at her as if she had betrayed him. Why, she asked herself, hadn't she sat with him and prepared him? At that moment she hated herself. All her life she had held it against her father that he had allowed others to control her life and now she was doing the same to her son.

She went with him to the sleepout to help him pack. He put everything he owned in the suitcase his grandfather had brought. He turned to go, then suddenly doubled back and grabbed his bible, the one his father had given him for his birthday. This was all he had of his father and he wasn't leaving it behind. She watched him reach the back door and open it angrily. Annie and Alec were screaming. She wanted to grab him and tell her father it was all a mistake but she knew this was right. Her heart was thumping.

"We will be in Rochester before the year is out, William, and we will all be together again," but her words faded into the air, following her father and son walking down the bricked path that Alexander had built with William.

After they had left and Sarah composed herself enough to explain to the sulking Annie and crying Alec what was happening, she took herself off to a corner of the allotment where she knew the workers would not be. It was then, for the first time since Alexander died, that she cried. It welled up from the pit of her stomach and broke through in sobs, sobs that she could not control. The workers heard her, looked over, knew what was happening and went back to work. Just another woman mourning the loss of her husband.

The sobs continued for some time and left her exhausted and empty. She lay down on the nearby bench which Alexander and William had built for them to have their smoko, and closed her eyes. Did she do the right thing by letting William go? Was it history repeating itself, like her father let her go? No it was not the same. It was only for a little while and he was with family, his grandfather.

Sarah was not religious like her father, or even like Alexander. Her religion was in the here and now of the people in her life, but as she lay on the bench, muscles aching as if she had worked a full day in the fields, she prayed for the first time in years.

"O God, please keep William close to you and bring him peace. And keep Annie, Alec and Agnes safe from illness or accidents. And please, God, help me to go on because I don't feel much like it at the moment."

When she came back into the house, Annie had made her a cup of tea and Alec had got a cushion to put behind her on the chair. Agnes climbed up onto her knee and snuggled into her bosom.

She embraced them all and knew that God had answered her prayers.

Chapter Sixteen

Rochester
1885

Sarah had never been to Rochester, the town nearest Bamawm, where her grandfather farmed. In fact she had never lived in the country since she left England at the age of eighteen months. The city of Melbourne was the only place she had ever known. The children were excited about the train journey and not too unhappy about leaving Hartwell. Since their father died, everything had been different and they were pleased to be going to live in the country.

"Will William be there to meet us?" said Annie as she struggled to carry a suitcase with all her worldly possessions." She had missed William since he went to live with his grandfather.

"I hope so," Sarah replied as she lifted Agnes onto the train. She tried not to think about what they were leaving. She tried to centre her thoughts on the children and their needs. But her heart was heavy and she wondered if she would ever feel any differently. She was a different person from the girl who had gone to live at *Shrublands*. She had known love and lost it.

It was the first time the children had experienced a country train and they loved it. They eyed all the other passengers and Sarah had to chastise Alec who was making faces at the ladies in the next seats, who told her not to worry as they had grandchildren themselves and understood the antics of small boys.

As they drew to a stop at Kyneton, she told Annie and Alec the story of Mrs Chisholm who was the reason she had come to Australia from England. The Chisholm family had settled in Kyneton, running a general store, selling provisions to the diggers journeying to the goldfields. "Your grandfather thought she was wonderful," she told Annie who was listening to the story while Alec was climbing under the seat.

The visit to the railway café in Kyneton was a treat for the children. They couldn't believe they could order a drink and a cake and the waitress would just bring it to them. Sarah had decided she would treat them to the rather expensive service instead of packing a lunch as the children had not had much to be happy about since their father died.

"Look Mama," said Annie, "we're sitting here with all the rich people."

Sarah didn't eat but had a hot cup of tea and thought of the times when she and the girls from *Shrublands* had ordered afternoon tea in the city in the hope of meeting a beau. Those days were gone. Now she was the mother of four children whose father had died. Life would not be easy.

Back on the train, Alec was getting restless so Sarah challenged him to watch for the stations. Annie joined in as she needed something to occupy her as well. They set up a chant. "Kyneton, Malmsbury, Elphinstone, Chewton, Castlemaine, Harcourt, Kangaroo Flat, Bendigo, Eaglehawk, Elmore, Goornong and finally, Rochester."

They repeated it so many times, Sarah thought she would scream. Finally the rain slowed as they neared Rochester.

"Rochester!" said Annie. "We're here, Alec!"

Sarah took a deep breath and prayed to God that all would be well. She carried Agnes and told Annie to look after Alec. Then they pulled down their cases and struggled off the train hoping that it wouldn't start to move off before they had completed the process.

The first thing she noticed was the space and the smell, not an unpleasant smell but strong nether-the-less. She saw a pretty town with palatial looking hotels dotted along the wide, main street opposite the station. She had been told the population was seven hundred and wondered if everyone knew everyone else, and if so, would they soon know her. Annie and Alec looked for William to meet them but instead, there was their grandfather.

"William wanted to come but there was no room for him," said Thomas in a matter of fact way which forbade any complaints. He did not hug them or even acknowledge the children, instead addressing everything to Sarah. The plan was to take them to his farm in Bamawm 13 miles away. Sarah knew he wanted to show the children where he lived, his farm and his vineyard. She knew he was proud of what he had achieved and couldn't blame him for wanting to show it off.

She would have preferred to go straight to their house in Mackay street, a hop skip and a jump from the station in Rochester and get settled in after the long journey. She wasn't really up for a guided tour, either physically or emotionally. The children, however, were in good spirits and she tried to look happy.

As the cart rolled along the road, Sarah was amazed at the flatness of the land. The paddocks, as the locals called them, seemed to stretch forever, broken up by a clump of trees that had escaped the clearing process, or a house. She wasn't sure she could survive in such an uninteresting place. Her father had spoken glowingly of it but to her it was more like a desert.

She saw William as soon as they turned in the drive. He looked taller and his skinny frame had filled out, giving the impression of health and strength. Annie and Alec jumped from the cart before it even stopped and ran to him, yelling with delight. Their big brother! She knew he was pleased to see them but he was holding himself back, trying not to show emotion in the presence of his grandfather.

Sarah was surprised that her hug was reciprocated by him. He seemed genuinely pleased to see her. Maybe the move to Bamawm had been a good one after all and her worries were ill founded. She heard him telling Annie about school.

"It's different from Camberwell, more fun. The headmaster is Mr Collins and I think he likes me because we both share the same name, William."

He told them how he walked a mile along a flat, dusty road to school which had some of the biggest trees he had ever seen and Mr Collins allowed the boys to climb them. If the girls tried to climb, however, he would come down on them like a ton of bricks, giving them a lecture about being 'ladylike.'

"Pooh," said Annie. "Why can't girls climb trees?"

"I think Grandfather agrees with Mr Collins," said William dismissively.

"Grandfather scares me," said Annie softly, looking around as if she expected to be overheard. "Is he really that bad?"

"He's not like Father," said William sadly as he watched Thomas Bradshaw approaching them.

Sarah smiled to herself. Did William feel about her father the way she had felt all her life, anxious to please but a little afraid? She knew he would want to come and live with his brother and sisters again but her father had convinced her of the wisdom of leaving him in Bamawm, where it had so obviously agreed with him.

"William," said Annie. "Are you coming to live with us in Rochester?"

"No, Grandfather spoke to me yesterday and told me I was staying here until I finish school. And, Annie, Grandfather is a man you don't argue with. I don't think even Mother would disagree with him." He smiled warmly at Sarah, " I don't mind it here and Marriott is kind," he added quickly as he saw Annie's glum face, " but I will come into town to see you every chance I get."

Sarah had wanted William to come to live with them but she could see that the farm life was good for his health. He seemed more grown up, more interested in what was happening around him. Could she insist that he return to the family? Was that fair? It was going to be hard for all of them as they had very little money and the food would not be as plentiful as what her father could provide. One less mouth to feed would certainly help.

She would need to find work, even if it were only taking in laundry. The children would need school books, clothes and enough food to grow. She was determined that they would want for nothing. Her father would help out but she did not want to be dependent on him.

After a wonderful meal prepared by Thomas' housekeeper, Marriott and William showed them around the farm. "We grow wheat, vegetables and grapevines," said Marriott." We have sheep and a few milk cows, chooks and of course lots of dogs." As he said this as a kelpie, Dusty, joined them. Annie stopped and patted Dusty who licked her all over.

"He's only a pup," explained Marriott. "Hasn't been trained for work yet."

Sarah watched her daughter fall in love with Dusty. Annie didn't want to see any more farm things, she just wanted to play with Dusty. He didn't mind the attention and played up to her. "I wish we could take him home."

"What about Ginger?" said Alec. "He wouldn't want a dog around the place."

"Ginger would love a playmate, Alec, especially as he is in a new town."

"Maybe if you asked Father, he might let you have him," said Marriott watching his niece with affection.

"Oh Uncle Marriott, could you ask him, please? I would love that."

William felt a pang of jealousy. He had secretly hoped that Dusty would be his dog. He had learnt, however, in the last year that he wasn't someone who had any power at all, over where he lived, who he lived with and it stood to reason that he would not have the power of choice over whether he could own a dog or not.

They finished their tour and turned towards the homestead, Sarah happy to see all her children together again. They left their footprints in the dust of the Bamawm Plains, Dusty playfully nipping at Annie's heels. The mist was closing in around the farm as Marriott brought the cart to take them to Rochester. As Sarah hugged William goodbye, she told him how happy she was that he was closer. Did she see a tear in his eye?

Marriott drove faster than his father and the journey to Rochester seemed to take half the time it had from the train. When they arrived at the house, their new home, Sarah thanked him for his trouble as he helped with the luggage. She noticed an affectionate smile on his Irish face. He must take after his mother, she thought.

"It's great that I have a sister in town. Now I'm not an only child. Sometime we must get together and talk about our father! He's a bit of a handful you know!"

Sarah didn't quite know how to react to such an intimacy. It was true that Marriott was her half-brother but she hardly knew him. "Yes," she said and could think of nothing to add.

The house in Mackay street was bigger than their cottage in Hartwell, a solid timber design that Thomas had built himself when he first came to the area. Sarah helped the children, and Dusty, get settled before she dragged herself to bed. There was much to do in the house, but that could wait until tomorrow.

"Oh Alexander," she said as she sat on the bed and tried to compose her conflicting emotions. "I wish you were here."

Chapter Seventeen

Sarah settled into a routine and slowly the sharpness of grief gave way to an evenness of life. She took in laundry which gave her enough money to pay the rates, settled Annie and Alec into school and tended to Agnes who was entering the toddler stage and had to be watched all the time.

While Sarah was working in the laundry at the back of the house, Agnes would play in the backyard with Dusty, talking to him and pretending he was a horse. Sarah wondered if she should teach her the bushrangers/troopers game she used to play all those years ago in North Melbourne. It was funny, she thought, how her mind returned to the happiness of her childhood in North Melbourne so long ago. Agnes was as old as she was when her mother died and the irony did not escape her.

When customers had collected their laundry, she and Agnes would sometimes walk down to the Campaspe River two blocks away and sit and watch the birds. After rain, the river would be brown and puddles would appear on the flats. Agnes loved to jump in the puddles and see what sort of a splash she made. Sarah never chided her for getting dirty, she just loved seeing her happy. Oh, thought Sarah. If only I could be happy again.

Alexander was never far from her thoughts. She wished he could be here watching the children grow. She could imagine them all on their own farm because despite her initial dislike of rural life, she found the life agreed with her and she knew Alexander would have loved it. She had come to know townspeople who had been kind to her when they found that her husband had died and also that she was

Thomas Bradshaw's daughter. It seemed he had quite a reputation in the area as an innovative farmer. A 'gentleman' they called him. Sarah had to admit that he always dressed nicely and carried himself as a man of importance but she had never thought of her father as 'a gentleman!'

Living here, she thought, was different from the city. She had never known a bushfire before, nor floods nor drought. In Hartwell, the creek was always running and the Yarra River was nearby. Here in northern Victoria, it rarely rained, but, when it did, the Campaspe River flooded. The sandbags would come out and the whole town, children included, would work into the night sandbagging the shops and the houses. Schools were closed and the children would play in the flooded waters, some even making their own boats. After the water had receded, the dank mustiness permeated everything and the smell was dreadful.

Sarah could put up with the floods but she hated the summer. Every day was hot and you didn't get the relief of a cool change like in Melbourne. The scorched earth cried out for water, cracking in response. She had grass in the back yard and in an effort to keep it green, she would save the water from cooking and laundry and tip it on the grass. All in vain. Dusty would sit, tongue hanging out, on the brittle growth they called grass, pleading for a drink. The same grass, however, would burst forth in lush greenery when the rains finally came.

She loved the peace and quiet of Rochester. When darkness came, she would walk outside, sometimes down to the river, and watch the stars. She would listen. Silence. It was beautiful. She was never lonely in the silence. She felt whole, as if she were in tune with the universe. And she liked the people.

One of these was Mavis, the rough talking woman next door whom Sarah thought must have been at least eighty years old.

"Come and join me for a cuppa, luv. You're living next door and I don't even know your name."

Her manner relaxed Sarah and she agreed with a smile. She was never the first one to make a move so was pleased with the forthrightness of Mavis. She reminded her of an older Kitty. When Sarah told her she was born in England, near Leamington, Mavis grew very excited.

"Well whaddya know! I was born just down the road, in Coventry. I came to this country when I was not much more than a girl, courtesy of the Guv'ment of England!" And with that she screeched laughing.

Sarah didn't know what that meant and didn't ask. She found herself telling Mavis about her mother and Alexander and ended by saying: "I suppose you know my father, Thomas Bradshaw?"

"Nope, never heard of 'im, but then luv, I don't get out much now."

Even though they had very little in common, Sarah felt accepted and that night, when she went to bed, she felt better than she had for a long time.

Time passed. Alexander was still in her thoughts but now she celebrated the fact that she had known and loved him rather than the crippling pain of loss. Agnes turned five and started school. Sarah hated the laundry work so was pleased to accept a position as housekeeper to a local doctor with a huge house. The house had been built by a Scotsman who had struck it rich on the goldfields but was killed soon after in a fight over a woman. It had been empty for some time and was the talk of the locals who said it may have been haunted by the Scotsman's ghost.

The doctor and his wife had left wealthy families in Britain to come to Australia and whereas he loved Australia, she hated it. 'This dreadful backward country,' she called it. Most of her days were spent lying in bed or sitting in the garden sewing. Their two daughters, aged 8 and 10, had a nanny, in the English fashion, and they hardly ever saw their mother. Sarah was interviewed by the doctor's wife in a way that made it quite clear that she was a servant, a lower category of human species. After outlining Sarah's responsibilities, the doctor's wife withdrew into her own little world.

"What's she like?" said Annie. "The girls at school think she's a snob.!" Sarah didn't mince words with her eldest daughter who had become more a friend than a daughter. "I think she is lazy and rude. Fancy having such a beautiful house and not even bothering to look after it yourself. But I don't think I'll have much to do with her and I'm grateful to have the work."

She had never experienced the stringent English Class system in her life at *Shrublands* as Mr Taubner had treated his staff with dignity. At *Shrublands,* everyone knew their place but they were proud within that place. No-one looked down on anyone else.

The doctor was different altogether. In contrast to his wife, he treated Sarah well and occasionally would stop and have a chat, seemingly interested in her as a person. She thought him good looking, not like the foreign visitor, but with something of the same charm about him. He had hazel eyes and brown, thick hair but it was his smile that Sarah loved. It was the smile of a cheeky little boy caught stealing an apple.

She noticed the way he looked at her and wondered if she were attractive. Alexander had often told her that she was beautiful but she thought he saw her inner beauty rather than her appearance. The foreign visitor had called her beautiful but she dismissed him as a liar. No-one else had ever complimented her. In fact, she believed herself to be quite plain. The Littles had discouraged mirrors in the house and their religion saw vanity as one of the worst sins.

Since her encounter with the foreign visitor she had been too afraid to flirt with anyone and had not really made an effort with her appearance. Now that she was almost thirty eight, she thought any decent looks she had would be fading. But every time she met casually with the doctor, she became more and more self-conscious.

At home, she stood in front of the mirror, turned sideways, and then the other way. She wasn't fat and the curves were still there, hidden, however, behind the shapeless dress she wore. Her hair was drab but she could do something about that and apart from the sadness in her eyes, she quite liked what she saw. Not beautiful, but pleasing enough.

She cracked an egg and used the yolk to wash her hair, giving it a sheen. She altered the seams in her dress so that it showed her figure. She applied cream on her soft, English complexion to hide the wrinkles and she smiled. The smile was the key, she thought. She had to learn how to smile again.

Why was she doing all this, she thought guiltily, when the doctor was a married man? Just to see if he notices me, she said to herself, to know if I can still be seen.

It certainly worked.

The doctor kept turning up in the very place where she was working. "We seem to be running into each other all the time lately," he said as if it were a coincidence. "Here, I'll help you move that chair. It's heavy."

As they were placing the chair on the newly swept floor, their hands touched and she felt the stirrings of desire.

They talked easily, person to person, about nothing in particular and when he walked away, she knew her cheeks were flushed.

After that meeting, she seemed to be constantly 'running into him.' He always stopped and chatted, asking about her children, commenting on the weather, talking about England. Sarah knew he looked forward to these chats as much as she did and this alarmed her. She saw him almost every day.

Sarah was no longer the young maiden who had fallen for the foreign visitor years before. She recognised exactly what was happening. A spark had been rekindled. She looked forward to seeing the doctor and occasionally, when they touched, she knew that it would be not too much longer before making a choice would not be possible.

He was married. What was she doing? She wanted to be loved again, but he was married. How strong was she? Since Alexander's death she had been lonely. Had she then, made her choice?

She relied on the fact that the doctor knew where the limit was.

At home, one evening, as she and Annie were cooking dinner, Annie remarked on the change in her mother.

"You look younger, Mama and so happy." Nearing 13 and almost ready to go into service herself, Annie was an astute young girl. Sarah was anxious to find her a place where she would find happiness and advancement. She couldn't bear for Annie to work for someone like the doctor's wife, nor did she want her to stay home and become a servant to her younger siblings. William had found a new life and so too should Annie.

Once a month, the doctor's wife would go away to Melbourne to stay with her cousin and indulge herself with parties, theatre shows and conversations about England. "Home," was what she called it. Her husband had agreed that she needed this time and for that purpose had bought a house in Eastern Hill big enough for his wife and the children to stay. She always took the girls with her as she liked to show them off to friends and family, as well as shop for them in the latest fashion houses of Melbourne. The nanny went as well making it possible for the doctor's wife to attend her social functions at any time of day or night. It was on one of these regular 'holidays' that it all happened.

"Well Sarah, you will have peace and quiet for the next two weeks. The family are all away."

"Do you miss them?" She called him by his first name now but had to be careful who was listening.

"I do," he said sheepishly, "but part of me sees it as a holiday for me as well. My wife, as you've probably gathered, is not the easiest person to live with. I don't think being a doctor's wife in a little country town like Rochester was quite what she had in mind when we left England."

"I left England when I was 18 months old," said Sarah, "so I don't hanker for it at all, although one day I would like to see all the things my mother used to talk about, like the Spa at Leamington."

"That's all gone now," said the doctor, settling in for a good chat. "They have filled in the pool and are in the process of turning it into a community space. We were there last year and I was a bit sad to see what they have done."

"I can't say I really remember it, just that it was a special place for my mother."

"Is your mother still alive?" said the doctor realising that he knew very little about this lovely creature who had wandered into his life.

"She died having my little sister, when I was three. It was a long time ago."

Before they both knew it, an hour had passed and the doctor had to open his surgery. He didn't open till 10am as he worked quite late in the evening. These hours suited the people of the town as they often came after work to see about their ailments. As he was leaving Sarah, however, he wheeled around, grabbed her hands and said:

"Sarah, I shouldn't say this but I really like you. See you tomorrow?" and he stumbled downstairs to where his surgery was located.

And so it was, every morning from 9 till 10, Sarah and the doctor would spend an hour together. At first, they would just talk. Sarah told him about her life and he of his. He and his wife had both inherited money from family in England, enough to buy property, travel to

England every two years, hire staff for their homes and have the finest clothes. Their marriage was more or less arranged by their families who were old friends and right from the start they were misaligned. Coming to Australia and facing the 'frontier' they thought the experience would form a bond between them but his wife's idea of being in the 'frontier' was doing without a lady's maid! He, on the other hand, thought Australia a wonderful new country with potential for anyone who had ideas and was prepared to work hard.

"I know your father Sarah. He and I have often cracked a bottle of his wine together. He is quite the businessman, is Thomas Bradshaw."

He was a thoroughly decent man, Sarah knew that. His patients spoke of him in glowing terms and she had never heard a word against him. She was convinced that their friendship was genuine and he was not just playing with her in order to seduce her but she knew, also, that talking was not enough for either of them. He seemed to create opportunities to brush against her or take her hand and she didn't discourage it.

She felt like she did when Alexander came into her life, thinking of nothing else but him, how he looked, the stirrings inside her and how much she wanted to get closer. She took more and more trouble with her appearance, made new clothes that flattered her figure and thought about what she would say, becoming interested in things he was interested in. She walked around the house dreaming of him touching her, ignoring the children who thought she was just tired.

"Mama. Are you listening?" said Annie when her mother didn't reply to her question.

Did she feel guilty? Did she think of her thoughts as sinful? Did she think about his wife at all?

Of course she felt guilty. She knew that she should put a stop to it and she also knew that if he did, the doctor would respect her decision. She couldn't count the number of times she resolved on this course of action.

But then she would see him coming and…

The physical contact started with a five to ten kiss one morning as they were taking leave of each other. The kiss was the line and they had crossed it. It was so easy.

Both of them entered into the affair with enthusiasm and, at the time, no regrets.

It was wonderful. Sarah was once again in that euphoric state she had experienced with Alexander. It was good. It had to be right.

"Sarah, I am not one bit sorry this has happened but we will have to be very careful. It's a small town and we both have too much to lose."

With the doctor's wife home, being together was difficult. Sometimes Sarah would go down to the surgery when there were no patients, other times he would make a 'house call' to one of her 'sick' children.

I can't give this up, thought Sarah. I can't.

Chapter Eighteen

She knew the signs. How could she not, after four children? What could she tell people? She was too honourable to tell the truth because she truly loved the doctor and would not want to taint his reputation. Her reputation did not matter, except for the children and maybe her father. She remembered how reluctant he was to offer her accommodation when she was pregnant with William. What would he think now?

So she remained silent, even as the situation became obvious. People talked. Of course they did. Country towns in Australia were like towns and villages everywhere. People loved to be scandalised. She told the children and her father that she was happy about her confinement, that she wanted this child and that they were to ask no more questions.

"What the hell are you playing at woman? Who is the father?" Thomas' anger disarmed her.

"I want this child, Father, and that is all I will say." She wanted to say so much more but didn't trust herself in the face of his anger. He threatened to cut off money for the children's schooling and to increase the token rent for their house. He said horrible things to her and even cast doubt on her story about the foreign visitor which he said he had been 'fool enough' to believe.

Sarah was hurt, and angry. How dare he suggest that she had been a willing partner to the foreign visitor's evil. This baby would be born out of love.

Sarah had a visit from William not long after she told her father. "Is it true, Mother? What Annie told me?" He was angry. What should she tell William? He was now almost 16, working as a farmhand on a neighbour's farm, a Mrs Gilmer. He was happy there and had told the Gilmers about his mother and the death of his father. They were strong Catholics and good people and she was grateful to them for making William part of their family but she feared he didn't want them to know that his mother was having a child out of wedlock. He was ashamed of her. She could see it in his face.

This saddened her. More than anything she wanted William to think well of her. She tried to say what she had said to her father, that she wanted this child but halfway through explaining, William stormed out, slamming the door as he went.

The doctor arranged to give Sarah a sum of money 'for the child' and also because she would be finishing as his housekeeper. She offered to stay as long as possible but his wife insisted that she didn't want a women of loose morals anywhere near her children. It hadn't occurred to her that her husband might be the father. She just presumed it was one of the town 'tomcats' who preyed on single women. After all Sarah was only a servant!

When Amy was born, she was registered as Amy Hamilton and Sarah was relieved that she had her mother's colouring and features. She thought she would have been strong enough to withstand the town gossip but it had worn her down and apart from Mavis next door, who couldn't have cared less that there was no visible father, she no longer had any friends. Many people who had been kind to her in the past, withdrew their friendship. Her father was distant and had made it clear that he was very, very disappointed in his daughter.

She longed to see the doctor. She sent Agnes with a message to the surgery for the doctor to make a house call. The last thing she needed in her state of mind was to run into the doctor's wife who had been working as her husband's receptionist, to everyone's amazement, as she had never done a day's work in her life.

"She's a beautiful, healthy little girl Sarah," he said, as he cradled her in his arms, looking for any resemblance to his other children. "Are you all right for money? I can give you more."

Sarah looked at him. He had changed. Nobody, she thought, breaks the rules of society without it having an effect on them. "I can manage. So far my father has not gone through with his threat to increase the rent and I am taking in laundry again. Amy is a good baby and I am feeling well, although the children have been teased about me. I don't like that."

"It doesn't seem fair," he winced, "that you should carry all the burden." He stopped short of saying what Sarah wanted to hear, that he would leave his wife, but she knew there was no chance of that happening. She watched him with his daughter and longed for him, wishing it could be different.

Even in Australia, where class consciousness was not what it was in England, there were still rules. Men from wealthy old moneyed families did not leave their wives and marry woman from the working class. She was a woman, she had played with fire and she had been burnt. She was a woman of loose morals. He was a respectable man.

Occasionally she thought, what if I should tell people that he is the father? What then? Why shouldn't he be the subject of gossip as well? But she knew that she, Sarah Hamilton, would not betray him. She was too good a person. The doctor returned to his wife, his work and his children. She cared for the baby and thought of the doctor all the time.

She took it for granted that Annie would understand but she was wrong. Annie was as angry as William and told her that she had been teased around town about her mother and she didn't appreciate being the brunt of jokes.

"I can't wait to leave Rochester," said Annie bitterly. "I hate this place."

But it was William's attitude that Sarah found unbearable. He was her beautiful, oldest boy. People who met him were impressed. He walked with an upright posture, his permanent scowl actually adding to his dark good looks. 'He is so like his father,' she thought, 'definitely not a Bradshaw.' He had a reputation as being a young man of integrity, as honest as the day was long.

She knew he was ashamed of her and wouldn't be seen with her in public, only visiting when the two of them could be alone. He would bring fresh produce from the farm and give her some money, spending most of the time with his brother and sisters, especially little Amy whom he had a real affection for.

"There's some vegetables for you, Mother, and Grandfather has sent a bottle of wine." He no longer called her 'mama' she noticed, but the more formal 'mother' as if to put some distance between them.

"Do you like his wine, William?" She struggled to make conversation.

"I don't drink Mother. You know that."

The two of them, mother and son, fell into a conversation of strained politeness and small talk. William did not say what he really thought, and Sarah, who so desperately wanted to reach out to her son and soothe his confusion, played the passive mother feigning interest in every word her son spoke.

"Mrs Gilmer's got new fences."

"They would have cost a lot," said Sarah, "Did you and Patrick Gilmer put them up?"

"It was hard work but we managed."

Small talk. Polite small talk.

Whatever Sarah did, she could not run the risk of losing her son as she felt they were already walking on eggshells.

She knew that by allowing him to live with his grandfather when he was only a boy, she ran the risk of losing him, but she had done it for his sake, for his health. If she had been selfish, William could have followed his father to the grave. Better that he be a stranger to her. And, even though she had never met Mrs Gilmer or her son Patrick, she resented them for the influence they had over William hoping he didn't become a Catholic as well, although she really didn't know what difference it would make!

William was stubborn and Sarah just had to hope that time would restore the once strong bond between them. When she looked at William, she thought about Alexander, a man who may not have been his true father but in every way was the finest father a boy could have known. She didn't want him to leave.

"William, thank you for what you have brought. Tell Mrs Gilmer and your grandfather that I appreciate it very much. The children and I will have a feast for the next few days."

William returned to the farm where he worked long hours. Sarah went back to a world where she washed other people's laundry and cared for the children at home. Her only joy came from watching her baby grow and her conversations with the doctor. She would visit the surgery or he would attend one of the children with an illness, real or contrived, and their love for each other continued to grow.

Chapter Nineteen

"My wife is taking the children to England for the winter," he told her one day. " I cannot leave the surgery as, at the moment, I am the only doctor in town, so she is taking the girls and going without me." The only other doctor in town, Dr Stokes, had had a heart attack at the district races some weeks before. "Maybe we can see more of each other?"

He was like a drug for her. She was lonely and he loved her. She knew what the consequences of 'seeing more of each other' might be but when she weighed up having another child against the loneliness of the life of a widow, she knew which one she would choose.

The doctor's wife sailed to England with the two girls and the nanny. Sarah spent all the time she could spare with the doctor and as a consequence, when Amy was weaned and 15 months old, Sarah found herself pregnant again. She wasn't devastated. In fact she was almost pleased.

"Ya there luv?" called Mavis over the fence which had many more palings missing since Sarah moved in. "I've got some pickles for ya. Got to do something with all those tomatoes that grow wild in the backyard."

Mavis looked at Sarah through the hole in the fence, her eyes travelling to Sarah's belly.

"What! Another one? Gawd."

Sarah couldn't be offended by the honesty of this woman who quickly invited her in for a 'cuppa'. She didn't want to know who the father was. She was simply concerned for her neighbour.

"Now don't you be lifting those heavy sheets, luv. Get that boy of yours to help you."

She was referring to Alec who, at twelve, was having to shoulder the work of a man around the house. That he hadn't gotten around to fixing the palings in the fence was hardly surprising.

The doctor was not quite so pleased about Sarah's pregnancy.

"This is not good, Sarah. People will be joining the dots. They know I do too many 'house calls' to Mackay Street."

Sarah was hurt at his tone. She thought he loved her. She thought he respected her. Was he just using her? She knew he wouldn't leave his wife and she had told him she understood that. But she could not believe that he thought the whole thing was her fault. She grabbed a dishcloth and flung it in his direction.

"Think nothing of it. People have such a low opinion of me that they will never think of you as the father. You are far too respectable."

Her touch of sarcasm jolted the doctor and he apologised, at the same time realising that this was getting far too serious. He knew he had to put a stop to it.

Francis James was born, giving William and Alec a little brother. He was the sweetest child one could possibly imagine but Sarah was worried when she saw in him the doctor's puppy dog eyes. She would have to make sure that his hair was cut differently so that people would not look at him and know.

To Sarah's surprise and delight, William visited often to play with his little brother. For an eighteen year old lad, he was surprisingly affectionate and gentle. It was as if the birth of this little boy, his half-brother, had triggered something in William, a softness. She thought he suspected that Amy and Francis were fathered by the same man and somehow, this made things better. She wondered what he would do or say if she told him the truth about his own parentage. Would he be less condemning of his mother? Or would it make things worse between them?

"Grandfather says he is glad it is a boy but he is not coming to visit."

"You are here, William. That's all I care about."

William gave his mother some money and kissed her on the cheek. "Goodbye Mother."

Mavis was in the garden, dressed as if she were going to a party, pulling up non-existent weeds, as Sarah closed the front gate behind William.

"Sarah, your children are so lucky to have such a wonderful mother. And you're doing it all alone, love, which ain't easy!" Such people were an antidote to the vitriol of others.

Francis and Amy were as close as two siblings could be. They didn't look to be sickly children but their constant visits to the doctor would suggest otherwise! Francis was the doctor's first son and he was besotted with him. Sarah would sometimes find him just staring at him, and had to remind him to be careful when other people were around that he didn't give himself away.

"Does your wife suspect?" said Sarah watching two year old Frank chasing Amy round the surgery and wondering how people would not know whose son he was.

"I don't think so," he said, "but she is pressuring me to go back to England. She says we have been here long enough and she wants the girls to finish their education at home."

"And you'll go?" There was panic in her voice. "Yes Sarah," he said sadly, "I will."

How could he? Just up and go back to England when he had two children here. Just up and leave her, the woman he said he loved. No, No, this couldn't happen. She was almost hyperventilating. "Sarah, are you all right?" She didn't answer. She couldn't. She clumsily gathered the children and left, leaving people in the waiting room wondering whether or not she had just been given bad news.

Outside she roughly tucked Francis into his pram and told Amy to hang onto the side. She was crying and hoped she would not see anyone she knew. The thought of not seeing the doctor again threw her into a spin. He was her world. She turned the corner into Mackay street and Amy began to cry. She had been walking far too fast for the little girl and she couldn't keep up.

Sarah stopped and scooped her into her arms.

"Mama's here, darling. We'll go home and have a nice drink of milk."

Amy stopped crying and cuddled into her mother oblivious of the fact that her father was moving to the other side of the world never to be seen again.

Once she had got Amy settled and she, herself, had calmed down, Sarah gave herself a good talking to. This was how it had to be. The doctor would return to England, to his world, no matter what she said or did, and she to hers. She did not want to part on bad terms. She loved him.

That night she sat in the kitchen waiting. She knew he would come. When Annie saw him at the front door, she wondered if her mother were sick. That would explain why she was acting so strangely. She made sure the younger children were in bed and hoped the doctor could fix whatever was wrong with her mother.

"I'm sorry, Sarah," he said when he sat down. "I must have sounded so callous."

Sarah kissed him. He was like a little boy who wanted absolution. She had had time to resign herself to the inevitable and had no more tears left.

"I don't want you to go," she said. "I know you have to but don't expect me to be happy about it."

He was relieved. He didn't want to part on bad terms, either, although he knew that for him, there were no real consequences, unless she revealed their secret.

"Will you ever tell the children about me?"

"I don't know. But I will think of you every time I look at them, especially Francis who is the image of you." She took his hand and put it on her cheek. " And I am glad we met even though I hate you for leaving." He wasn't sure of her tone but when he looked up, she was not angry, just sad, very sad.

Because the children were in the next room and because anything else would have been inappropriate, they hugged. He told her that she was the best thing that had happened to him in Australia and she knew it didn't matter if she believed him or not.

She did not see him again and as he walked out she was hit with the realisation that it was different for him. People talked about the sudden exit and gossip spread about how he had had an affair with his former receptionist, or how the wife was very ill, or that they had been summoned home by ailing parents. Another doctor came and he was soon forgotten although every now and then people would say what a lovely doctor he was.

And so, she was now, once again, Sarah Hamilton, the widow of Alexander Hamilton with six children!

Chapter Twenty

After the doctor left, Sarah spiralled into a deep melancholy. She no longer took pride in her appearance and the children were looking unkempt. The doctor had brought light into her life after Alexander's death and now the light had been extinguished. Something had shrivelled inside her when he sailed to England with his family. The loneliness that had haunted her for so much of her life resurfaced.

The money from the laundry did not pay well and even though Alec was paying board and William gave her money when he could, she never had enough. She couldn't ask her father for more as the memory of their last encounter was fresh in her mind.

"Sarah, this is the last straw. Another child out of wedlock. You won't tell me who the father or fathers are, if indeed there is more than one, so all I can say is that you can ask him, or them, to support you. I refuse to pay money to support the children of a man who is not your husband."

And with that, she was cast off.

The years that followed felt like she was in a tunnel with fog at each end, a tunnel she could never leave. Amy and Francis were perfect babies and Alec and Agnes still loved her as their mother. This is what kept her going when she felt like throwing herself into the Campaspe. She drew on all her strength to be a mother to them and love them.

Annie had left, gone to Melbourne to look for work and she didn't expect she would return. They had not parted on good terms.

These were bad years for her as she neared forty five. After a great deal of effort, she managed to procure a cleaning job for the local water board director, and when she saw a pound note lying on the floor, she pocketed it. 'He wouldn't miss it,' she thought, 'and I really need it'. But she was wrong. He did miss it and what's more he knew who took it. It was a trap. He took her to court.

Oh the shame of it all. She knew the townsfolk judged her badly but nothing compared with standing in front of a magistrate, with reporters writing in their note pads her every word. She was found guilty.

Sarah Hamilton now had a criminal record. As she stood before the judge who pronounced her guilty and committed her to pay twelve shillings court costs as well as repaying the one pound note, she felt hollow. She had completely lost all respect in the community as well as her own self-respect.

Her father and William had different reactions to Sarah's conviction.

Thomas paid the fine. It was that or see his daughter in jail. But he made it known that short of disowning her, he didn't want anything more to do with her.

William visited his mother a few days after the court case.

"William, I am so sorry. I don't know why I did it. I have never stolen anything in my life before but it has just been so hard."

She tried hard to hold the tears back as she did not want to break down in front this impressive young man, her son. What he said next surprised her greatly. "Grandfather was partly responsible. He should never have insisted on the market rent for this house as a punishment. The money Alec and I gave you just wasn't enough for you to live on. I understand that." She went to hug him but he took a step back and stood, ill at ease.

"I'm going to Melbourne, Mother. I leave tomorrow. Mrs Gilmer has found work for me at a bakery called Hennessey's in Armadale, not far from where we lived in Hartwell. They want someone who can learn accounting and will pay for me to go to night school. Mrs Gilmer has recommended me."

Sarah felt her heart pounding. William was leaving her again and this time it was his choice. She desperately wanted him to stay but knew she could not be so selfish. She grabbed hold of the arm of the chair and eased herself into it.

"I'm so proud of you William and your father would be also." At the mention of Alexander, Sarah could see a tear forming in William's eye. There wasn't much more she could say without herself dissolving into tears. William kissed her on the cheek and said "Goodbye, Mother, I'll write when I get settled."

He turned and walked out.

Chapter Twenty-one

The Rochester streets were being decorated for Christmas as Sarah turned 44. She decided she would treat Frank and Amy to a cake. With one child on each hand, balancing a basket, she walked along Moore Street to the baker. Some people nodded to her in acknowledgement and smiled at Frank who was one of those adorable toddlers who evokes a smile from even the grumpiest of people. Amy ran on ahead, anxious to choose which cake she would have.

Since Sarah's court appearance, strangely enough, people had been more sympathetic towards her. The Depression of the nineties was fading but for a while it had been severe and many townsfolk had found themselves worrying about where their next meal would come from.

"The children are adorable, Mrs Hamilton, and so well behaved." This from a woman who had been a source of malicious gossip in the past. Perhaps time makes for forgiveness.

The doctor had been gone from the town for three years. She had heard nothing from him, no letter, no money, nothing. Was she bitter? A little. It would have been comforting to know that he hadn't forgotten her. Did she regret ever knowing him? She looked at her two children and knew that she could regret nothing.

Opening the heavy door of the baker's, Sarah and the children were greeted with the yeasty smell which makes one immediately hungry. Francis ran to the glass cabinet, eyeing a cream bun whilst Amy couldn't make up her mind and went from one to the other. The shop was crowded and Sarah fell into an easy conversation with the women there. She knew most of them and they talked about their children, a topic about which they shared so much.

"I see Agnes and Alec at the sports ground often, Sarah. They have grown so much. Alec is quite a young man now."

Sarah acknowledged their comments and asked after their own children, all the time wondering what they would say if they knew she was with child again!

She had suspected it for a while but had had it confirmed this morning on her visit to the new doctor in town who was cold and clinical and told her that she was too old to have any more children. He said it in such a way that he had listened to all the gossip about her and was issuing not just a medical opinion but a judgement as well.

Sarah dreaded her father finding out. She wouldn't tell him because they had hardly spoken since the court case but the gossip would reach his ears soon enough. What she dreaded most was telling her children. Would they understand? She had heard nothing from Annie since she went to Melbourne and very little from William. But it was Alec and Agnes whom she worried about most as they had become such a strong support to her and were with her every day. She couldn't bear for them to disown her like William and Annie had.

However harshly they would judge her it could never be as harshly as she had judged herself. She'd taken in a boarder, a traveller. It was good money and she found his company refreshing. He was like a gypsy, here today and gone tomorrow but his tales of the places he had visited filled the cold, lonely nights for her and when he invited her into his bed, she didn't refuse. She wondered whether there was something wrong with her that she needed someone's arms around her and would sacrifice so much to achieve it.

"And what's it to be for you young man?" The baker was speaking to Francis who hadn't moved away from the cream bun with jam and cream oozing out of its crevices. She paid for the cakes as well as a loaf of bread, said goodbye to the women still waiting and opened the door for the children to spill onto the footpath, begging their mother to allow them to sink their teeth into their cakes.

"Not till we get home and have lunch first," she said as Amy slipped her chocolate éclair obediently back into the paper bag.

When the trees had lost their leaves and the wood fires were filling the town with smoke, Nellie Hamilton was born. It was a difficult labour, the first Sarah had ever experienced and during it, she thought of her mother and wondered whether or not she would die. And did she care if she did?

She had a dream.

Her mother was beside her holding her hand but she was only a little girl. Her mother was quite beautiful and when the little girl looked into her eyes and pleaded with her to stay, her mother shook her head and smiled, disengaging her hand as she did so.

Was it real? Was her mother speaking to her? She thought most likely it was the result of what the doctors gave her to kill the pain. But what if she did die? How would that affect her children? Would Francis and Amy be given to strangers and wonder all their life who they were? Would this new baby survive or would it be left to be buried with her?

After registering Nellie's birth, with 'father unknown' entered into the column describing father's name, and settling a new member of the family into her daily routine, Sarah knew that this was a moment when she needed to make some difficult choices.

She took the baby, Nellie, to her favourite spot on the Campaspe. To get there, she passed St Joseph's Catholic church, built on the back of gold money and far too big for the parish it served. She guessed it was a statement. The church was the last building before the river scrub and she was always sure of complete privacy. No-one ever came here.

She loved it at this time of year. It was cold but the worst of winter was over and the green of the river bank was refreshing for the eyes. The dead trees which decorated the billabong spoke to her of desolation and loss but they also provided the bird life with a home. Everything has a purpose, she thought.

Meandering around the billabong she came to the actual river. After the recent rains, it was flowing quite swiftly and this is where she loved to sit. She took off her cape and lay it on the grass where she placed Nellie, such a tiny person, she thought, and so defenceless.

Sarah knew that the new respect she had gained from the community would be tested after this birth. That didn't worry her as she knew how fickle people were, although it saddened her. She liked it when people thought well of her.

She was struggling to find enough money for the rent and to feed the children. Six year old Amy and four year old Frank were active children who were always hungry. Agnes was thirteen and whereas she could have gone into service, Sarah needed her at home. She was feeling the loss of her youth and energy and Agnes was the rudder that kept the ship sailing. Both Alec and Agnes had been wonderful supports to her and her concern that they would reject her had been unfounded.

Alec was a good boy and helped out whenever he could but when it came to practical things, he wasn't much help. Without his board money, however, Sarah would be destitute. The laundry work was physically exhausting. Getting up early in the morning to light the copper and the heavy lifting of the sheets into the tub of blue water and weaving them through the ringer was taking its toll on Sarah. She wished she could earn her money some other way but with little Nellie still at the breast, it was an impossibility.

Sarah stared at the flowing current and imagined jumping into the water with Nellie. The river would take them quickly along its swollen banks and they would not be found for some days. She played out the scene in her mind. People finding the bodies, the children being told, their lives disrupted by being separated and sent to orphanages, their utter sorrow. How could she do that to Alexander's children, or the doctor's?

And what of her father? Although he had hurt her with his judgments and remonstrations, she knew he loved her and would feel guilty for not supporting her more. His reputation would suffer even more than it already had. People would blame him.

Nellie stirred and Sarah gathered her into her arms, holding perhaps too tightly. She really was a dear little girl who had no idea what her mother had been thinking. 'I am all you have,' said Sarah, 'and I won't let you down.' Then she prayed.

God help me. Help me to find a way.

Chapter Twenty-Two

It was Mavis who came to her rescue. Her neighbour was out walking and saw Sarah appear on the river pathway with Amy. She knew straightaway that all was not right.

"Ah luv," she said as she put her arms around Sarah's drooping shoulders, "ya must be feelin' the world is agin ya."

Sarah allowed herself to be comforted, crying into the older woman's substantial bosom.

"I've bin there meself, luv, and I can tell ya, there ain't gunna be a knight in shinin' armour comin' along any time soon. Ya gotta face the world and be your own shining knight. Tell the world ta go ta hell!"

The words hit home. Mavis was right. Sarah had to pull herself out of her misery. There was no-one else, not even her father. As she walked home with Mavis, listening to her quaint turn of phrase, she knew what she had to do. She weaned Nellie and placed her in the care of Agnes, who at 14 was as capable as any adult and set about to find a well-paid job.

For the first time since the doctor left, she concentrated on her appearance. The mirror came out and told her that she had aged but she still had good skin. The egg yolks reinvigorated her hair where the grey hairs weren't too prominent as yet. Her best dress was repaired. She polished her shoes and she practised smiling.

After some effort, she found a cleaning job with the local solicitor, Mr Conleth Gorman.

Mr Gorman was not likely to be a temptation to Sarah. He was elderly, gruff and Sarah suspected a whisky drinker, but he was fair, professional and paid well. The money was enough for Sarah to run her household and even to pay for music lessons for Amy and Frank who demonstrated quite a talent. The only disappointment for Sarah in this rebuilding of her life, was that William and Annie were in Melbourne and she was estranged from her own father whom, although living so close, she never saw — but still loved.

After the incident at the river, she sought Mavis' company more often and found she could talk to her. For all her eccentricity, she had what Sarah needed most, wisdom. What had been a polite acquaintance had become a true friendship formed by the fact that both were outsiders. Mavis gave her cuttings from her rose bushes and Sarah developed great solace from her garden. As she planted vegetables, Alexander's spirit was with her and she smiled as she remembered the happy years they spent together.

It was on one of these days, when she was deep in thought, that she was brought back to reality by three words.

"William's getting married." Alec had found her in the garden trying to stake the roses. She looked at her son and for a while couldn't register what he was saying. He looked so much like his father. 'William getting married.' It started to sink in.

Her first reaction was hurt, hurt that William hadn't told her, but then she supposed she should be happy for him, happy that he had found his life partner. But she was struggling to overcome the hurt and wished she could be less selfish. She heard herself asking Alec who the woman was.

"Her name is Margaret O'Brien, and it's at St Joseph's Catholic Church in Malvern in two weeks' time."

Sarah asked Alec how William and Margaret had met. "William works with Margaret's brother, John," said Alec. " He will be best man."

Sarah was sad for Alec that he wouldn't be best man but she supposed the fact that it was a Catholic wedding ruled him out. The O'Brien family, she heard, was one of the most prominent Catholic families in Melbourne.

That night she cried for the loss of William. He hadn't even told his mother he was getting married.

Chapter Twenty-Three

The year 1900 saw wonderful celebrations in Rochester. Sarah and the children partied with the rest of the town as the new century rolled in. Twenty-two year old Alec joined eighteen year old Agnes, twelve year old Amy, ten year old Frank and five year old Nellie as they picnicked on the dry soil of the Showgrounds. Marriott called in for a while and apologised for his father who wasn't feeling very well.

As Sarah sang Auld Lang Syne with the whole of the Rochester Township, she was at last content, happy to say goodbye to the nineteenth century and to the suffering that she had experienced in the fifty years that she spent there. Now, as she looked at five of her seven children, she thought of Alexander and the doctor whom she had loved. She thought of her father who had tried to be a good father and whom she would always love.

The candles on the makeshift stage were lit heralding in a new century.

She thought of William and Annie and hoped in the years to come that they would make peace with her.

Chapter Twenty-Four

Rochester
November 1913

Sarah was struggling. Her breathing was laboured and she needed to stop. A log by the side of the road beckoned and she succumbed. It was hot, the late Spring temperatures boding ill for the summer ahead. She took her shoes off and rubbed her feet, not because they were sore but she needed to concentrate her concerns somewhere. The perspiration was building on her forehead, and life, at that moment, seemed all too hard.

The Dingee Road stretched out ahead, proud in its desert — like way but not inviting. No-one would be enticed to travel on such a road in the hope of riches ahead. It was there so that people could go from one point to another, nothing more. The trees were leaning inwards begging for a drink, their leaves ripe for a fire to tear through them.

Sarah tried to remember the last time it rained. She thought it would have been some months ago and yet, not so long ago, the town of Rochester flooded!

Just as she was mounting the energy to continue her journey, she heard an unfamiliar sound followed by an alarm of some kind. She jerked her head around in fright only to be confronted by a miraculous sight. It was a motor car. She had seen them around, from time to time, but they were still a source of fear and amusement.

This one was green and apart from the dust of the road, looked shiningly new. The driver stopped.

"Mrs Hamilton, isn't it?" shouted the driver loudly so he could be heard above the engine, not wanting to turn it off.

Sarah stood and hurriedly tried to get her feet into her shoes, feeling embarrassed to be caught out like this.

"You look a bit done in," he continued. "I suppose you'd be heading out to the Wilson Farm so why don't you get in and I'll drive you the rest of the way."

Small country towns. Not only do people know you but they know where you are going, thought Sarah, but she accepted the invitation and secretly was excited about her first ride in a motor car.

"Thank you Mr Colliver," she said as she climbed in the chugging contraption, "Yes I am going out to help Agnes with the new baby."

"What do you think of MY new baby?" said Mr Colliver patting his Model T Ford with great reverence.

Mr Colliver was a kind man, a farmer who didn't judge Sarah like so many of the townspeople did. To him, she was just a person who needed a lift, a mother who was on her way to help her daughter.

Sarah affirmed his choice of motor car as well as she knew how, making sure she hung on as they turned the corner. She suspected Mr Colliver was going faster than usual to impress her.

"I saw your father last week, Mrs Hamilton, as I was out at Bamawm. Forgive me for saying this but he seemed to get very confused about things. I'm not sure he even knew who I was."

For the sake of the conversation, Sarah agreed with Mr Colliver that her father was not as sharp as he usually was, but really how would she know? She had not seen her father for so long. At the mention of him, she felt a pang of the heart. She missed him, even if things were strained between them. He was her father and she loved him.

As they approached the Wilson farm, Sarah thanked her rescuer and climbed down onto the sideboard and then onto the road. She began to walk up the drive towards the house hoping that Agnes' husband, Robert, would not be there. She did not like him and suspected that he treated Agnes badly.

Almost as soon as she entered the house and greeted Agnes, the baby was thrust into her arms. Could she could take her for a few hours as the house was untidy and dinner was not cooked? Sarah knew that Robert would make Agnes suffer if she didn't have everything spic and span for him when he came in from the farm.

Sarah placed baby Clarice in the pram and wheeled her down to a far corner of the paddock, where there was a patch of green fed by an underground spring. Clarice was unsettled so Sarah cuddled her and sang to her until she closed her eyes, then tucked her into the pram with a summer weight blanket, knowing that babies like to feel secure no matter how hot it is.

The shady nook away from the burning sun and the soothing green grass had a soporific effect on Sarah. She could just sit here, as long as Clarice was asleep, watching the animals resting under the shady gums, thinking. As she looked lovingly at her grand-daughter, she talked to her, knowing that the words would drift away into the atmosphere. No-one was listening.

"I was not much older than you when my mother died, Clarice. You know, I can't even remember what she looked like but I remember her smell and her arms around me and the stories. I loved hearing about England — Leamington Spa, Hinton, Priors Marston, my grandparents and cousins. She said we would go back one day and see everything."

Clarice was fast asleep. In repose, thought Sarah, she looked like Agnes as a baby. Sarah could have watched her for hours but was distracted by a nagging pain in her back which she was finding harder to ignore as it hurt every time she drew breath. She leant back on the decrepit wooden bench, wondering why the weather was this hot in November.

Clarice stirred as if she were having a dream. Her little mouth puckered up and she gave a squeal. Sarah patted her and moved the pram further into the shade. Even that small exertion sent a pain through her and Sarah flopped back onto the bench drifting into a deep sleep. The last thing she remembered was the sight of a magpie watching her from the roof of the shed.

"Mama! Mama!"
Sarah heard the baby first, crying.
Was that Nellie?
She struggled to open her eyes.
And focus. Where was she?
Agnes was nursing the crying baby. It wasn't Nellie. How could it be? Nellie was grown up. It was Clarice. She remembered now. She was looking after her. How long had she been crying? Wasn't she asleep? Sarah saw a blurry little girl standing beside Agnes, looking worried.

It was Agnes speaking: "Lenna, take the horse and go into Rochester for the doctor."

Who was sick? thought Sarah. Why is the doctor being called? She tried to stand but the pain in her back shocked her. "Come on Mama. Let's get you into the house." And with that, she lent on Agnes and allowed herself to be guided.

It was 1913 and the dark clouds of war had yet to descend upon Australia but for Sarah, her own dark cloud was hovering in the Rochester sky.

PART THREE

WILLIAM HAMILTON

Australia: 1873 – 1969

Chapter One

Armadale, Melbourne 1913

The telegram arrived.

William. Mother very sick. Doctor says few days. Alec

He wanted to go. He planned to go but didn't. It wasn't just the money of two day's lost pay. It was something else. Margaret did not understand his decision. She was trying to manage their lives and the house, with three young children and dominating sisters breathing down her neck, telling her what she was doing wrong.

And then the second telegram:

Mother died. Burial on Wednesday. Alec

He was too late.

Margaret tried to console him but as was his way with things of the heart, he pushed her aside, instead walking to St Peter's in Eastern Hill where he worshipped every Sunday. The city was busy but inside the church, all was silent. The candles glowed on the altar, beckoning passers-by to come forward. William put his hand in his pocket and retrieved a penny, a penny to light a candle for his mother.

Was that all she was worth? A penny? William felt hollow.

He shuffled inconspicuously into a pew and rested his head in his hands. She was gone and he would never have the chance to say sorry. He would never talk to her again.

Images floated through his mind, the good times when his father was alive and his mother had told him that there was a special place in a mother's heart for the oldest – not that she loved him more than the others, but differently.

He was the oldest. He had helped his mother with the younger ones, Annie, Alec and Agnes. He had helped his father build the chicken coop in the yard, and felt so proud of himself when his father said. "William, you handle a hammer well."

He remembered the day they got their first chickens and the excitement of collecting the first eggs. He stoked the copper on washing day, chopped wood for the fire and prepared the vegetables for the market run to Malvern on Saturday.

His mother would sit on his bed and tell him stories, exciting stories about her sea journey to Australia from England, an England which he imagined to be all green with people like in the story books he and Annie loved to read.

"One day, William, we will go to England and see it for ourselves."

The hours passed. Several people came, prayed and left, sending curious glances in his direction. He tried not to catch their eye.

Why hadn't he started school earlier? Why was he still home till he was nine years old? They had told him he was 'sickly' but he didn't remember that. He had stayed home and worked alongside his father. Was that another lie, that he was too sick to go to school? Another betrayal?

William felt the paralysis of depression although he could never identify it as such. He felt hollow, empty, and tired. He wanted to be angry but couldn't muster enough energy. Sitting here in this timeless church, an imitation of countless churches around the word testifying to people's belief in something greater than themselves, he wondered if he could ever return to his life which now seemed pointless and dead.

When had he last seen his mother? It was over fifteen years ago. He recalled the moment he told her he was leaving Rochester to go to Melbourne. She didn't say much but he knew she was hurt. They had never been good with words, she or him, and the tension between them was never named. The only one of his family he had seen in that time was Alec, whom he met regularly in the city. Margaret liked Alec and had consented to his being a godfather to their second son.

His mother had sent William away when he was a child, sent him to live with his grandfather whom he hardly knew, a man he didn't like much and who treated him harshly. He had loved his father and hated the fact that he had died. He had prayed for him to get better but his prayers fell on deaf ears.

His father believed that God had a plan for everyone and we had to accept that plan. William didn't much like the plan God had for his father or for him. He remembered the present his father had given him for his tenth birthday. It was a bible.

"Carry this with you everywhere you go William. The answers are all there."

But he was wrong. The answers were not all there. What was the answer to the despair he was feeling? Was it good that he felt this way?

He looked at the crucifix and wondered if the despair that Jesus felt was anything like what he was feeling. But Jesus was good. William knew that he was anything but good. He was forty years old, fit, healthy, happily married with three sons. Why couldn't he shake the guilt that he felt? Why had he acted as he did? Why hadn't he contacted his mother? Why did he not invite her to attend his wedding?

Surely she was to blame. She had sent him away as a child and then embarrassed him with her shameful lifestyle. What hope did he have in Rochester with a mother like that? Anybody would have acted like him in the same circumstances, wouldn't they?

Oh why didn't he go to her when he received the first telegram?

A woman wandered into the Church with a bucket of flowers. She looked at William, saw that he was upset, and touched him on the shoulder as she walked past towards the altar. He was embarrassed. He didn't like other people giving him sympathy.

Not far from this church, he had spent his first ten years, happy years, when his father was alive. He remembered the creek which ran at the back of their garden. He and Annie and Alec would spend hours playing there, pretending to be pirates or convicts. When it rained, the creek would flood and they would float a piece of bark downstream and be sailors. Once Alec got caught beneath a branch and William and Annie used all their strength to get him out before he drowned. They never told their parents about that.

He loved working beside his father and listening to his stories. When it was time for a break, and the weather was nice, Sarah would bring them some freshly baked scones. She would wink at Alexander and say. "It's apricot jam!" and he would smile back. He loved that smile and would give anything to see it again.

It was on one of those breaks that Alexander told William the story of how he landed in Victoria and 'jumped ship' to find gold.

"And did you find gold?" William asked, imagining his father bumping his toe on a huge nugget of gold.

"One thing I want you to remember William," said Alexander. "There's no such thing as getting rich quickly. If people tell you about an easy way to make money, ignore them. There's only one way to make a success of your life and that's to work for it. I learnt that the hard way."

William loved these stories of the early days. He had a vivid imagination, and sometimes pictured himself on the goldfields with his father, being hoisted down the mine and finding gold to the praise of all those 'characters' that his father spoke about.

PART THREE WILLIAM HAMILTON

His father could make anything. Once, he made a contraption from bits of wood he had collected and wheels from an old dog cart. It had a flat piece of timber for sitting on and ropes for steering. The children called it a 'race-cart' and spent hours of fun speeding dangerously down Burke Road. It was exhilarating and as soon as it stopped, the cart was pulled up the hill as quickly as possible for the next ride.

His mother used to worry that they might collide with a horse and cart and was not happy about it but his father was always on hand to pick up the pieces when they crashed. At first it was just William and Annie who took part in the escapades but it was not long before Alec became part of the team as well. The neighbourhood children, especially the Eddy children next door, thought the 'race-cart' the best thing they had ever seen and begged for a turn. Annie thought she would take advantage of their enthusiasm and charged them each a penny for a turn.

When William thought of their cottage, it was always night-time. In winter the fire would be burning and the kettle would be sitting on the stove, steam floating to the rafters. His mother would sing songs that she had learnt as a child. He knew she had not lived with her parents but with another family but she never spoke about them much, except to say they had a piano and her Aunty Helen taught her to play. She had a beautiful voice and William loved to close his eyes and listen to her, although she sang a few too many sad songs for his liking.

The market garden in Hartwell was not a gold mine but was more lucrative than any gold Alexander had ever discovered in his time as a miner. William remembered the smell of the peas, beans, potatoes, carrots and radishes as they sat in the shed waiting to be sorted. His father would take him with him when he went to the markets and he loved the excitement of people pushing and shoving to buy food for their families. With the money they got, they would buy meat and a bun for William. The taste of that, he still remembered, with the icing and sultanas melting in his mouth.

Like every person who lived in Victoria at the time, William had heard of Ned Kelly and his gang. The exploits of robbing banks and holding whole towns ransom fed the children's imagination and they couldn't get enough of the stories. The story of the Glenrowan siege spread quickly through every household. Some were glad Ned Kelly had been captured and the other gang members killed, but for William and the other children, there was a sense of disappointment.

It was one of William's special memories. His father hoisting him onto his shoulders at Coburg, outside Pentridge, trying to glimpse the famous bushranger. After a while, however, it became apparent that Ned Kelly was not going to appear. The word went around the crowd that he had arrived elsewhere because authorities were afraid of the behaviour of the enormous crowd which, apparently, they were not expecting. William was bitterly disappointed and very tired after waiting for so long but when his father suggested an ice-cream on the way back to the station, his disappointment eased. He had had a whole day with his father, just the two of them, so he thanked Ned Kelly for making that possible.

And then everything changed. William noticed the change in his father. He coughed a lot and started work later in the morning. No longer did he laugh and wrestle with him. In fact he hardly smiled at all. Surprisingly, his mother kept him home from school and asked him to do more in the garden. Normally he would have been happy about this but it was different. He wasn't working alongside his father. He was doing his father's work.

His father got sick, really sick, gradually becoming so ill that he couldn't work at all. William and Sarah did as much as they good, though the physical work played havoc with William's health, while Annie looked after Agnes.

The worst part was that the doctor said they had to stay away from him. Whatever was wrong could be spread to them. When he visited his father, lying in his bed, he had to stand at the door. He hated doing this and wanted everything to go back to the way it was.

"William," said his father one October day, "I am not going to get better. You will be the man of the house and you must look after your mother. I know you will do it well. You have always been a good boy, the best son a man could have."

William didn't reply with any reassuring words. He couldn't. He ran from the house, down to the creek, angry, hurt and confused. He threw stones at the nearest gum tree as hard as he possibly could until his arm hurt and he sat on a log and cried.

That November day was seared in his memory. He and his father should have been together, planting tomatoes. But instead, he was with his mother in the market garden when Alec came crying to tell them that his father, whom he loved with all his heart, had died.

The woman with the flowers was walking towards him. He couldn't face talking to her so he hastily got up from his reverie, beating a retreat into the sunshine of Albert Street, where people moved with heads down, hastening to get where they were going. William blinked at the sudden light and felt exposed.

The sensible William was returning, the forty year old accountant known for his reserve and caution. No longer was he the little boy sitting by the creek but a grown man who needed to return to his wife and discuss with her his journey to Rochester to attend his mother's burial. William was exhausted from the emotional upheaval since receiving the telegram so decided to catch the tram home instead of walking. Maybe he could take his son, Jack, with him.

Chapter Two

He settled into a corner seat of the tram away from the stares of those who might notice him. Even though he was in his forties, he had the childhood excitement of riding in one of the new electric trams and focused on the view out the window, watching the men in suits hurrying to appointments and women in their finery moving towards the shops. At one point he saw two little boys darting towards the river with a yabby net. Once upon a time that would have been him.

When his father died, William could not recall his mother crying but it was almost as if a light went out in her. She dealt with all the details and explained to him and Annie that it was up to them now to help her with the younger children. Alec was too young to know what had happened but he sensed the sadness in the atmosphere and retreated into himself.

He wondered how his mother coped for the next few months financially. How she fed and clothed them, he didn't know. Maybe his father had saved some from his meagre wage. Here sitting on the tram thirty years later, William guessed it had, more likely, come from his grandfather. His grandfather! The thought of Thomas Bradshaw jolted him physically, reminding him of one of the worst days of his life.

It was one of those bleak Melbourne days when the sun shines insipidly through the heavy clouds. It must have been June or July. His father had been dead little more than six months. A man appeared in the doorway of their little Hartwell house. He was well dressed, like a gentleman from the nearby manor. William wondered who he was but there was something in his face which reminded him of his mother. It was his eyes. They were the same. He had a vague memory that he had met him before but couldn't place where.

"Children, this is your grandfather – my father."

His mother had spoken of their grandfather. He lived somewhere on a farm but he couldn't remember meeting him.

His 'grandfather' stood by the door, apart. His clothes seemed ill at ease with the cottage. "William," said Sarah, "Say hello to your grandfather."

He had mumbled a weak hello, the sound dying on his lips. Why was she focusing on him and not Annie or Alec? He felt uneasy and wished his father were here sitting in the kitchen chair grinning at him and assuring him that everything was all right.

And then the words that shattered his life. "William," said his mother, "Your grandfather is going to take you to his farm in the country to live with him. You know you have not been well and the city is not a good place for you. You need good food and fresh air. At your grandfather's farm, you will have horses to ride and lots of space to run around. You are a very lucky boy!"

But the shakiness of her voice betrayed her words. Annie blurted out from the corner of the room where she was cuddling the family cat, always accepted to be William's. "He's not taking Ginger with him is he?"

He looked at Annie. She looked frightened and Alec withdrew under the table, not knowing why everyone was acting so strangely. It was at that moment that Agnes woke up crying from her sleep. His mother picked her up and held her towards the gentleman, suggesting he might like to hold her, but his hands remained by his sides.

His grandfather spoke.

"Your mother can't look after you all now that your father is no longer here, William, and we need to get you strong so you can get a job and help your mother. We have a good little school in Bamawm and you can finish your schooling there. Soon your mother will move to Rochester, and you can see your brothers and sisters then." An almost affectionate smile softened his face as he looked at Annie, "No Annie, we are not taking Ginger with us. You can bring him with you when you all come."

He had spoken to William as if he were grown up but William felt anything but grown up. The tears were welling up within him and he turned to face his mother. She was crying too but managed to take the suitcase from his grandfather's grasp and thrust it towards him. "Your grandfather has bought you a brand new case, William. Here, take it and pack your things. You are going on this afternoon's train."

He went to the bedroom that he shared with Alec and Annie, opened the drawers and packed his belongings. They easily fitted in the case. As he glanced around the space which had been his home, he blinked back the tears, not able to believe what was happening. He moved towards the door but then remembered his bible, the one his father gave him for his birthday. He turned back towards the bed, picked it up and put it in the case. It was all he had left of his father.

When he got back to the kitchen, his grandfather was talking to his mother in a low voice. He noticed some money in her hand. This was not right. The world was spinning and he couldn't make it stop. His mother was sending him away and he was only ten years old.

Why was she doing this? Wouldn't he be more help at home with her? He knew he hadn't been in the best of health but he needed his family more than fresh air and good food.

His grandfather took his case, smiled warmly at Annie who was cuddling Ginger to within an inch of his life, and ushered him out the door. William turned to see Alec come out from under the table and scream, "I want William! Where is he going?" Annie took Ginger and moved over to Alec where she offered him the cat. His mother's shoulders were hunched and she was trying to smile at him. William knew now, that her heart was breaking but then he just saw the whole thing as a massive betrayal.

Chapter Three

The tram reached the Glenferrie Road tram stop and William ambled home dreading the reproval he would receive from his sister in law, Kate, for running off like he did. Margaret would be understanding. She always was, and he looked forward to a time when there was no distraction so they could talk. The sisters lived next door and seemed to think it their right to barge in on William and Margaret at any time of day. He knew they were protective of their younger sister whose struggle with polio had made her dependent on them but he just wished they would take a step back.

As he turned into Stanhope Street, he was happy to see Margaret walk towards him. He guessed she too needed to escape her sister's domination.

"William," she said, as she hugged him, "I am so sorry."

William hugged her tight and thanked God he had met such a wonderful woman. She was eight years older than him and seemed to be endowed with the wisdom and compassion her sisters lacked. One of her brothers, John, was his best friend and the other, Terence Joseph, or 'T.J.' as he was known, was his partner in business so he was inextricably linked to the family. It was only the sisters who drove him to distraction.

"I'll catch the morning train to Rochester." Then he paused, hesitant about Margaret's reaction, "Will I take Jack with me?"

"He has an interschool cricket game tomorrow against Xavier. I don't think he would like to miss that. And William," she didn't quite know how to say this, " he didn't know her."

He agreed, secretly relieved as he knew Jack would ask questions about the grandmother he had never met. "I'll go alone. It's probably for the best anyway."

Margaret's sister, Kate, who had been watching from the window, appeared at the front gate in the style of someone on the attack. Her whiny voice was not loud but did not allow argument. "I hope you're not thinking of leaving your poor wife and going to that woman's funeral. She was never a mother to you and she doesn't deserve any grief you may think you have for her."

A horrified Margaret was about to say something when William angrily pushed past Kate, stepping on her toe accidently in the process. He was cranky and knew unless he got away he would not be responsible for anything he said or did.

When they were alone and the children were in bed, Margaret began the conversation they had been avoiding for fifteen years.

"Kate should not have said those things, William. Whatever scandals your mother was involved in, she loved her children. And yet you hardly ever talk about her." William hung his head and cried, something Margaret had never seen before, even after the birth of their children.

He knew he could never explain to this guileless woman why he had rejected his mother. Margaret was the youngest of five sisters and dominated by all of them. Her family was everything to her but she couldn't see the power the O'Brien family had on the way she thought about life. And he, William, had been drawn into their narrow way of looking at the world.

They wanted him to convert to Catholicism but he refused. He conceded that the boys could be brought up Catholics – that was non-negotiable if he wanted to marry Margaret, but holding onto his Anglican faith was important to him, of who he was and who his mother, father and grandfather were.

He honoured his part of the bargain, making sure the boys were woken, dressed and on time as altar boys at Mass during the week and on Sundays. The two oldest were at Catholic schools, even though it was a financial sacrifice, and he never spoke to them of his own religion. That, he kept private.

The sisters made fun of him, how he walked into Eastern Hill every Sunday, to St Peter's while the rest of the family went to St Joseph's Catholic Church, less than 200 yards away. He gave everything to this new family but they would not take his religion.

He loved them all, in a way. They had been good to him when he arrived in Melbourne fifteen years ago. T.J, as the oldest brother, had invited him into his firm after he qualified as an accountant and John, the younger brother, had become his best friend.

He loved the fact that the family were united and strong. They were part of the Catholic community of Melbourne which knew prejudice from the dominant English, Protestant establishment and had developed a siege mentality against it. The trouble was that William was part of that protestant establishment. He fell between two worlds and sometimes he felt as if he were suffocating.

Margaret was different, soft and warm. She thought well of everyone.

"Whoever she was, William, she was your mother."

He wanted to scream at his wife. But you didn't know her. She was a woman of loose morals and the talk of the town but he knew how that would sound.

He lifted his tear stained face and looked at Margaret. He was calm.

"I never got the chance to say sorry."

Chapter 4

The train left Spencer St Station at 8am. Margaret had packed a flask of tea and some sandwiches which fitted neatly into his bag. He would arrive into Rochester in time for the burial and be on the late afternoon train back to Melbourne.

He was apprehensive but knew that some things just had to be got through, and this was one of them. His anxiety was relieved somewhat by the excitement of a long train trip. He was like a kid when it came to travelling on trains.

The journey with his grandfather nearly thirty years earlier had not been exciting, although it should have been. He was numb then and he thought the trip would never end. They had stopped twice at railway cafes, once at Kyneton and once in Bendigo. His grandfather had ordered milk and buns for him but they remained un-eaten when the whistle went to re-join the train.

The rhythmic rattling rocked him to sleep and when he woke, the train was pulling into Bendigo. He pulled out the lunch Margaret had packed for him and prepared his thoughts for the final stage of the journey.

As he approached Rochester station, William felt the strangeness that affects all who return to a world they thought they had left forever. Everything was the same – except him. The past tugged at his soul and returned him to his insecurities and discomfort and he couldn't do anything about it. It was a disconcerting experience.

He was eleven years old when his family moved to Rochester. He could still see Annie hugging Ginger, scared to let him out of her clutches. Alec was all agog at the excitement of his first train trip and Agnes was gripping Sarah's hand overwhelmed by the whole experience.

And his mother. She looked unhappy. He guessed she didn't want to move to Rochester but she had no choice. He had been glad to see his family again but by then, he had a different life and he found the experience confusing.

The train stopped at Rochester station and William noticed Alec through the window. For a split second he thought it was his father. He reached up to the overhead compartment, grabbed his bag, then queued to leave the train.

The brothers embraced and walked the two hundred metres to the family home. William expected his mother to be at the front gate, waiting, but of course she wouldn't be. She was dead. Most likely lying in the front room. He braced himself for the viewing of a woman he could never imagine dying.

"She looks peaceful," said Alec as if he could read William's thoughts. They were brothers and had always seemed to know what the other was thinking. Alec had been William's contact with the family. They met at least twice a year when Alec came to Melbourne and even though William had made it quite clear that the O'Briens were his family now, he was hungry for the news which came with Alec.

He had hardly gotten to know his younger brother, Frank and sisters, Amy and Nellie who were born in Rochester after he went to live with his grandfather and Mrs Gilmer. His mother had never disclosed the identity of their father or fathers and this made her the subject of gossip. William had been ashamed of her.

"Good to have you here, William."

"I was too late."

"She talked about you a lot."

"I wish I'd come, Alec."

"I told her you were on your way. She seemed happy with that. And William, she went quickly in the end."

"Did she suffer?"

Alec told him how she had collapsed at Agnes' farm and been brought home in Robert's new horse and cart. "The doctor said it was most likely pneumonia but she refused to go to hospital. She had pain in her back and her breathing was bad. Nellie was here, William. She is a gem. I think she should be a nurse."

"Did grandfather visit?" This was important to William. He wasn't sure why.

"No. We told him but he said he wasn't well enough. Things have been a bit prickly with him over the last few years. I don't think he ever got over the court case. To have children out of wedlock was one thing, but to steal and go before the Magistrate's court was the last straw. He'll be glad to see you though."

William winced. His feeling of guilt increased.

"She never met my boys"

"She knew about them though." She used to tell everyone about her clever grandsons in Melbourne."

The house in Mackay Street had the curtains drawn. They walked into the front room where Sarah lay. Alec stayed a few seconds and then left William alone. The undertaker would arrive shortly.

She looked peaceful and quite beautiful and for the first time he could see a strong resemblance to Annie. What is it about people when they die, that they recover their inner beauty? He had never really thought about his mother's looks, but standing with her, he could see that she was a good looking woman who would turn men's heads. He tried to recall the last time he had seen her and with a shudder remembered the awkward exchange. He pulled a chair over so that he could sit and be close to her as his legs were feeling slightly wobbly.

"Mother, I'm sorry. I'm sorry." He paused and sniffled, feeling the pain in his gut.

He wanted to say so much but he couldn't find the words. Instead he just sobbed with the sobs coming from deep within his tortured soul. Since he had received the telegram, he had chided himself with guilt and regret and knew that it would stay with him until the day he died.

The burial was carried out in the Rochester way. He knew what to expect. The cart proceeded down the main street where shops closed their doors and the shopkeepers stood out front with their heads bowed. He knew many of the people who now showed the convention of respect would have been the very ones who gossiped about his mother while doing business. But could he be critical? He, of all people?

The procession followed, all dressed in black, behind the cart, until the town bridge whereby they needed to find other transport to the cemetery. Most of the crowd were women, he noticed, and was glad that Australians had broken with the tradition that women did not attend burials. Alec suggested that these women, while not openly friendly with Sarah in her lifetime, had obviously deemed her, a fellow mother, worthy of their respect. Maybe they were far more understanding of her sins than he was.

"Mother would have enjoyed this," whispered Alec to his brother as they approached the bridge. Frank had organised a friend he knew who had a motor car to take them the remainder of the distance to the cemetery and they saw him waiting up ahead.

William couldn't wait to tell his boys about the motor car which was now solemnly proceeding along the Kyabram Road behind horse drawn carriages. He smiled as he thought of how impressed they would be.

As the cemetery came into view, he saw his grandfather with his uncle Marriott, sitting in the shade of a blue gum trying to ward off the blistering sun. Thomas was frantically waving the flies away, without much success. William hardly recognised him as the man he had last seen and it was hard to maintain his dread of him as he now looked like an old man who couldn't quite understand what was going on around him.

They alighted from the motor car and made their way to the Anglican section where the crowd had gathered, some with parasols to ward off the searing sun. He recognised a few people but tried not to make eye contact. The last thing he wanted was a sympathetic conversation adding fuel to his already festering guilt.

The minister looked around, surprised at the crowd, and launched into the formal prayers in a booming voice which was not necessary as everyone had crowded together around the freshly dug hole.

"Lord we commend this woman to your care. May she enter your kingdom and enjoy eternal life……."

William prayed his own prayer:

That God would be merciful.

That his mother would forgive him, that he could forgive her.

That they would meet again.

What had her life been, he thought as he watched the coffin lowering into the grave. What had she done with the 62 years allotted to her? What have any of us done? He looked at his younger brother Frank whose face told the story of a grief stricken young man who had grown up with no father, and for whom Sarah was the only parent he knew. He was, thought William, the best looking of all of them.

As each person threw their allotted handful of dirt on the coffin and walked away, William felt the tears behind his eyes. He couldn't cry. He wouldn't cry. He had no right to cry.

Alec saved him. "Come and talk to Grandfather, William." William walked across to the shade of the blue gum where his grandfather was seated, glad to get out of the sun.

"Grandfather," he said shaking his hand. "You are well?" It was a stupid question, he realised, because his grandfather was quite obviously not well.

"Don't think it will be long before I join your mother, William, but how is everything in the big smoke? You certainly look as if you have done well for yourself." Was there a hint of pride in his grandfather's voice?

"Alec tells me you're selling the farm and moving to Torrumbarry."

"I haven't decided yet!" snapped Thomas. "The work has got a bit much but we have a boy out there who's practically running the place. Maybe I'll give the farm to him!"

This comment was meant to stir Marriott who just winked at William and said. "He often calls the lad William, thinking he's you." William wondered if his grandfather was kinder to the lad than he had been to him, but today was not the day to harbour bitter memories. They talked for a while, Thomas continually mopping his brow and heaving great sighs. They were both glad that Marriott was there. Neither he nor his grandfather found the conversation easy. Marriott was a story teller, a raconteur, and because he was so comfortable with himself, he inspired an ease in others as well.

William was hurt that his grandfather had not asked after his wife or his children. It was a reminder to him that the two families were separate and would never meet. Perhaps he was still wanting his grandfather's approval, after all these years. Perhaps he was not as grown up as he thought.

He spent more awkward minutes making small talk with people who approached him. It was as if he were watching himself play a part and he was not connected with the person he observed. When the driver of the motor car suggested he needed to leave for the station, he was relieved.

He had enjoyed seeing his siblings again. Their grief for the mother they loved shocked him, making him feel more like an outsider. The stories Nellie and Frank related were of a woman he didn't know, a warm, loving, good person. Alec had them all laughing as he related the story of the cat, Ginger, they brought with them to Rochester.

"He ran off when we arrived and the Eddys told us he turned up in Camberwell at our old house, with bleeding paws. He walked all the way from Rochester to Camberwell, nearly a hundred miles!" As the place seemed more important to Ginger than the people, the Eddys agreed to keep him, much to Annie's disappointment.

Nellie didn't believe it. She said a cat couldn't walk that far and wouldn't know where to go. Alec insisted it were true and only wished Annie were there to corroborate his story. His heart was heavy as he had laughed along with the others. There was a bond between them but it did not include him. When he'd left Rochester for Melbourne, his mother was still nursing Nellie and had just been through a nasty court case which gave her a criminal record. Later, Alec told him, she settled down quite considerably and there were no more scandals.

He had sent her money every month hoping that the little he sent would be enough to make stealing unnecessary ever again. It wasn't easy for him to do this as his family was growing and he didn't earn a great deal but it was his wife, Margaret who insisted. She thought it was the right thing to do. His mother had written to thank him many times and he knew he should write back but he didn't. Truth be told he hadn't thought about her much at all.

He thought about his youngest sister, Nellie, whom he hardly knew. She had had rheumatic fever recently and still looked fragile. There was something about her, though, that tugged at William's heart strings. She told him she loved animals and hated Alec's story about Ginger because she couldn't bear to think of the poor cat walking all that way to find his old home. William listened intently when she spoke of Sarah, her poetic language giving back to him the Sarah he remembered when he was a boy. Something ethereal about her, he thought, as if she belongs to another world. He wondered what would become of her.

He supposed he was jealous of the closeness of Nellie, Frank and Amy. They had been nice to him but he knew he did not belong. Frank was an honest, sincere young man who worked for Cobb & Co as a painter and told William of his great love, music. William wondered where he got that ability from. He liked Frank for his sincerity and honesty and listened as he described the work he did for Cobb & Co. and what they were like as a company to work for. He said it was just a job, though, as what he really loved was playing the cornet in the Foundry Band. Most of his friends were from the Band and they met and practised in a mate's house three times a week followed by a drink at the Criterion.

"I'd love to travel," said Frank in a dreamy way. "When I've saved enough money, I'd love to get a passage on a ship, working my way round the world. Mother used to say she wanted me to visit England, especially a place called Leamington. I think that's where she had come from."

It had not been easy for the Hamilton children growing up in Rochester, the younger three not knowing who their father was and having a mother with a 'reputation.' But William admired how well they had balanced their love for their mother with the gossip they must have experienced. It made him feel ashamed. At the same time he rejoiced in the fact that, at least he knew who his father was.

Chapter Five

William had spent his life watching new buildings growing up in the city of Melbourne and loved it. Sometimes, on his lunch hour he would just stand and watch the men working. Maybe, he thought, he should have been an architect or a builder, like his grandfather. The Rochester Train Station was one such building, a grand testament to the industry of the last century when the State of Victoria grew from a colonial outpost to a sophisticated centre of industry. The trip to Melbourne took four hours when just thirty years earlier it would have taken two days.

William stood with Alec and Frank waiting for the train to arrive from Echuca. He had said goodbye to Agnes, Amy and Nellie at the cemetery.

"What will you do now?" asked William already feeling removed from any decision process.

Alec picked up William's bag as the train approached. "Frank will go to live with Amy after her wedding and Nellie will live with Agnes. They'll be all right." William took his bag and shook Alec's hand. Then he turned to Frank and did the same.

"Give our love to Margaret and the boys," yelled Alec amid the sound of the steam engine, "especially my Godson!"

"He's the clever one!" said William, "has read every book in the house and knows everything."

"Of course," grinned Alec. William called to Frank that the same boy also shared both their names, William Francis, but the words were drowned out and Frank did not hear them.

William was a lather of sweat. He found a seat as far away from other passengers as he could and slid down into the leather seat. He felt like a wound up spring. He placed the package of leftover food that Nellie had packed him on the empty seat next to him. He waved as the train began to move. He knew he would see Alec again in Melbourne as they met regularly but an uneasiness unsettled him when he looked at Frank. What was that about? he wondered,

All he knew was that the decision to attend his mother's funeral was the right one. He had done it for Alec but had not counted on the bonus of reuniting with his brother, Frank and his sisters, Agnes, Amy and Nellie. Where was Annie? he wondered. Of all his siblings, she was the one he loved the most. They were close in age and had shared so much together when his father was alive. Annie reminded him of the happy times, when they shared a bed and would talk and talk until their father would enter the bedroom and pretend to be cross. He knew there was trouble between Annie and his mother but he didn't know the details and he knew his mother grieved for her daughter, not knowing where she was or what had happened to her. He'd love to see her again.

For a while after he went to Bamawm, they wrote to each other. She was eight years old and doing the work of an adult. He felt sorry for her. When they moved to Rochester, she seemed to lose her way and mix with the wrong sort of people. Whereas he had his grandfather and the Gilmers, Annie had no-one except her mother who was struggling to make ends meet. He wished he had done more for her.

The four hour train trip would be a chance to process the past six hours, in fact, more importantly, the past forty years. Something was niggling him and he couldn't work out what it was. He had a wonderful wife and three healthy, bright boys. He had a responsible job which he liked and enough money to live a comfortable life. His wife's sisters were annoying with their bossiness but they weren't so bad really.

Margaret had been the best thing that ever happened to him, she was one in a million. He knew the polio she had contracted before he met her had left its legacy. He sometimes felt her wincing in pain beside him in bed but she rarely complained. He wondered how much his mother had suffered in those last weeks before she died. Alec had said she had borne her pain gallantly and this didn't surprise him. In death, his mother was becoming far more real to him.

The train was slowing to a halt in Bendigo, a town he knew well. His wife and her family came from here. A cup of tea, he thought, at the railway café, to go with Nellie's sandwiches.

It was crowded as he pushed through the swinging doors and looked around for a table. There was none, but an older woman indicated a spare chair beside her. I hope she doesn't want to talk, he thought but accepted the invitation, sitting down in such a way that didn't invite conversation. The woman took the hint and went on reading her book.

Still uneasy, he ordered a strong tea and tried to unravel his feelings. Was he angry at meeting his grandfather again? No it wasn't that. His grandfather had done what he thought was right and he couldn't hold a grudge against him for the harsh treatment he dealt out to William when all he was crying out for was affection. His grandfather thought that he needed a strong hand and had certainly given him that.

Was it that he felt guilt for not having seen his mother for eighteen years? Partly, he thought, although he had sent her money. The warning train whistle sounded, and the violence of the sound acted like a shock. He knew what his feeling of unease was about. He downed the remainder of the stale tasting tea and said to himself. Hold that thought.

He helped a woman onto the train with her two little children and acknowledged her thanks before resettling in his seat. He didn't feel like eating the food Nellie had packed until he deciphered the thought he had had in the tea room. He closed his eyes and tried to empty his mind of everything around him, the smell of the engine, the hustle and bustle of passengers, the rattling along the track and the sun searing through the window.

The train was drawing into Castlemaine when it all became clear.

He was living a double life! The William Hamilton of Stanhope Street, Armadale, partner and accountant, middle class, father of three Catholic boys and husband of Catholic Margaret was a completely different person from William Hamilton, Anglican, eldest son of Sarah Hamilton and older brother of Annie, Alec, Agnes, Amy, Frank and Nellie, a working class Rochester farm boy.

How could he reconcile the two Williams? He had spent the last fifteen years pretending that one didn't exist, had never existed. Was this why he sometimes felt a rage that he couldn't explain and that others around him were puzzled by? Was this why he sometimes was far too strict on the boys? Was this why he became more devoted to his Anglican faith than he ever had before? Was this why he often shut Margaret out from his thoughts, sometimes cruelly? She didn't deserve such treatment and he knew it hurt her but he seemed unable to control his behaviour.

It was true he resented being taken from his home and sent to Bamawm at the age of 10, not just being taken away from his mother but his brother and sisters as well. And whereas he was nearby when his mother had the other three children, he wasn't living at home and had not been able to form a bond with them. Until now. Or was he kidding himself? Was it a gap too wide to bridge?

William's eyes were moist when the train stopped at Kyneton and a woman got on and sat down beside him. He moved closer towards the window and pretended to be sleeping so that he wouldn't have to talk to her. She looked pleasant enough and seemed the sort that would be telling you her life's story before they arrived in Woodend and he certainly did not want that.

In order to survive, he had to reconcile the two Williams and decide which one he was going to be. His mother was now gone. He was no longer responsible to her or for her. He had enjoyed the kinship of his brothers and sisters but as the train steamed towards Melbourne, he felt that bond disintegrating. It could not survive their history. The others had their own lives and whereas he cared about them all, he knew they lived in different worlds. Too much time and history had elapsed. Yes, he would still see Alec when he came for his twice yearly visit to Melbourne, but that would be his only involvement with his family.

It had to be that way.

He knew what his wife's family thought of the Hamiltons. They had heard the stories of his mother, how she had three children out of wedlock and been in court for stealing from her employer. They weren't interested in the complexities of the situation, just that she wasn't a 'respectable' person. He knew, also, that their faith dictated that non-Catholics were an inferior species and not to be encouraged. He, William, was accepted, but with certain reservations.

It would be too difficult to try to maintain the two Williams. He knew that. He knew that when he walked in the door of his house in Stanhope Street, the sisters would be there. They would ask him how it all went but would not be interested in the answer. Margaret would want to know but there was no way he could make her understand how he was torn.

William Hamilton returned to his life in Melbourne. He was a married accountant, married to Margaret with three sons. The

O'Brien family were his family. For the rest of his days on this earth, this would be his life.

Chapter Six

Armadale
1964

His grandchildren insisted on a celebration to mark his 90th birthday. He didn't want any fuss and retreated to his room as soon as it was polite to do so. They meant well and certainly they were the only meaning he found in life anymore but sometimes he found their exuberance tiring.

His room was one of the many small bedrooms in the Edwardian house in Armadale, built almost seventy years earlier. On bluestone foundations and on a corner block, it demonstrated the majesty and optimism of the era. Next door, towering over the backyard was a similar red brick building belonging now to the Tramways but which once housed the school his sons had attended. Across a busy Glenferrie Road was the Catholic church where he had married. His own house, where he had raised his three sons and lived with his wife, Margaret, who was dead thirty years, was thirty metres along the same street. Across the road was a house which had once belonged to his friend and best man, John O'Brien. Not far were the houses where the sisters had lived.

He had not moved far in the seventy years since he left Rochester.

The house belonged to his youngest son, Leo, and his family. He had lived here since Margaret's death. His grand-daughter, Elizabeth, was doing a school project, sitting in his room, squashed between the door and the bed, pen and paper in hand, ready to ask him questions. She wanted to know about the Australia of his childhood. He guessed he was a substitute for a history book.

"Tell me, Pappy, about the feud between Henry Lawson and Banjo Paterson. Our teacher said that people at the time used to buy the Bulletin just to get the latest instalment."

He answered her questions as well as he could. He knew she loved it when he quoted whole poems by heart, especially *The Man from Snowy River*. He told her about life on the farm in Bamawm, when he worked for Mrs Gilmer, how he had several falls from horses and decided he never, ever wanted to buy a farm.

He told her about his grandfather and how he finished his schooling in Bamawm, but the story she loved the most was the one about Ned Kelly. "I told the girls at school that story and they didn't believe me."

Elizabeth and the other grandchildren found his stories exciting and spent hours listening to him. He was a window to the past, to history and fuelled their love of it.

But he never mentioned his mother.

Once, he mentioned his brother, Alec, whom he met in the city, a 'wild fella' he called him. Never did he mention the others.

Since his visit for his mother's burial, in 1913, he had become more and more ensconced into his wife's family. He had become the family accountant and since all of them were investors, or stock brokers, there was much work to do. The Hamiltons of Rochester had become a distant memory, resurrected from time to time by announcements of deaths.

His grandfather, Thomas Bradshaw, had died a few months after William's mother. This was not a surprise as he was nearing ninety and William had the impression he had had enough. What was a shock, however, was Nellie's death, twelve months to the day after her mother. She was only nineteen.

William had chosen not to return to Rochester for either of these funerals.

Each death, however, caused him immense grief. His grandfather, Thomas Bradshaw, had been a huge part of his life and his death took something of William with him. After all, he had been his father figure for much of his childhood. He often thought of the man who had tried to become a father to him but whose methods belonged to another world. His death had softened William's memories of him.

Nellie's death affected him much more, however, because she was such a pure human being who wanted nothing more than harmony in the world. Maybe, it was true, that 'only the good die young'. William could see her at the cemetery telling him about her dreams and he found it hard to imagine such a beautiful person no longer existing. He was glad his mother was not alive to grieve for her youngest, beautiful little girl.

Nellie's death in 1914 coincided with an event that would have major repercussions on the country and on the Hamilton Family. Australia, though now an independent country, pledged its allegiance to the British Empire against the Germans when war was declared.

Frank was among the first to enlist from Rochester and Agnes sent William a picture of him in his uniform looking optimistic and handsome. He was sent to Gallipoli to relieve the Anzacs who were holding desperately onto ground against a determined Turkish Force, then onto France, where, at Pozieres, he was nominated for a military medal for 'bravery under intense fire', carrying wounded soldiers to safety. But trench foot, shell shock and finally the spanish influenza took their toll and the Frank who returned to Australia in 1920 was a shell of the man in that photo, the man who had waved William off at the station.

Alec and William met often. They had lunch together at the same café in Collins Street. The besuited accountant and the country farmer, an odd couple in the tea room where women with delicate white aprons waited on them and gave them curious looks. William thought Alec had aged but watching him hoe into the corned beef sandwich, all he could see was his father. He was the image of him. William wondered why he had not inherited any of his father's looks.

Alec conveyed the news of the family and Rochester, but mostly they talked about Frank.

"Many of his friends were killed, William, and he only just survived."

"What will he do?"

"He's been given a settlement farm, in Strathallan. You know Frank, he's hardly a farmer, but he says he'll make a go of it. Everyone's trying to help but he's not right. I'm concerned about him." After a pause to swallow the last of the sandwiches, he added, "I'm glad Mother died when she did, William. She was spared so much suffering."

William felt ashamed. Alec was taking on the worries and responsibility of the family when it really should be him. Alec hid his worries behind a mask of bonhomie and storytelling and for that William was grateful but here he was, the one who couldn't keep up with Annie and William on the makeshift carts in their childhood but the one keeping the family together.

The waitress cleared their table and asked them if they wanted anything else. There was a queue at the door waiting to be seated so she was anxious to hurry them up. William took the bill and waved off Alec who offered to pay his share.

"They all send their love," said Alec as they stood at the corner of Swanston Street and Collins. William knew they probably hadn't sent their love but accepted Alec's words as a polite formality.

When Agnes died from diabetes in 1934, after bearing eleven children, William mentioned it at the dinner table. They hadn't even known he had a sister called Agnes, and were surprisingly interested. Alec had sent him a telegram with the details of the funeral in Elmore. Of course, he told Margaret and the boys, he wouldn't be able to go.

"Why don't you go, Father," said Leo who was twenty three. "I can borrow Gerry Nolan's car and drive you myself." This would be no sacrifice on Leo's part as he was crazy about cars and would love any excuse to take his mate's car for a country drive. After much umming and ahhing, William agreed.

They set out before dawn so as to make it in time. He and Leo were not close but when his son asked questions about Agnes and why he had never heard about her before, or her eleven children who would be his cousins, William, lulled into the intimacy of a road trip, told him the story of his family. Leo listened as if it were a fairy tale and when William made him promise not to tell the others, Leo shrugged as if it were of no import and told him he would collect him after the service as he did not want to meet a whole lot of strangers, even if they were relatives.

What a different experience Agnes' burial was for William, so different from his mother's burial in 1913.

He felt a stranger.

Agnes' family didn't know who he was, Nellie wasn't there and he was shocked at the difference in Frank. If people can be a shadow of their former selves, it was Frank. His self-assurance was gone and he found it difficult to maintain a conversation. Amy was living in Deniliquin and the mother of six children. She and William were pleased to see each other but the conversation was focused on Agnes.

"It's a relief, really, William. She suffered so much."

"Because of the diabetes?"

"Yes and because of her husband. He made life miserable for her."

'Bastard!' thought William. He didn't understand men who treated their wives badly. It was foreign to him. He couldn't imagine treating Margaret badly. He looked over to Robert Charles whom he had spoken to as he arrived. Looks deceive, he thought, he seems like such a nice bloke.

Still no word of Annie. She had disappeared off the face of the earth. No-one had heard from her. William hoped she was all right. There was no way of tracing her and he just presumed that she didn't want to be traced. He thought he understood her more now that he had come to terms with his own life and where he belonged. Maybe Annie had felt the same. Still, thought William, in my mind she will always be the one who charged the kids from the neighbourhood a penny for a ride in our homemade cart.

William had lost touch with Marriott but heard from Alec that he died, penniless in Bendigo. He was sad about that as he remembered him as someone who was always kind to him when he landed on his grandfather's property as a young, confused boy.

In the space of the next twenty years after Agnes died, he attended three more significant funerals. Frank, whom he hoped was finally at peace, his own wife, Margaret, without whom he felt lost and finally Alec, the brother with whom he had formed a close and loving bond. After Alec had gone, he lost touch with Amy and never spoke to her again.

I am an old man, he thought as he looked out his window to the Armadale street, at the constant traffic, realising that this is where he would die. For some reason his thoughts went back to Bamawm, to his grandfather, to the farm and to his mother.

Would he see her again? Did he really believe that he would?

He looked at his grand-daughter who still sat waiting for him to answer her last question. He wanted to tell her about his mother and how he had loved her.

But instead, a tear came to his eye and he said nothing.

Conclusion

I am at the St Kilda cemetery
I need no map
The burial place is known to me
And visible
Just inside the gates off Dandenong Road
Turn right to the Catholic section
A large gravestone and written in Italics, on the front

Hamilton
In loving memory of Margaret Hamilton, died 7/7/1945
and her beloved husband, William. Died 9/5/1969.
Requiescat in Pace.

Notes to the reader

I have wanted to write the story of my great-grandmother, Sarah Hamilton, since I discovered her. She was my grandfather's mother and yet I didn't even know her name was Sarah until my cousin, Joan, found her. There she was lying in an unmarked grave in the town where I had lived for 5 years and yet I did not know it. I had been to many funerals there and probably walked across her grave.

She was lying there with her nineteen year old daughter, Nellie, of whom I had no knowledge. She had seven children, three to Alexander Hamilton, to whom she said she was married for ten years. (However, no record exists of their marriage) The other four, including my grandfather, all have, in the space for the father's name on their birth certificates, 'father unknown'.

She was a single mother with seven children and yet she kept them together as a family and, with two exceptions, they were close and supported each other through life.

One of those exceptions was my grandfather, William Hamilton, Sarah's first born. He lived with my family in Melbourne from the time before I was born. He had a bedroom next to mine, watched my brothers, my sister and I grow, told us stories of the early years of Victoria's white settlement, excited us with tales of going to see Ned Kelly, recited the poems of Lawson, Paterson and C.J Dennis at length and provided us with a model of a thoroughly honest and decent man. We all loved him dearly though my father often said he was a much gentler grandfather than he was a father!

When I asked my mother why we knew nothing of his birth family, she said she guessed it had something to do with religion, as he was an Anglican and he married into a conservative Catholic family. She thought his family may have 'cut him off' as so many families did when a 'mixed marriage' took place. After much research and consideration, however, I do not think it was as simple as that.

I was fortunate to be joined in my research by my sister-in-law, Mauri Hamilton, whose appetite for accuracy and historical facts complemented my sometimes romantic search.

In order to understand William and his mother, Sarah, it was necessary to go back in time to the mid nineteenth century to England.

The English Connection

Once we had found where Sarah's parents, Thomas Bradshaw and Sarah Fairbrother, had come from in England, it seemed important to go there. The most significant villages were all in the English Midlands, between Warwick and Northampton: Priors Marston, Byfield and Woodford Cum Membris. Priors Marston, where we stayed, is now a dormitory suburb with houses, a pub and a population of about five hundred. But it is very beautiful and so full of history. My husband, Peter, and I were lucky to have the wisdom and knowledge of Peter Jackson to guide us through that history.

He took us to *The Butcher House*, where Thomas Bradshaw grew up and where Thomas' father, and later his brother, operated their shop. I would have been happy to observe it from the outside but Barbara Flint, who lives there now, welcomed us into the house with a smile and many cups of tea. She showed us the original hooks in the ceiling where the meat would have hung. It was very special.

In Byfield, Pam Hicks showed me how illustrious the Fairbrothers were, with graves set apart and several stained glass windows in their honour.

I was getting a picture of who Thomas and Sarah Jane were and how they fitted into their communities.

We explored in other villages and towns such as Chipping Warden, Priors Hardwick, Charwelton, (where Thomas' sister, Mary, lived with her family), Napton on The Hill, Daventry, Southam, Leamington and Warwick, all of which had some significance to Thomas and Sarah. For some reason Sarah declared on an official certificate that she was born in Leamington, but official records discount this. On one such certificate, someone had written "Lymington' which resulted in an earlier wild goose chase to Hampshire!

My main aim in writing this story was to 'redeem' Sarah, a woman who under very difficult circumstances, some through no fault of her own, had to make choices and live with the consequence of those choices. It would have been so easy for her to place her children in 'care' as so many single mothers did at that time. But, instead, she didn't and what resulted was a close knit family whose members looked after each other. If she were alive today she would be proud of her seven children, twenty seven grand-children and who knows how many great-great-grandchildren and so on.

To write the story of Sarah, it was necessary to create plausible stories to fill the many blanks. I researched life in Melbourne and Rochester at the time and fitted the characters into that context as well as I could, staying faithful to the facts as much as possible.

What follows is a listing of what is fact and what is fiction.

Thomas and Sarah Jane (Jane)

- Thomas was born in 1824 in Priors Marston. He was the third child of Thomas and Mary (Marriott). He was a carpenter.
- Mr Hart was the headmaster of the school at Priors Marston. He planted the two Lebanese cedar trees named after the Napoleonic battles. It is plausible that Thomas was one of the children who helped.
- Sarah Jane (Jane in the book) was born in 1822 in Woodford, the oldest child of William and Maria Fairbrother. She was a milliner. Her parents married four months before she was born.
- Thomas and Sarah Jane married in Luton in 1848.
- *The Hat Box* in Lancrets Path in Luton is a real place that existed in 1848.
- The cholera epidemic of 1848 was real. A new cemetery outside the town was created to cope with the thousands of deaths.
- Thomas and Sarah Jane returned to the Woodford area where Sarah, my great grandmother was born in December 1850.
- Although we do not know where Thomas did his carpentry apprenticeship, the conditions of the Indenture Agreement are copied verbatim from a historical document supplied by Peter Jackson.
- Thomas' brother, John, took over his father's butcher business but dabbled in bee keeping and tried innovative measures to extract better honey.
- The Marriott family still operate butcher shops in Woodford.
- Thomas and Sarah Jane left England in July 1852 on *The Ballengeich*, arriving in December 1852. They took advantage of the Family Colonization Scheme run by Caroline Chisholm who was concerned that the white population of Australia was predominantly single men. She requisitioned ships and canvassed for young families and single women to emigrate,

targeting people 'of good character.' She campaigned in many places, including Northampton, offering a loan to make the journey possible. She also 'grouped' families into family groups. This is how Thomas met his future business partners.
- They lived in North Melbourne where Thomas was a partner in a construction firm with James Russell, Joseph Little, Henry Swindale and William Pickersgill, (Arthur in the book). All, with the exception of Henry Swindale, he had met on the ship.
- Sarah Jane died in childbirth in January 1854, four days after delivering a baby girl. The baby lived for four days but was buried with her mother the day Sarah Jane died. The cause on the death certificate says: 1. Childbirth and 2. Dysentery.
- Thomas is unaccounted for from 1854 – 1859, but there is some evidence that he was living in St Kilda, in Pakington street, in a house which he may have built.
- In 1859, he bought land in Laanecoorie on the Loddon river. Adjoining his land was that of the pioneer of the district, Peter Lyon.
- In 1860, Thomas married Catherine Lyon, daughter of Peter, in Creswick. On the marriage certificate he declared that his wife had died but says he has **no children**. Yet, Sarah was ten years old at this stage.
- In 1861, Thomas and Catherine had a son, Marriott. Marriott was his mother's maiden name.
- In 1869, Catherine died, most likely of ovarian cancer in Sandridge. (Cause of death was Ovarian dropsy). Her death certificate is signed by the surgeon, Robert Charles Curtis.
- In 1873, Thomas was living in Bamawm, working at Rest-down station and building houses in the district, some of which he owned.

- From 1874 until he went to live with Marriott sometime between 1910 and 1914, he owned land in Bamawm and according to newspaper reports was an 'innovative farmer' and a 'respected gentleman.'
- He had 25 acres of vines under cultivation and won prizes at the local shows, some as far as Ballarat, for his red wine.
- He died in 1914 in Torrumbarry where he had moved to be with his son, Marriott.
- 'The boy' is entirely fictional.

Sarah

- Sarah Bradshaw was born in Daventry in the Midlands of England in 1850 and left England to come to Australia in 1852, when she was 19 months old.
- Her mother, Sarah Jane Fairbrother, died in childbirth, 13 months after arriving in Melbourne. (NB: Her name was in fact Sarah Jane but for obvious reasons, I have called her Jane throughout in the book).
- After the death of her mother, Sarah did not stay with Thomas but she was **not** sent to an orphanage. She must have been 'looked after' by someone. As Thomas had no family in Australia, it must have been someone he knew and trusted. His business partners, with whom he had travelled from England, were a possibility. Was it James Russell or Joseph Little? Both had young families and could have taken Sarah. James Russell is ruled out as his whole family drowned off the coast of Wales when they returned to England for a visit! He alone survived. That left Joseph and Helen Little and it is entirely plausible that they took Sarah into their family.

- Sarah died as a 'charwoman,' so it is likely she went into service at a young age. *Shrublands* in Camberwell is a possibility as it was near where she lived, and being a huge estate with extensive gardens and vines, it would have needed many staff including gardeners. Alexander Hamilton was a gardener and this is a likely place where he and Sarah could have met. *Shrublands* was built in 1861 by Ernst Carter, a dentist, who was one of the first wine makers in the colony and the first meeting of the Victorian Winemakers' Association was held on the premises.
- Frederik Taubner is entirely fictional.
- We have no real knowledge of where Sarah was from the age of three until the age of twenty-two when she appears to register the birth of my grandfather as William Bradshaw (Father unknown) in 1873 in Hartwell.
- Sarah Bradshaw and Alexander Hamilton were together not long after William was born.
- Alexander Hamilton had the lease of a house and 4 acres of market garden in Hartwell from 1873 until his death in 1883. The Landlord was John Pool. Alexander's name is on the rates notice until September 1883, two months before his death, when Sarah Hamilton is listed as the rate payer for the following year.
- Sarah had 7 children, but only three with Alexander:
  - William Hamilton (1873-1969) Father – unknown. Born in Hartwell
  - Annie Hamilton (1875 — ?) Father – Alexander Hamilton. Born in Hartwell
  - Alec Hamilton (1878 – 1952) Father – Alexander Hamilton. Born in Hartwell
  - Agnes Hamilton/Wilson (1882 – 1934) Father – Alexander Hamilton. Born in Hartwell

- ▷ Amy Hamilton/Scott (1889 – 1976) Father – unknown. Born in Rochester
- ▷ Francis Hamilton (1891 – 1943) Father – unknown. Born in Rochester
- ▷ Nellie Hamilton (1895 – 1914) Father – unknown. Born in Rochester
- The 'foreigner', 'the doctor,' and the 'boarder', are entirely fictional.
- Sometime after 1884, Sarah moved her family to Rochester and worked as a charwoman. She had three more children.
- In 1898, she was before the court for stealing one pound. She was found guilty.
- In 1913, she died of bronchitis.
- In 1914, Nellie died suddenly of heart failure. She was nineteen and lived with Agnes after her mother's death.
- In 1915, Frank was among the first men to enlist in WW1. He listed his sister, Amy Scott, as his next of kin.
- In 1934, Agnes died of diabetes in Rochester after having had 12 children. She is buried in Elmore.
- In 1936, Marriott died in Bendigo at the Benevolent Asylum and is buried in Kangaroo Flat.
- In 1943, Frank died in Tongala leaving his wife Elsie and four children. Alec and Frank's son, Jim, were with him the day he died.
- In 1953, Alec died in Tongala. Agnes and Frank's sons were pall bearers.
- In 1969, William died in Melbourne, leaving three sons.
- In 1976 Amy died in Deniliquin leaving eight children.
- Annie is an unknown.

William
(based on stories he told and family memories)

- William Hamilton was my "pappy."
- William had only three years schooling because he was a 'delicate child', starting in Camberwell and finishing in Bamawm where his grandfather lived. The Bamawm school was where the Bamawm Golf Course is now.
- He thought he was born in March 1874, but, according to his birth certificate, he was born exactly a year earlier. These dates were obviously doctored by his parents to 'legitimise' his birth.
- Although he went to Bamawm after his father died, he didn't speak of the death of his father to us.
- The man whom he believed to be his father, Alexander Hamilton, had 'jumped ship' in Melbourne when he arrived from Scotland and disappeared to the goldfields.
- William's brother, also called Alexander, (Alec) and whom he called a 'wild fella', was in contact with William but we never met or saw him. We thought him a 'myth.'
- William's father took him to see Ned Kelly when the bushranger was supposed to arrive at Pentridge in 1880. He remembered sitting on his father's shoulders and the crowd being annoyed that Ned didn't turn up.
- William finished his schooling at the Bamawm school (which was on the site where the Bamawm golf course now is) in 1887.
- He worked on a farm in Bamawm owned by Mrs Gilmer and her brother Mr Curran. Mrs Gilmer's son, Patrick, had a tremendous influence on my grandfather and he spoke about him often, saying he was the most decent man he ever met. William stayed on the farm until he went to Melbourne sometime between 1894 and 1897

- He never spoke to us of his mother.
- My mother remembered that my father, Leo Hamilton, took William to 'his sister's funeral' in Rochester (it was, in fact, Elmore) some time before my parents were married in 1941. As Agnes died in 1934, this would tally with the fact.
- My father never spoke about this, not even when I moved to Rochester. I believe he knew far more than he ever told us.
- There is no record of Annie. She seems to have vanished from the face of the earth although we know she was alive in 1913 when her mother died.

The title of the book, *Redeeming Sarah*, sums up my reason for writing it. My wish is that it will be read by the many people who are here on this earth because of Sarah. Her perseverance and dedication to her family, despite difficult circumstances, are valued by all of us.

www.ingramcontent.com/pod-product-compliance
Lightning Source LLC
Chambersburg PA
CBHW032028290426
44110CB00012B/714